.NET Framework 4.5 Expert Programming Cookbook

Over 50 engaging recipes for learning advanced concepts of .NET Framework 4.5

A.P. Rajshekhar

BIRMINGHAM - MUMBAI

.NET Framework 4.5 Expert Programming Cookbook

Copyright © 2013 Packt Publishing

All rights reserved. No part of this book may be reproduced, stored in a retrieval system, or transmitted in any form or by any means, without the prior written permission of the publisher, except in the case of brief quotations embedded in critical articles or reviews.

Every effort has been made in the preparation of this book to ensure the accuracy of the information presented. However, the information contained in this book is sold without warranty, either express or implied. Neither the author, nor Packt Publishing, and its dealers and distributors will be held liable for any damages caused or alleged to be caused directly or indirectly by this book.

Packt Publishing has endeavored to provide trademark information about all of the companies and products mentioned in this book by the appropriate use of capitals. However, Packt Publishing cannot guarantee the accuracy of this information.

First published: January 2013

Production Reference: 1110113

Published by Packt Publishing Ltd.
Livery Place
35 Livery Street
Birmingham B3 2PB, UK.

ISBN 978-1-84968-742-3

www.packtpub.com

Cover Image by David Gutierrez (bilbaorocker@yahoo.co.uk)

Credits

Author
A.P. Rajshekhar

Reviewers
Wei Chung, Low
Jason De Oliveira

Acquisition Editor
James Jones

Lead Technical Editor
Ankita Shashi

Technical Editors
Jalasha D'costa
Worrell Lewis
Varun Pius Rodrigues

Copy Editors
Brandt D'Mello
Aditya Nair
Laxmi Subramanian
Ruta Waghmare

Project Coordinators
Priya Sharma
Abhishek Kori

Proofreader
Lawrence A. Herman

Indexer
Rekha Nair

Production Coordinator
Shantanu Zagade

Cover Work
Shantanu Zagade

About the Author

A.P. Rajshekhar, Senior Developer with Red Hat, has more than 7 years of experience in IT, having worked on applications ranging from enterprise-level web applications and game development to android applications. His endeavors include development of Learning Management System, Health Systems, Supply Management Solution, and Xbox-based games. He has extensive knowledge of different technologies (SOA, Portal, Java Persistence, and .NET Persistence) and platforms (Sharepoint and JBoss EAP). He is also the author of *Building Dynamic Web 2.0 Websites with Ruby on Rails, Packt Publishing*, that was in Amazon's top 50 in Web 2.0 for 6 months. Apart from that he has also contributed to DevShed Portal on topics ranging from server-side development (JEE/.NET/RoR) to mobile (Symbian/Android-based development) and game development (SDL and OpenGL) with a total readership of more than 3 million. He is currently ranked among the top 10 authors on DevShed. You can find out about his interests on his blogs – http://aprajshekhar.wordpress.com and http://sententiasupervicis.wordpress.com.

> Authoring a book is not an easy feat. However, the help and guidance from my family and friends helped me to author this book. First, I would like to thank Packt Publishing for providing me an opportunity to work on such an exciting project. I would like to thank my parents for their constant encouragement. Special thanks to my friends Shrikant Khare and Sormita Chakraborty for their support, encouragement, and initial research on the topics to be covered.

About the Reviewers

Wei Chung, Low is a Business Intelligence Manager, a .NET developer, and a MCT, MCPD, MCITP, MCTS, MCSD.NET. He works with IPG MediaBrands (NYSE: IPG) at its Kuala Lumpur, Malaysia campus. He is also a member of PMI, certified as PMP. He started working on Microsoft .NET early in his career and has been involved in development, consultation, and corporate training in the areas of business intelligence, system integration, and virtualization. He has worked for the Bursa Malaysia (formerly Kuala Lumpur Stock Exchange) and Shell IT International previously, which gave him rich integration experiences across different platforms.

He strongly believes that a good system implementation delivers precious value to businesses, and integration of various systems across different platforms shall always be a part of it, just as diverse people from different cultures live together in harmony in most of the major cities.

Jason De Oliveira works as CTO for Cellenza (`http://www.cellenza.com`), an IT Consulting company specializing in Microsoft technologies and Agile methodology in Paris, France. He is an experienced Manager and Senior Solutions Architect, with advanced skills in Software Architecture and Enterprise Architecture.

Jason works for big companies and helps them to realize complex and challenging software projects. He frequently collaborates with Microsoft and you can quite often find him at the Microsoft Technology Center (MTC) in Paris.

He loves sharing his knowledge and experience via his blog, by speaking at conferences, writing technical books, writing articles in the technical press, giving software courses as a Microsoft Certified Trainer (MCT), and coaching co-workers in his company.

Microsoft has awarded him the Microsoft® Most Valuable Professional (MVP C#) Award since 2011 for his numerous contributions to the Microsoft community. Microsoft seeks to recognize the best and brightest from technology communities around the world with the MVP Award. These exceptional and highly respected individuals come from more than 90 countries, serving their local online and offline communities and have an impact worldwide. Jason is very proud to be one of them.

Please feel free to contact him via his blog if you need any technical assistance or want to exchange information on technical subjects (`http://www.jasondeoliveira.com`).

Jason has worked on the following books:

- *WCF 4.5 Multi-tier Services Development with LINQ to Entities, Packt Publishing*
- *Visual Studio 2012 - Développez pour le web, ENI Publishing*

www.PacktPub.com

Support files, eBooks, discount offers and more

You might want to visit www.PacktPub.com for support files and downloads related to your book.

Did you know that Packt offers eBook versions of every book published, with PDF and ePub files available? You can upgrade to the eBook version at www.PacktPub.com and as a print book customer, you are entitled to a discount on the eBook copy. Get in touch with us at service@packtpub.com for more details.

At www.PacktPub.com, you can also read a collection of free technical articles, sign up for a range of free newsletters and receive exclusive discounts and offers on Packt books and eBooks.

http://PacktLib.PacktPub.com

Do you need instant solutions to your IT questions? PacktLib is Packt's online digital book library. Here, you can access, read and search across Packt's entire library of books.

Why Subscribe?

- Fully searchable across every book published by Packt
- Copy and paste, print and bookmark content
- On demand and accessible via web browser

Free Access for Packt account holders

If you have an account with Packt at www.PacktPub.com, you can use this to access PacktLib today and view nine entirely free books. Simply use your login credentials for immediate access.

Instant Updates on New Packt Books

Get notified! Find out when new books are published by following @PacktEnterprise on Twitter, or the *Packt Enterprise* Facebook page.

Table of Contents

Preface	**1**
Chapter 1: Core .NET Recipes	**5**
Introduction	5
Implementing the validation logic using the Repository pattern	6
Creating a custom validation attribute by extending the validation data annotation	10
Using XML to generate a localized validation message	16
Extending the validation attribute for localization	19
Creating custom attributes	22
Processing custom attributes via reflection	27
Using asynchronous file I/O for directory-to-directory copy	33
Accessing JSON using dynamic programming	38
Chapter 2: Application Events and Windows Forms	**45**
Introduction	45
Creating an event that can have generic values as payload	46
Creating a table layout that can dynamically add or remove rows based on the size of the collection	52
Creating DataGridView dynamically	61
Creating a video player using DirectX and Windows Forms	71
Chapter 3: Threading and Parallel Programming	**77**
Introduction	77
Creating a shared resource	78
Handling Producer-Consumer race conditions	82
Handling background threads in Windows Forms	88
Handling threads in WPF	93
Using parallel programming to make bulk image processing faster	98
Chaining two parallelized bulk image processing operations	101

Table of Contents

Chapter 4: ASP.NET Recipes – I — 105
Introduction — 105
Creating a user registration page using HTML5 controls — 105
Saving a draft of a user registration page using HTML5 client storage — 109
Binding objects to controls using strongly-typed data controls — 114
Implementing communication between an ASPX page and a Silverlight application — 119

Chapter 5: ADO.NET Recipes — 129
Introduction — 129
Saving large files (BLOB) in MS SQL Server using ADO.NET — 129
Retrieving large files (BLOB) from SQL Server using ADO.NET — 134
Using transactions to maintain database consistency when saving multiple files — 138
Using DataSet to modify custom XML configuration files — 145

Chapter 6: WCF Recipes — 151
Introduction — 151
Implementing custom binding in WCF — 151
Creating a WCF REST service — 157
Handling exceptions using FaultContract and FaultException — 162
Uploading files using Stream — 166
Securing a service using role-based security — 173

Chapter 7: WPF Recipes — 179
Introduction — 179
Implementing the Model and Repository patterns — 180
Implementing View Model — 187
Implementing View commands and binding data to View — 190
Using the live data shaper for live sorting — 196
Playing videos using MediaElement — 199
Using Ribbon control to display the video player controls — 203

Chapter 8: ASP.NET Recipes – II — 209
Introduction — 209
Preventing cross-site injection using the anti-XSS library — 210
Adding Google Map functionality using Map Helper — 213
Third-party authentication of users using Google — 216
Implementing unobtrusive validation — 218

Chapter 9: Silverlight Recipes — 223
- Introduction — 223
- Using Pivot control to present asset data — 223
- Accessing webcams — 227
- Using client-side storage for saving a draft of the user registration data — 231

Chapter 10: Entity Framework Recipes — 235
- Introduction — 235
- Joining two entities using LINQ — 236
- Uploading files using Entity Framework and stored procedures — 240
- Managing connections manually for long-running tasks — 244
- Using functions that return tables as return values — 247

Index — 255

Preface

.NET is an architecture-neutral programming language and agnostic framework that caters to the varying requirements from desktop application, to business solutions, to multiplayer online three-dimensional games. The Version 4.5 added many new features and enhanced the existing ones that help in the development of robust and user-friendly solutions more easily. *.NET Framework 4.5 Expert Programming Cookbook* takes a hands-on approach in teaching you how to use the new as well as advanced features of the .NET Framework 4.5. Each topic will teach you how to use a specific feature of .NET to solve a real world problem or scenario.

This is a concise and practical cookbook with recipes which demonstrates advanced concepts with all the new functionality of the .NET Framework 4.5.

What this book covers

Chapter 1, Core .NET Recipes, will cover the core concepts in .NET, which include metadata programming, reflection, asynchronous I/O, and dynamic programming.

Chapter 2, Application Events and Windows Forms, covers topics such as event handling, dynamically generating controls, and layouts as well as creating video players using Managed DirectX.

Chapter 3, Threading and Parallel Programming, will cover multi-threading, thread-safety, and the parallel framework extensions to avoid threading pitfalls in your Windows Forms, WPF, and Silverlight applications.

Chapter 4, ASP.NET Recipes – I, explains the new features of ASP.NET applications including strongly-typed controls, HTML 5 controls, and client-side storage as well as passing data between Silverlight and the ASPX page.

Chapter 5, ADO.NET Recipes, covers saving and retrieving files of big size (BLOB) in SQL Server, managing transactions, and using DataSet to operate upon XML data.

Preface

Chapter 6, *WCF Recipes*, explains uploading files using streamed mode, implementing REST services, handling exceptions using FaultContract, implementing custom binding, and securing services using role-based security.

Chapter 7, *WPF Recipes*, will cover design patterns that include MVVM, repository pattern, and Data Mapper as well as new controls such as Ribbon control and live data shaper. It will also cover creating a video player using WPF Media API.

Chapter 8, *ASP.NET Recipes – II*, covers the new features of ASP.NET websites such as enabling Google/Facebook, SSO-based authentication, adding unobtrusive validation, embedding maps in websites, and protecting against cross-server scripting attacks.

Chapter 9, *Silverlight Recipes*, explains the new pivot control, accessing webcams, and client-side storage.

Chapter 10, *Entity Framework Recipes*, will cover using LINQ to join multiple entities, calling stored procedures using Entity Framework, handling long-running tasks, and using table-valued functions of MS SQL Server.

What you need for this book

You will need Visual Studio 2012, MS SQL Server 2008 or higher, Windows 7 or higher, and hardware compatible with Windows 7 or higher. A webcam will be required to run certain recipes.

Who this book is for

This book is for those who have basic to intermediate knowledge about the .NET Framework and want to understand its advanced features and features new to .NET 4.5. Each advanced feature covered in this book assumes that the reader has the basic knowledge of the concept being discussed.

Conventions

In this book, you will find a number of styles of text that distinguish between different kinds of information. Here are some examples of these styles, and an explanation of their meaning:

Code words in text are shown as follows: "The core of the validation logic lies in the `IsUsernameUnique` method of the `MockRespository` class."

A block of code is set as follows:

```
public interface IRepository
{
  void AddUser(User user);
  bool IsUsernameUnique(string userName);
}
```

When we wish to draw your attention to a particular part of a code block, the relevant lines or items are set in bold:

```
foreach (string filename in Directory.EnumerateFiles(sourceDir))
{
   using (FileStream sourceStream = File.Open(filename, FileMode.Open))
   {
   }
}
```

New terms and **important words** are shown in bold. Words that you see on the screen, in menus or dialog boxes for example, appear in the text like this: "Then click on the **Copy** button to start copying."

> Warnings or important notes appear in a box like this.

> Tips and tricks appear like this.

Reader feedback

Feedback from our readers is always welcome. Let us know what you think about this book—what you liked or may have disliked. Reader feedback is important for us to develop titles that you really get the most out of.

To send us general feedback, simply send an e-mail to feedback@packtpub.com, and mention the book title through the subject of your message.

If there is a topic that you have expertise in and you are interested in either writing or contributing to a book, see our author guide on www.packtpub.com/authors.

Customer support

Now that you are the proud owner of a Packt book, we have a number of things to help you to get the most from your purchase.

Downloading the example code

You can download the example code files for all Packt books you have purchased from your account at http://www.packtpub.com. If you purchased this book elsewhere, you can visit http://www.packtpub.com/support and register to have the files e-mailed directly to you.

Errata

Although we have taken every care to ensure the accuracy of our content, mistakes do happen. If you find a mistake in one of our books—maybe a mistake in the text or the code—we would be grateful if you would report this to us. By doing so, you can save other readers from frustration and help us improve subsequent versions of this book. If you find any errata, please report them by visiting http://www.packtpub.com/support, selecting your book, clicking on the **errata submission form** link, and entering the details of your errata. Once your errata are verified, your submission will be accepted and the errata will be uploaded to our website, or added to any list of existing errata, under the Errata section of that title.

Piracy

Piracy of copyright material on the Internet is an ongoing problem across all media. At Packt, we take the protection of our copyright and licenses very seriously. If you come across any illegal copies of our works, in any form, on the Internet, please provide us with the location address or website name immediately so that we can pursue a remedy.

Please contact us at copyright@packtpub.com with a link to the suspected pirated material.

We appreciate your help in protecting our authors, and our ability to bring you valuable content.

Questions

You can contact us at questions@packtpub.com if you are having a problem with any aspect of the book, and we will do our best to address it.

Core .NET Recipes

In this chapter we will cover:

- Implementing the validation logic using the Repository pattern
- Creating a custom validation attribute by extending the validation data annotation
- Using XML to generate a localized validation message
- Extending the validation attribute for localization
- Creating custom attributes
- Processing custom attributes via reflection
- Using asynchronous file I/O for directory-to-directory copy
- Accessing JSON using dynamic programming

Introduction

This chapter will cover recipes related to core concepts in .NET, which will include the following:

- **Metadata-driven programming**: The first six recipes will cover how to use attributes as metadata for specific purposes such as validation and localization.
- **Reflection**: The *Processing custom attributes via reflection* recipe will tell you how to use reflection to create metadata processors such as applications or libraries that can understand custom attributes and provide the output based on them.
- **Asynchronous file I/O**: This is a new feature for file input/output introduced in .NET 4.5. The *Using asynchronous file I/O for directory-to-directory copy* recipe will cover this feature.

Core .NET Recipes

> ▸ **Dynamic programming**: .NET 4.0 introduced the concept of dynamic programming, in which blocks of code marked as dynamic will be executed directly, bypassing the compilation phase. We will look at this in the last recipe, *Accessing JSON using dynamic programming*.

Implementing the validation logic using the Repository pattern

The **Repository pattern** abstracts out data-based validation logic. It is a common misconception that to implement the Repository pattern you require a relational database such as MS SQL Server as the backend. Any collection can be treated as a backend for a Repository pattern. The only point to keep in mind is that the business logic or validation logic must treat it as a database for saving, retrieving, and validating its data. In this recipe, we will see how to use a generic collection as backend and abstract out the validation logic for the same.

The validation logic makes use of an entity that represents the data related to the user and a class that acts as the repository for the data allowing certain operations. In this case, the operation will include checking whether the user ID chosen by the user is unique or not.

How to do it...

The following steps will help check the uniqueness of a user ID that is chosen by the user:

1. Launch Visual Studio .NET 2012. Create a new project of **Class Library** project type. Name it `CookBook.Recipes.Core.CustomValidation`.
2. Add a folder to the project and set the folder name to `DataModel`.
3. Add a new class and name it `User.cs`.
4. Open the `User` class and create the following public properties:

Property name	Data type
UserName	String
DateOfBirth	DateTime
Password	String

    Use the automatic property functionality of .NET to create the properties. The final code of the `User` class will be as follows:

    ```
    namespace CookBook.Recipes.Core.CustomValidation
    {
        /// <summary>
        /// Contains details of the user being registered
    ```

```
    /// </summary>
    public class User
    {
        public string UserName { get; set; }
        public DateTime DateOfBirth { get; set; }
        public string Password { get; set; }
    }
}
```

> **Downloading the example code**
> You can download the example code files for all Packt books you have purchased from your account at http://www.packtpub.com. If you purchased this book elsewhere, you can visit http://www.packtpub.com/support and register to have the files e-mailed directly to you.

5. Next, let us create the repository. Add a new folder and name it `Repository`.
6. Add an interface to the `Repository` folder and name it `IRepository.cs`.
7. The interface will be similar to the following code snippet:

```
public interface IRepository
    {
    }
```

8. Open the `IRepository` interface and add the following methods:

Name	Description	Parameter(s)	Return Type
`AddUser`	Adds a new user	User object	`Void`
`IsUsernameUnique`	Determines whether the username is already taken or not	string	`Boolean`

After adding the methods, `IRepository` will look like the following code:

```
namespace CookBook.Recipes.Core.CustomValidation
{
    public interface IRepository
    {
        void AddUser(User user);
        bool IsUsernameUnique(string userName);
    }
}
```

9. Next, let us implement `IRepository`. Create a new class in the `Repository` folder and name it `MockRepository`.

Core .NET Recipes

10. Make the `MockRepository` class implement `IRepository`. The code will be as follows:

    ```
    namespace CookBook.Recipes.Core.Data.Repository
    {
        public   class MockRepository:IRepository
          {
              #region IRepository Members
              /// <summary>
              /// Adds a new user to the collection
              /// </summary>
              /// <param name="user"></param>
              public void AddUser(User user)
              {

              }
              /// <summary>
              /// Checks whether a user with the username already
              ///exists
              /// </summary>
              /// <param name="userName"></param>
              /// <returns></returns>
              public bool IsUsernameUnique(string userName)
              {

              }

              #endregion
          }
    }
    ```

11. Now, add a private variable of type `List<Users>` in the `MockRepository` class. Name it _users. It will hold the registered users. It is a `static` variable so that it can hold usernames across multiple instantiations.

12. Add a constructor to the class. Then initialize the _users list and add two users to the list:

    ```
    public   class MockRepository:IRepository
          {
              #region Variables
              Private static List<User> _users;

              #endregion
              public MockRepository()
              {
                  _users = new List<User>();
                  _users.Add(new User() { UserName = "wayne27",
    DateOfBirth = new DateTime(1950, 9, 27), Password = "knight"
    });
    ```

```
            _users.Add(new User() { UserName = "wayne47",
DateOfBirth = new DateTime(1955, 9, 27), Password = "justice"
});
        }
        #region IRepository Members
        /// <summary>
        /// Adds a new user to the collection
        /// </summary>
        /// <param name="user"></param>
        public void AddUser(User user)
        {
        }
        /// <summary>
        /// Checks whether a user with the username already exists
        /// </summary>
        /// <param name="userName"></param>
        /// <returns></returns>
        public bool IsUsernameUnique(string userName)
        {

        }

        #endregion
    }
```

13. Now let us add the code to check whether the username is unique. Add the following statements to the `IsUsernameUnique` method:

    ```
    bool exists = _users.Exists(u=>u.UserName==userName);
    return !exists;
    ```

    The method turns out to be as follows:

    ```
    public bool IsUsernameUnique(string userName)
    {
        bool exists =
        _users.Exists(u=>u.UserName==userName);
        return !exists;
    }
    ```

14. Modify the `AddUser` method so that it looks as follows:

    ```
    public void AddUser(User user)
    {
            _users.Add(user);
    }
    ```

Core .NET Recipes

How it works...

The core of the validation logic lies in the `IsUsernameUnique` method of the `MockRespository` class. The reason to place the logic in a different class rather than in the attribute itself was to decouple the attribute from the logic to be validated. It is also an attempt to make it future-proof. In other words, tomorrow, if we want to test the username against a list generated from an XML file, we don't have to modify the attribute. We will just change how `IsUsernameUnique` works and it will be reflected in the attribute. Also, creating a **Plain Old CLR Object** (**POCO**) to hold values entered by the user stops the validation logic code from directly accessing the source of input, that is, the Windows application.

Coming back to the `IsUsernameUnique` method, it makes use of the **predicate** feature provided by .NET. Predicate allows us to loop over a collection and find a particular item. Predicate can be a static function, a delegate, or a lambda. In our case it is a lambda.

```
bool exists = _users.Exists(u=>u.UserName==userName);
```

In the previous statement, .NET loops over `_users` and passes the current item to `u`. We then make use of the item held by `u` to check whether its username is equal to the username entered by the user. The `Exists` method returns true if the username is already present. However, we want to know whether the username is unique. So we flip the value returned by `Exists` in the return statement, as follows:

```
return !exists;
```

Creating a custom validation attribute by extending the validation data annotation

.NET provides **data annotations** as a part of the `System.ComponentModel.DataAnnotation` namespace. Data annotations are a set of attributes that provides out of the box validation, among other things. However, sometimes none of the in-built validations will suit your specific requirements. In such a scenario, you will have to create your own validation attribute. This recipe will tell you how to do that by extending the validation attribute. The attribute developed will check whether the supplied username is unique or not. We will make use of the validation logic implemented in the previous recipe to create a custom validation attribute named `UniqueUserValidator`.

How to do it...

The following steps will help you create a custom validation attribute to meet your specific requirements:

1. Launch Visual Studio 2012. Open the `CustomValidation` solution.
2. Add a reference to `System.ComponentModel.DataAnnotations`.

Chapter 1

3. Add a new class to the project and name it `UniqueUserValidator`.
4. Add the following using statements:

   ```
   using System.ComponentModel.DataAnnotations;
   using CookBook.Recipes.Core.CustomValidation.MessageRepository;
   using CookBook.Recipes.Core.Data.Repository;
   ```

5. Derive it from `ValidationAttribute`, which is a part of the `System.ComponentModel.DataAnnotations` namespace. In code, it would be as follows:

   ```
   namespace CookBook.Recipes.Core.CustomValidation
   {
       public class UniqueUserValidator:ValidationAttribute
       {

       }
   }
   ```

6. Add a property of type `IRepository` to the class and name it `Repository`.
7. Add a constructor and initialize `Repository` to an instance of `MockRepository`. Once the code is added, the class will be as follows:

   ```
   namespace CookBook.Recipes.Core.CustomValidation
   {
       public class UniqueUserValidator:ValidationAttribute
       {
           public IRepository Repository {get;set;}

           public UniqueUserValidator()
           {
               this.Repository = new MockRepository();
           }
       }
   }
   ```

8. Override the `IsValid` method of `ValidationAttribute`. Convert the `object` argument to `string`.
9. Then call the `IsUsernameUnique` method of `IRepository`, pass the string value as a parameter, and return the result. After the modification, the code will be as follows:

   ```
   namespace CookBook.Recipes.Core.CustomValidation
   {
       public class UniqueUserValidator:ValidationAttribute
       {
           public IRepository Repository {get;set;}
   ```

```
            public UniqueUserValidator()
            {
                this.Repository = new MockRepository();
            }
            public override bool IsValid(object value)
            {
                string valueToTest = Convert.ToString(value);
                return this.Repository.IsUsernameUnique(valueToTest);
            }
        }
    }
```

We have completed the implementation of our custom validation attribute. Now let's test it out.

10. Add a new **Windows Forms Application** project to the solution and name it `CustomValidationApp`.
11. Add a reference to the `System.ComponentModel.DataAnnotations` and `CustomValidation` projects.
12. Rename `Form1.cs` to `Register.cs`.
13. Open `Register.cs` in the design mode. Add controls for username, date of birth, and password and also add two buttons to the form. The form should look like the following screenshot:

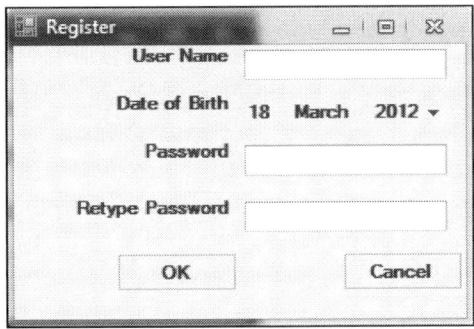

14. Name the input control and button as given in the following table:

Control	Name
Textbox	txtUsername
Button	btnOK

Since we are validating the `User Name` field, our main concern is with the textbox for the username and the **OK** button. I have left out the names of other controls for brevity.

15. Switch to the code view mode. In the constructor, add event handlers for the Click event of `btnOK` as shown in the following code:

    ```csharp
    public Register()
    {
      InitializeComponent();
      this.btnOK.Click += new EventHandler(btnOK_Click);
    }

    void btnOK_Click(object sender, EventArgs e)
    {
    }
    ```

16. Open the `User` class of the `CookBook.Recipes.Core.CustomValidation` project. Annotate the `UserName` property with `UniqueUserValidator`. After modification, the `User` class will be as follows:

    ```csharp
    namespace CookBook.Recipes.Core.CustomValidation
    {
        /// <summary>
        /// Contains details of the user being registered
        /// </summary>
        public class User
        {
            [UniqueUserValidator(ErrorMessage="User name already exists")]
            public string UserName { get; set; }
            public DateTime DateOfBirth { get; set; }
            public string Password { get; set; }

        }
    }
    ```

17. Go back to `Register.cs` in the code view mode.

18. Add the following `using` statements:

    ```csharp
    using System.ComponentModel;
    using System.ComponentModel.DataAnnotations;
    using CookBook.Recipes.Core.CustomValidation;
    using CookBook.Recipes.Core.Data.Repository;
    ```

19. Add the following code to the event handler of btnOK:

    ```
    //create a new user
    User user = new User()
    {
    UserName = txtUsername.Text, DateOfBirth=dtpDob.Value
    };
    //create a validation context for the user instance
    ValidationContext context = new ValidationContext(user, null,
    null);
    //holds the validation errors
    IList<ValidationResult> errors = new List<ValidationResult>();

    if (!Validator.TryValidateObject(user, context, errors, true))
    {
     foreach (ValidationResult result in errors)
         MessageBox.Show(result.ErrorMessage);
    }
    else
    {
      IRepository repository = new MockRepository();
      repository.AddUser(user);
      MessageBox.Show("New user added");
    }
    ```

20. Hit *F5* to run the application. In the textbox add a username, say, `dreamwatcher`. Click on **OK**. You will get a message box stating **User has been added successfully**.

21. Enter the same username again and hit the **OK** button. This time you will get a message saying **User name already exists**. This means our attribute is working as desired.

22. Go to **File | Save Solution As...**, enter `CustomValidation` for **Name**, and click on **OK**.

 We will be making use of this solution in the next recipe.

How it works...

To understand how `UniqueUserValidator` works, we have to understand how it is implemented and how it is used/called. Let's start with how it is implemented. It extends `ValidationAttribute`. The `ValidationAttribute` class is the base class for all the validation-related attributes provided by data annotations. So the declaration is as follows:

    public class UniqueUserValidator:ValidationAttribute

This allowed us to make use of the public and protected methods/attribute arguments of `ValidationAttribute` as if it is a part of our attribute. Next, we have a property of type `IRepository`, which gets initialized to an instance of `MockRepository`. We have used the interface-based approach so that the attribute will only need a minor change if we decide to test the username against a database table or list generated from a file. In such a scenario, we will just change the following statement:

```
this.Repository = new MockRepository();
```

The previous statement will be changed to something such as the following:

```
this.Repository = new DBRepository();
```

Next, we overrode the `IsValid` method. This is the method that gets called when we use `UniqueUserValidator`. The parameter of the `IsValid` method is an object. So we have to typecast it to string and call the `IsUniqueUsername` method of the `Repository` property. That is what the following statements accomplish:

```
string valueToTest = Convert.ToString(value);
return this.Repository.IsUsernameUnique(valueToTest);
```

Now let us see how we used the validator. We did it by decorating the `UserName` property of the `User` class:

```
[UniqueUserValidator(ErrorMessage="User name already exists")]
public string UserName {get; set;}
```

As I already mentioned, deriving from `ValidatorAttribute` helps us in using its properties as well. That's why we can use `ErrorMessage` even if we have not implemented it.

Next, we have to tell .NET to use the attribute to validate the username that has been set. That is done by the following statements in the **OK** button's Click handler in the `Register` class:

```
ValidationContext context = new ValidationContext(user, null, null);
//holds the validation errors
IList<ValidationResult> errors = new List<ValidationResult>();
if (!Validator.TryValidateObject(user, context, errors, true))
```

First, we instantiate an object of `ValidationContext`. Its main purpose is to set up the context in which validation will be performed. In our case the context is the `User` object. Next, we call the `TryValidateObject` method of the `Validator` class with the `User` object, the `ValidationContext` object, and a list to hold the errors. We also tell the method that we need to validate all properties of the `User` object by setting the last argument to true. That's how we invoke the validation routine provided by .NET.

Core .NET Recipes

See also

- The *Implementing Model and Repository pattern* recipe discussed in *Chapter 7, WPF Recipes*

Using XML to generate a localized validation message

In the last recipe you saw that we can pass error messages to be displayed to the validation attribute. However, by default, the attributes accept only a message in the English language. To display a localized custom message, it needs to be fetched from an external source such as an XML file or database. In this recipe, we will see how to use an XML file to act as a backend for localized messages.

How to do it...

The following steps will help you generate a localized validation message using XML:

1. Open `CustomValidation.sln` in Visual Studio .NET 2012.
2. Add an XML file to the `CookBook.Recipes.Core.CustomValidation` project. Name it `Messages.xml`. In the **Properties** window, set **Build Action to Embedded Resource**.
3. Add the following to the `Messages.xml` file:

   ```xml
   <?xml version="1.0" encoding="utf-8" ?>
   <messages>
    <en>
     <message key="not_unique_user">User name is not unique</message>
    </en>
    <fr>
       <message key="not_unique_user">Nom d'utilisateur n'est pas unique</message>
    </fr>
   </messages>
   ```

4. Add a folder to the `CookBook.Recipes.Core.CustomValidation` project. Name it `MessageRepository`.
5. Add an interface to the `MessageRepository` folder and name it `IMessageRepository`.

Chapter 1

6. Add a method to the interface and name it `GetMessages`. It will have `IDictionary<string,string>` as a return type and will accept a `string` value as parameter. The interface will look like the following code:

    ```
    namespace CookBook.Recipes.Core.CustomValidation.MessageRepository
    {
        public interface IMessageRepository
        {
            IDictionary<string, string> GetMessages(string locale);
        }
    }
    ```

7. Add a class to the `MessageRespository` folder. Name it `XmlMessageRepository`.

8. Add the following `using` statements:

    ```
    using System.Xml;
    ```

9. Implement the `IMessageRepository` interface. The class will look like the following code once we implement the interface:

    ```
    namespace CookBook.Recipes.Core.CustomValidation.MessageRepository
    {
        public class XmlMessageRepository:IMessageRepository
        {
            #region IMessageRepository Members

    public IDictionary<string, string> GetMessages(string locale)
    {
       return null;
    }

            #endregion
        }
    }
    ```

10. Modify `GetMessages` so that it looks like the following code:

    ```
    public IDictionary<string, string> GetMessages(string locale)
    {
        XmlDocument xDoc = new XmlDocument();
        xDoc.Load(Assembly.GetExecutingAssembly().GetManifestResourceStream("CustomValidation.Messages.xml"));
        XmlNodeList resources = xDoc.SelectNodes("messages/"+locale+"/message");
        SortedDictionary<string, string> dictionary = new SortedDictionary<string, string>();
        foreach (XmlNode node in resources)
    ```

```
        {
            dictionary.Add(node.Attributes["key"].Value, node.
    InnerText);
        }

        return dictionary;
}
```

Next let us see how to modify `UniqueUserValidator` so that it can localize the error message.

How it works...

The `Messages.xml` file and the `GetMessages` method of `XmlMessageRespository` form the core of the logic to generate a locale-specific message. `Message.xml` contains the key to the message within the `locale` tag. We have created the `locale` tag using the two-letter ISO name of a locale. So, for English it is `<en></en>` and for French it is `<fr></fr>`.

Each `locale` tag contains a `message` tag. The `key` attribute of the tag will have the key that will tell us which `message` tag contains the error message. So our code will be as follows:

```
<message key="not_unique_user">User name is not unique</message>
```

`not_unique_user` is the key to the `User is not unique` error message. In the `GetMessages` method, we first load the XML file. Since the file has been set as an embedded resource, we read it as a resource. To do so, we first got the executing assembly, that is, `CustomValidation`. Then we called `GetManifestResourceAsStream` and passed the qualified name of the resource, which in this case is `CustomValidation.Messages.xml`. That is what we achieved in the following statement:

```
xDoc.Load(Assembly.GetExecutingAssembly().GetManifestResourceStream(
"CustomValidation.Messages.xml"));
```

Then we constructed an XPath to the `message` tag using the locale passed as the parameter. Using the XPath query/expression we got the following message nodes:

```
XmlNodeList resources = xDoc.SelectNodes("messages/"+locale+"/
message");
```

After getting the node list, we looped over it to construct a dictionary. The value of the `key` attribute of the node became the key of the dictionary. And the value of the node became the corresponding value in the dictionary, as is evident from the following code:

```
SortedDictionary<string, string> dictionary = new
SortedDictionary<string, string>();
foreach (XmlNode node in resources)
{
   dictionary.Add(node.Attributes["key"].Value, node.InnerText);
}
```

The dictionary was then returned by the method. Next, let's understand how this dictionary is used by `UniqueUserValidator`.

Extending the validation attribute for localization

If you do not want to hardcode the message or embed it as a resource, the only approach left is to extend the attribute so that messages can be decided at runtime based on the locale used. Extending an attribute for this purpose can also help if you decide to fetch the message from the database or an external translation service.

In this recipe, we will modify the `UniqueUserValidator` code so that it can generate locale-based custom messages. The custom messages will be fetched from an XML file using the logic developed in the previous recipe.

How to do it...

The following steps will guide you as you generate locale-based custom messages:

1. Open `CustomValidation.sln` in Visual Studio .NET 2012.

2. Open `UniqueUserValidator` and add the following `using` statements:

   ```
   using CookBook.Recipes.Core.CustomValidation.MessageRepository;
   using CookBook.Recipes.Core.Data.Repository;
   ```

3. Then add a property of type `IMessageRepository` and instantiate it in the constructor:

   ```
   public IRepository Repository {get;set;}
   public IMessageRepository MessageRepo {get;set;}

   public UniqueUserValidator()
   {
      this.Repository = new MockRepository();
         this.MessageRepo = new XmlMessageRepository();
   }
   ```

4. Override the `FormatErrorMessage` method of `ValidationAttribute`. In the overridden method, get the current locale and call the `GetMessage` method of `IMessageRepository` with the locale value. Then, return the value corresponding to the `ErrorMessage` property. In code, it will be as follows:

```
public override string FormatErrorMessage(string name)
{
  string locale =
Thread.CurrentThread.CurrentCulture.TwoLetterISOLanguageName;
  return this.MessageRepo.GetMessages(locale)[this.ErrorMessage];
}
```

We have completed the modifications to `UniqueUserValidator`. Now let's see how to use it. Along with using the modified `UniqueUserValidator` code, we will also test whether it responds to the change in locale correctly.

5. Open the `User` class, which is in the `DataModel` folder of the `CookBook.Recipes.Core.CustomValidation` project.

6. Change the `ErrorMessage` parameter of the `UserName` property to the following:

```
[UniqueUserValidator(ErrorMessage = "not_unique_user")]
public string UserName { get; set; }
```

7. Next, open the `Register` class of `CustomValidationApp` in the design mode. Add a label and a combobox. Name the combobox `cmbLocale`. After adding the controls, the **Register** form will look as follows:

8. Next, open the `Register` class in the view code mode. Add the following code in the constructor:

```
cmbLocale.Items.Add("en-IN");
cmbLocale.Items.Add("fr-FR");
cmbLocale.SelectedIndex = 0;
```

Chapter 1

9. Add an event handler for the `SelectedIndexChanged` event of `cmbLocale` as follows:

    ```
    public Register()
    {
      InitializeComponent();
      cmbLocale.Items.Add("en-IN");
      cmbLocale.Items.Add("fr-FR");
      cmbLocale.SelectedIndex = 0;
      cmbLocale.SelectedIndexChanged += new
                EventHandler(cmbLocale_SelectedIndexChanged);

      this.btnCancel.Click += new EventHandler(btnCancel_Click);
      this.btnOK.Click += new EventHandler(btnOK_Click);
    }

    void cmbLocale_SelectedIndexChanged(object sender, EventArgs e)
    {
    }
    ```

10. Add the following code to the event handler for the `SelectedIndexChanged` event of `cmbLocale`:

    ```
    Thread.CurrentThread.CurrentCulture = new CultureInfo(cmbLocale.SelectedItem.ToString());
    ```

11. Press *F5* to run the application. Enter `wayne27` as username. Click on **OK**. You will get a message saying **User name is not unique**.

12. Select **fr-FR** from the locale combobox. Click on the **OK** button. You will get a message saying **Nom d'utilisateur n'est pas unique**, which is the French version of the message we have used in `Messages.xml`.

How it works...

The main change we did to the attribute is overriding the `FormatErrorMessage` method of `ValidationAttribute`. The validation framework / data annotation library calls the `FormatErrorMessage` method when it needs to output a message corresponding to a property. In short, by overriding it, we can provide a customized message.

To do so, we first need to find the two-letter ISO name of the current locale. Using the `CurrentCulture` property of `CurrentThread`, which is a static property of the `Thread` class, we can find the locale name. The following code did that and provided us with the two-letter ISO name of the current locale:

```
string locale = Thread.CurrentThread.CurrentCulture.TwoLetterISOLanguageName;
```

Next, we passed the locale to the `GetMessages` method of `IMessageRepository`. From the returned dictionary, we found the message we wanted using the `ErrorMessage` property/named parameter and returned it. The value in `ErrorMessage` acted as the key:

```
return this.MessageRepo.GetMessages(locale)[this.ErrorMessage];
```

`CustomValidationApp` performs two roles. First of all, it makes use of the `UserName` property of the `User` class decorated with `UniqueUserValidator` to pass the key of the message we want, as shown:

```
[UniqueUserValidator(ErrorMessage = "not_unique_user")]
public string UserName { get; set; }
```

The value we passed to `ErrorMessage` acted as the key in `FormatErrorMessage`. The other role the application performs is to provide us with a *test platform* for testing locales, in this case, English and French. This was done by the following code in the `SelectedIndexChanged` event handler of `cmbLocale` in the `Register` class:

```
Thread.CurrentThread.CurrentCulture = new CultureInfo(cmbLocale.
SelectedItem.ToString());
```

What we did in the preceding code is to set the current culture of the application to the culture selected in the locale combobox. When we set the `CurrentCulture` property of `CurrentThred` of the `Thread` class to a particular culture, the culture of the application is changed until the application is closed. Use this only for testing purposes.

Creating custom attributes

In the previous recipes we saw how to extend existing attributes to suit our needs. However, there are situations where you don't have an existing attribute to extend. In such cases, you will have to create your own attribute. In this recipe we will look at creating custom attributes. Our attribute will help you to keep track of bugs fixed within a class. It can be used to tag the class itself or methods within the class.

A **custom attribute** is a class extending from `System.Attribute`. However, its behavior is quite different from a class. And to make it to work as an attribute, extra steps such as creating another class that can process the attribute are required.

How to do it...

1. Launch Visual Studio .NET 2012. Create a project of type **Class Library** and name it `CookBook.Recipes.Core.DefectTracker`.
2. Delete `Class1.class` from the project.
3. Add a folder to the project and name it `Attributes`.
4. Next, add a class to the folder and name it `DefectTrackerAttribute`.

5. Derive the `DefectTrackerAttribute` class from `Attribute`.
6. Add the following properties as shown in the following table:

Name	Type
DefectID	Int
ResolvedBy	String
ResolvedOn	String
Comments	String

   Once the properties are added, our class will look as follows:

   ```
   namespace CookBook.Recipes.Core.DefectTracker.Attributes
   {
       public class DefectTrackerAttribute:Attribute
         {
             #region Public Properties
             public int DefectID {get;set;}
             public string ResolvedBy {get;set;}
             public string ResolvedOn {get;set;}
             public string Comments {get;set;}
             #endregion
         }
   }
   ```

7. Now, let's specify all the places where, within a class, we can use this attribute by decorating/tagging the class with the `AttributeUsage` attribute:

   ```
   [AttributeUsage(AttributeTargets.Class |
       AttributeTargets.Constructor |
       AttributeTargets.Field |
       AttributeTargets.Method |
       AttributeTargets.Property,
       AllowMultiple = true)]
     public class DefectTrackerAttribute:Attribute
       {
           #region Public Properties
           public int DefectID {get;set;}
           public string ResolvedBy {get;set;}
           public string ResolvedOn {get;set;}
           public string Comments {get;set;}
           #endregion

       }
   }
   ```

8. Next, add a constructor so that we can pass the values via the constructor. The `Comments` parameter will be optional. In code, the constructor will be as follows:

   ```
   public DefectTrackerAttribute(int defectID, string resolvedBy,
   string resolvedOn, string Comments = "")
   {
     this.DefectID = defectID;
     this.ResolvedBy = resolvedBy;
     this.ResolvedOn = resolvedOn;
     this.Comments = Comments;
   }
   ```

   That completes the steps in creating `DefectTrackerAttribute`. Let's see how to use it.

9. Add a project of type **Class Library** and name it `DefectTrackerTest`.
10. Delete `Class1.cs`.
11. Add a reference to the `CookBook.Recipes.Core.DefectTracker` project.
12. Next, add a class to `DefectTrackerTest` and name it `CurrencyConverter`.
13. Add the following import:

    ```
    using CookBook.Recipes.Core.DefectTracker.Attributes;
    ```

14. Add a `private` variable of type `double`:

    ```
    private double _value;
    ```

15. Add a parameterized constructor that will look as follows:

    ```
    [DefectTrackerAttribute(1042,"AP", "2012/02/11","Changed float
    param to double")]
    public CurrencyConverter(double value)
    {
      _value = value;
    }
    ```

16. Add `DefectTrackerAttribute` to the constructor.
17. Add a method that accepts a `double` argument and returns a `double` value.
18. Tag the method with `DefectTrackerAttribute`. The method will look as follows:

    ```
    [DefectTrackerAttribute(DefectID = 1042, ResolvedBy = "AP",
    ResolvedOn = "2012/02/11")]
    public double ToRupee()
    {
       return _value * 50;
    }
    ```

How it works...

As I mentioned earlier, a custom attribute is really a class that is inherited from `System.Attribute`. Our `DefectTrackerAttribute` class is no different. So, we inherit it from `Attribute`:

```
public class DefectTrackerAttribute:Attribute
{
}
```

Now, we have to pass information to the attribute. This can be done in two ways:

- Through a constructor
- As a named parameter of the constructor

Using a constructor to pass the parameter is similar to what we do for classes. However, for the constructor parameters to be used as named parameters, we will need properties. So we added properties and the constructor:

```
public class DefectTrackerAttribute:Attribute
    {
        #region Public Properties
        public int DefectID {get;set;}
        public string ResolvedBy {get;set;}
        public string ResolvedOn {get;set;}
        public string Comments {get;set;}
        #endregion
        public DefectTrackerAttribute()
        {
        }
        public DefectTrackerAttribute(int defectID, string resolvedBy, string resolvedOn, string Comments = "")
        {
            this.DefectID = defectID;
            this.ResolvedBy = resolvedBy;
            this.ResolvedOn = resolvedOn;
            this.Comments = Comments;
        }
    }
```

The members of the class to which we can apply the attribute is the most important aspect of that attribute. To specify this, we can use the `AttributeUsage` attribute. Since we want to apply our attribute to classes, constructors, methods, fields, and properties, we specify it as follows:

```
[AttributeUsage(AttributeTargets.Class |
  AttributeTargets.Constructor |
  AttributeTargets.Field |
  AttributeTargets.Method |
  AttributeTargets.Property,
  AllowMultiple = true)]
public class DefectTrackerAttribute:Attribute
  {
      #region Public Properties
      public int DefectID {get;set;}
      public string ResolvedBy {get;set;}
      public string ResolvedOn {get;set;}
      public string Comments {get;set;}
      #endregion
      public DefectTrackerAttribute(int defectID, string resolvedBy, string resolvedOn, string Comments = "")
      {
          this.DefectID = defectID;
          this.ResolvedBy = resolvedBy;
          this.ResolvedOn = resolvedOn;
          this.Comments = Comments;
      }
  }
```

The `AllowMultiple` argument specifies whether the attribute can be used more than once on a class or its members. As the same member may be modified multiple times for different defects, we will be using our attribute multiple times on that member. Hence, we passed `AllowMultiple` as true. With that we come to the end of this recipe.

In `DefectTrackerTest`, we have just one class, `CurrencyConverter`. We tagged its constructor and `ToRupee` with `DefectTrackerAttribute`:

```
public CurrencyConverter(double value)
{
   _value = value;
}

[DefectTrackerAttribute(DefectID = 1042, ResolvedBy = "AP", ResolvedOn = "2012/02/11")]public double ToRupee()
{
          return _value * 50;
}
```

Chapter 1

In the next recipe we will see how to create a processor for our attribute and how to use them both.

Processing custom attributes via reflection

In the previous recipe, we developed a custom attribute named `DefectTrackerAttribute`. However, the attribute, by itself, does not do anything. Unless there is an application or library that looks at the class and members tagged/decorated by the attribute, it is just a piece of code that does nothing. So, in this recipe, we will see how to process the class tagged by `DefectTrackerAttribute` using reflection.

How to do it...

1. Launch Visual Studio .NET 2012.
2. Open `CustomAttribute.sln`.
3. Open the `CookBook.Recipes.Core.DefectTracker` project in **Add a folder to the project**. Name it `Processor`.
4. Add a class to the folder and name it `DefectTrackerProcessor`.
5. Add the following imports:

   ```
   using System.Reflection;
   using CookBook.Recipes.Core.DefectTracker.Attributes;
   ```

6. Add the following methods to it:

Name	Parameters	Return type
GetDetails	String assmblyPath	String
	String className	
GetMemberDetails	String memberName	String
	IEnumerable<DefectTrackerAttribute> attributes	

7. To the `GetMemberDetails` method, add the following code:

   ```
   StringBuilder sb = new StringBuilder();
   sb.Append("\n");
   if (!sb.ToString().Contains(memberName))
     {
        sb.Append(memberName);
     }
   foreach (var attribute in attributes)
     {
   ```

```
                sb.Append("ID-");
                sb.Append(attribute.DefectID);
                sb.Append("\t");
                sb.Append("Resolved By-");
                sb.Append(attribute.ResolvedBy);
                sb.Append("\t");
                sb.Append("Resolved On-");
                sb.Append(attribute.ResolvedOn);


        }
    return sb.ToString();
```

8. To the `GetDetails` method, add the following code:

```
StringBuilder details = new StringBuilder();
Assembly assembly = Assembly.LoadFrom(assemblyPath);
Type type = assembly.GetType(className, true, true);

//check whether the constructors have the custom attribute
ConstructorInfo[] constructorInfo = type.GetConstructors();
foreach (var item in constructorInfo)
{
 IEnumerable<DefectTrackerAttribute> attributes =
        item.GetCustomAttributes<DefectTrackerAttribute>();
 details.Append(GetMemberDetails(item.Name, attributes));
}

//check whether the methods have custom attribute
MethodInfo[] methodInfo = type.GetMethods();

foreach (var item in methodInfo)
{
 IEnumerable<DefectTrackerAttribute> attributes =
    item.GetCustomAttributes<DefectTrackerAttribute>();
 if (attributes.Count() > 0)
 {
  details.Append(GetMemberDetails(item.Name, attributes));
 }
}

return details.ToString();
```

That completes the first step. Next, let us look at how to use the processor.

9. Add a project of type **Windows Forms Application** and name it `DefectTrackerApp`.
10. Add a reference to the `CookBook.Recipes.Core.DefectTracker` project.
11. Rename the `Form` class to `TrackDefect`.
12. Switch to the design mode. Design the form so that it looks like the following screenshot:

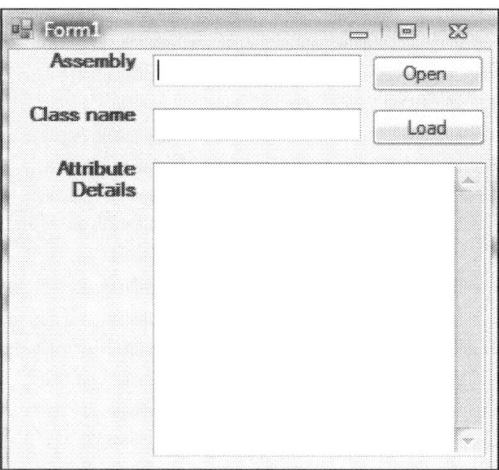

13. Name the textboxes and buttons as follows:

Control	Description	Name
Textbox	For the assembly path, that is, the path of the `.dll` or `.exe` file to be loaded	`txtAssembly`
Button	To display the file open dialog	`btnOpen`
Textbox	To enter the fully qualified class name to be loaded from the assembly	`txtClassName`
Button	To call `DefectTrackerProcessor`	`btnLoad`
Textbox	To display the details of the fixed defects in the class	`txtDetails`

14. Double-click on `btnOpen` to generate the Click event handler. In the event handler, add the following code:

```
if( diagOpen.ShowDialog() == System.Windows.Forms.DialogResult.OK)
txtPath.Text = diagOpen.FileName;
```

15. Switch to the design mode. Double-click on `btnOpen` to generate the Click event handler. In the event handler, add the following code:

```
if (!String.IsNullOrEmpty(txtPath.Text) && !String.IsNullOrEmpty(txtClassName.Text))
  {
```

```
            txtDetails.Text = new DefectTrackerProcessor().
        GetDetails(txtPath.Text,
                txtClassName.Text);
        }
```

16. Add the following import:

    ```
    using CookBook.Recipes.Core.DefectTracker.Attributes;
    ```

17. Set `DefectTrackerApp` as a startup project.
18. Press *F5* and run the application.
19. Click on the **Open** button. In the file dialog, navigate to the `bin` folder of the `DefectTrackerTest` project. Select `DefectTracker.dll`. Observe the full path being displayed in the textbox next to the **Open** button.
20. In the textbox next to the **Load** button, enter `DefectTrackerTest.CurrencyConverter`. Click on **Load**.
21. The multiline textbox next to the **Details** label will be filled with details of the constructor and the methods that make use of the attribute.

That completes the steps for creating a processor for the custom attribute and using it. Next, let us dive more into the code to understand what is happening.

How it works...

The core of the `DefectTrackerProcessor` class is the `GetDetails` method that uses reflection to find out whether the class whose name has been sent as the parameter contains `DefectTrackerAttribute`. The first step is to load the assembly containing the class using the `LoadFrom` static method of the `Assembly` class. The next step is to retrieve the class from the assembly and set it to the `Type` class variable. These two steps are achieved in the following statements:

```
Assembly assembly = Assembly.LoadFrom(assemblyPath);
Type type = assembly.GetType(className, true, true);
```

The `Type` class is the root of the functionality provided by .NET for reflection. It is the entry point to gain details regarding the members of a class or structure. In the preceding code, the `GetType` method looks into the assembly and returns the `Type` instance containing details of the class whose name has been passed via the `className` variable. The second parameter of `GetType` is set to `true` so that, if the class is not found, an exception is thrown and we can know that something is wrong. We want to find the class regardless of whether the class name is passed in upper- or lowercase. Hence, the last parameter is set to `true` to tell `GetType` to ignore the case of the class name.

Now that we have the `Type` instance containing the details of the class, we can check whether the members of the class are decorated with `DefectTrackerAttribute` or not. The first class member that we check is the constructor. The following statement provides the details of the constructors within a class:

```
//check whether the constructors have the custom attribute
ConstructorInfo[] constructorInfo = type.GetConstructors();
```

The `GetConstructors` method of `Type` returns an array of `ConstructorInfo`. Each instance of `ConstructorInfo` in the array contains details such as the name and attributes decorating that constructor, for each constructor of the class that `Type` represents. Next, we iterate through the array and get the list for `DefectTrackerAttribute` for the current constructor as shown in the following statements:

```
foreach (var item in constructorInfo)
{
  IEnumerable<DefectTrackerAttribute> attributes =
                  item.GetCustomAttributes<DefectTrackerAttribute>();
  details.Append(GetMemberDetails(item.Name, attributes));
}
```

Then, we passed the list to the `GetMemberDetails` method along with the name. In the `GetMemberDetails` method, we iterate over the list to get the defect details using the properties of `DefectTrackerAttribute` as shown:

```
foreach (var attribute in attributes)
{
  sb.Append("ID-");
  sb.Append(attribute.DefectID);
  sb.Append("\t");
  sb.Append("Resolved By-");
  sb.Append(attribute.ResolvedBy);
  sb.Append("\t");
  sb.Append("Resolved On-");
  sb.Append(attribute.ResolvedOn);

}
```

Similar to the constructor, we can get details of methods tagged with `DefectTrackerAttribute` using the `GetMethodInfo` method of the `Type` class. That is what we have done in the following statements:

```
//check whether the methods have custom attribute
MethodInfo[] methodInfo = type.GetMethods();

foreach (var item in methodInfo)
{
   IEnumerable<DefectTrackerAttribute> attributes =
            item.GetCustomAttributes<DefectTrackerAttribute>()
   if (attributes.Count() > 0)
   {
       details.Append(GetMemberDetails(item.Name, attributes));
   }
}
```

The `MethodInfo` class contains the details of a method of the class represented by `Type`. The array returned by `GetMethods()` contains details of all the methods within the class. We iterated over the array and determined whether the method is tagged with the attribute or not. If it is tagged, that is, the attribute list contains one or more elements, we fetched the details, just like we did for the constructor(s). Once we got the details of the constructor and the methods, we returned the details as a `string` value.

In the `TrackDefect` class of `DefectTrackerApp`, we called the instantiated `DefectTrackerProcessor` and called the `GetDetails` method with the assembly path and the class name that was entered via the UI. This is done in the Click event handler of the `Load` button.

```
private void btnLoad_Click(object sender, EventArgs e)
{
if (!String.IsNullOrEmpty(txtPath.Text) &&
           !String.IsNullOrEmpty(txtClassName.Text))
 {
   txtDetails.Text = new DefectTrackerProcessor().GetDetails(txtPath.
Text, txtClassName.Text);
 }
}
```

There's more...

We saw how `Type` helps us to get details of constructors and methods of a class. Similarly, we can get details of the properties of a class using the `GetProperties` method. It returns an array of `PropertyInfo`. Each `PropertyInfo` holds the details of a specific property of the class. If you want details of only a specific property, call the `GetProperty()` method and pass the property name as argument.

Using asynchronous file I/O for directory-to-directory copy

Asynchronous file I/O has been a feature of .NET from Version 1.1 onwards. However, the loops that the developer had to run to get it working were many. In Version 4.5, .NET introduced a new API that would make using asynchronous file operation easy. At the core of the API, we have two operators—`async` and `await`. This recipe will focus on using these operators to implement an asynchronous directory-to-directory copy utility.

How to do it...

The following steps will help you perform directory-to-directory copy using asynchronous file I/O:

1. Launch Visual Studio .NET 2012. Create a project of type **Class Library** and name it `CookBook.Recipes.Core.AsyncFileIO`.

2. Rename `Class1.cs` to `Utils.cs`.

3. Open `Utils.cs`. Make the class public and static as shown:

   ```
   public static class Utils
   {
   }
   ```

4. Add a `public static` method to the class and name it `CopyDirectoryAsync`. It will take two parameters – a string containing the source directory and another string containing the target directory. It will return a `Task` value of type `int`. The signature will be as follows:

   ```
   public static Task<int> CopyDirectoryAsync(string sourceDir,
   string targetDir)
   {
   }
   ```

5. Change the method signature to add the `async` keyword to it:

   ```
   public static async Task<int> CopyDirectoryAsync(string sourceDir,
   string targetDir)
   {
   }
   ```

6. Add a variable of type `int` to the method. Assign the count of the files in the target directory:

   ```
   int count = Directory.EnumerateFiles(targetDir).Count();
   ```

7. Next, add the following code:

   ```
   foreach (string filename in Directory.EnumerateFiles(sourceDir))
   {
     using (FileStream sourceStream = File.Open(filename, FileMode.Open))
     {
        using (FileStream DestinationStream = File.Create(targetDir +
                    filename.Substring(filename.LastIndexOf('\\'))))
        {
                await sourceStream.CopyToAsync(DestinationStream);
        }
     }
   }
   ```

8. Add the `return` statement as shown:

   ```
   return (Directory.EnumerateFiles(targetDir).Count() - count);
   ```

   Next, let us look at how to use the `Utility` class. To use the `Utility` class, we will create a **Windows Forms Application** project.

9. Add a project of type **Windows Forms Application** and name it `AsyncFileIO`.
10. Add a reference to `CookBook.Recipes.Core.AsyncFileIO`.
11. Rename `Form1.cs` to `FileUtility.cs`.

12. Open `FileUtility.cs` in the design mode. Design the form so that it looks like the following screenshot:

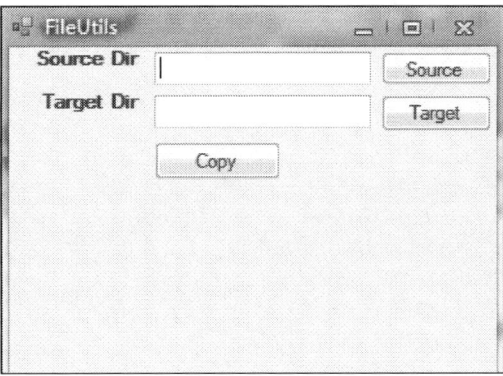

13. Name the controls as detailed in the following table:

Control	Description	Name
Textbox	To hold the path of the source directory	`txtSource`
Button	To display the directory chooser for choosing the source directory	`btnSource`
Textbox	To hold the path of the target directory	`txtTarget`
Button	To display the directory chooser for choosing the target directory	`btnTarget`
Button	To start copying from the source to the target directory	`btnCopy`
Folder Browser Dialog	To display the folder chooser	`diagFolder`

14. Double-click on `btnSource` to add the Click event handler for it. Add the following code to the event handler:

    ```
    if (diagFolder.ShowDialog() == System.Windows.Forms.DialogResult.
    OK)
    {
       txtSource.Text = diagFolder.SelectedPath;
    }
    ```

15. Switch to the design mode. Add the Click event handler for `btnTarget` by double-clicking on it. In the event handler, add the following code:

    ```
    if (diagFolder.ShowDialog() == System.Windows.Forms.DialogResult.
    OK)
    {
        txtTarget.Text = diagFolder.SelectedPath;
    }
    ```

16. Similarly, add the Click event handler for `btnCopy`. Then, add the following code to the handler:

    ```
    if (!String.IsNullOrEmpty(txtSource.Text) && !String.
    IsNullOrEmpty(txtTarget.Text))
    {
       Utils.CopyDirectoryAsync(txtSource.Text, txtTarget.Text);
    }
    ```

17. Press *F5* and run the application. Click on the **Source** button to choose the directory that you want to copy. Choose the directory to which you want to copy by clicking on the **Target** button. Then click on the **Copy** button to start copying.

That completes the steps to create directory-to-directory copy functionality, which does the copying asynchronously.

How it works...

The whole logic of asynchronous copy is implemented within one method: the `CopyDirectoryAsync` method of the `Utils` class. As you have already seen, both the class and the method are public as well as static. The reason for making the method static is that we have implemented it as a utility method. Utility methods are always implemented as public and static methods. In .NET itself, all the methods of the `Math` class are static methods, and the class itself is static.

Now let us look at how the logic works. If you observe the signature of the method, there are two things that make it different from other methods (or synchronous methods).

```
public static async Task<int> CopyDirectoryAsync(string sourceDir,
string targetDir)
```

First is the `async` keyword. It means that somewhere in the method an asynchronous task is going to be executed. Next is the return type. If you want to return any value from a method that has `async` in its signature, you will have to do it using the `Task` object. In our case, we wanted to return the number of files copied. So we have used `Task<int>` as our return type.

As we wanted to return the number of files copied, we will have to know the current number of files in the target directory. With the following statement we can achieve this:

```
int count = Directory.EnumerateFiles(targetDir).Count();
```

In the preceding statement, we have used the `EnumerateFiles` method of the `Directory` class to get a list of all the filenames within the target directory and then got the number of elements in that list. Next, we have to get the files we want to copy. For that, we iterate over the filenames returned by `Directory.EnumerateFiles`. To `EnumerateFiles`, we passed the path of the source directory as shown:

```
foreach (string filename in Directory.EnumerateFiles(sourceDir))
{
}
```

Then, we open each file for reading as a stream:

```
foreach (string filename in Directory.EnumerateFiles(sourceDir))
{
    using (FileStream sourceStream = File.Open(filename, FileMode.Open))
    {
    }
}
```

Once we have opened the file to be copied, we have to open another stream to the location where the file will be copied. To do that we created a file of the same name and then connected a new stream to it, as shown in the following highlighted code:

```
foreach (string filename in Directory.EnumerateFiles(sourceDir))
{
    using (FileStream sourceStream = File.Open(filename, FileMode.Open))
    {
        using (FileStream DestinationStream = File.Create(targetDir +
                    filename.Substring(filename.LastIndexOf('\\'))))
        {
        }
    }
}
```

Now comes the most important part of our code, the statement that makes asynchronous copy work. Once we open a stream to a file in the destination directory, we can transfer the contents. To do so, we used the `CopyToAsync` method of the `FileStream` class. However, what makes the content transfer statement important is the `await` keyword before it, as in:

```
await sourceStream.CopyToAsync(DestinationStream);
```

Core .NET Recipes

The `await` keyword in the preceding statement tells the framework that the execution of this method is suspended until the `CopyToAsync` method is done. Apart from that, the `await` keyword also tells the framework to return the control of the execution to the code that called this method, that is, `CopyDirectoryAsync`. In other words, until the current file is copied, the application can resume its normal operation and would not appear to the user as if the application is frozen.

In our case, the `FileUtils` class calls the `CopyDirectoryAsync` method when **Copy** is clicked. When the execution reaches the `await` statement, the control is returned back to the `FileUtils` class until the current file, as per the loop, is copied. Till the file is copied, the user can make use of any feature of the application. Once the file is copied, the file in the source directory is opened and the process continues. If the size of the files are huge, say 500 MB, you will be able to see the effect of the asynchronous transfer.

Accessing JSON using dynamic programming

In Version 3.5, .NET introduced the `var` keyword. With `var`, developers got the choice of not declaring the type of the variable. It became the task of the compiler to infer the type of the variable based on the value assigned. .NET 4.0 took this concept a step ahead by introducing the keyword `dynamic`.

When a variable is declared `dynamic`, its type is inferred only during execution. The compiler does not check for the type and type safety of a `dynamic` variable. This helps a lot when dealing with data whose type is either unknown or too complex to be bound to a compiled object. In this recipe, you will see how `dynamic` can access parsed JSON data without creating classes for the JSON elements. One thing to keep in mind is that in this recipe the implementation of logic and the application that uses the implementation are one and the same. In other words, the main application itself contains the logic.

How to do it...

The following steps will help you access JSON using dynamic programming:

1. In Visual Studio .NET 2012, create a new project of type **Windows Forms Application**. Name it `DynamicJsonParsing`.
2. Rename `Form1.cs` to `AccessJson.cs`.
3. Open `AccessJson` in the design mode. Design the form so that it looks like the following screenshot:

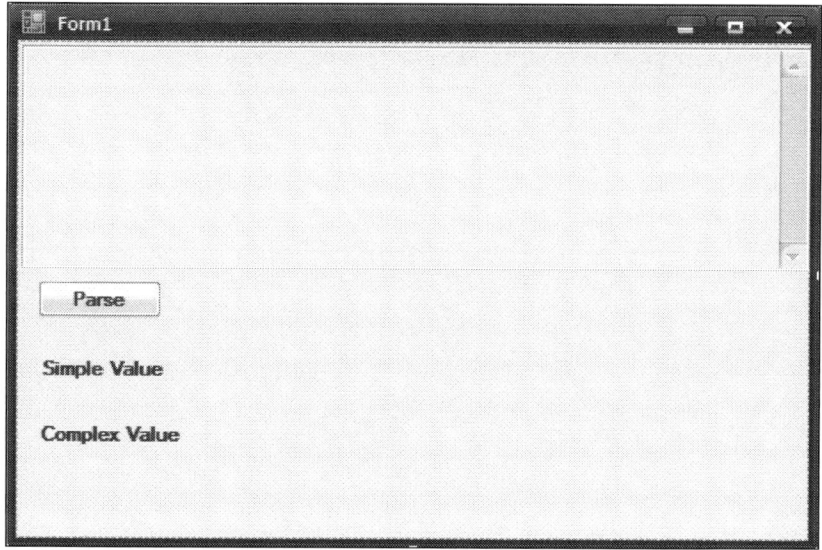

4. Name the controls as detailed the following table:

Control	Description	Name
Label	To display the name of the element whose value will be shown	`lblValueFor`
Label	To display the value of the element	`lblValue`
Label	To display the name of the complex element whose value will be shown	`lblComplexValueFor`
Label	To display the value of the complex element	`lblComplexValue`
Textbox	To display the JSON string being parsed and accessed	`txtJson`
Button	To parse, access, and display the values of JSON data.	`btnParse`

5. Add a reference to `System.Web.Extensions`.
6. Switch to the code view mode and add the following import:

   ```
   using System.Web.Script.Serialization;
   ```

7. Next, add the following `private` method to the class. It will return the JSON data.

    ```
    private string GetJsonString()
    {
            return @"{
                        'order':{
                                    'name':'testOrder',
                                    'value':'1000',
                                    'products':[
                                        {'name': 'testProduct',
                                            'expiry': '12 months'
                                        }]
                                },
                        'delivery':'at home'
                    }";
    }
    ```

8. In the constructor, add the following statement after the call of the `InitializeComponents` method:

    ```
    txtJson.Text = GetJsonString();
    ```

9. Switch to the design mode. Double-click on the `btnParse` button to add a Click event handler.

10. In the event handler, add the following statements:

    ```
    var serializer = new JavaScriptSerializer();
    var dictionary = serializer.Deserialize<Dictionary<string,
                                                dynamic>>(txtJson.Text);
    lblValueOf.Text = "Value of delivery";
    lblValue.Text = dictionary["delivery"];
    lblComplexValueOf.Text = "name of product of order";
    lblComplexValue.Text = dictionary["order"]["products"][0]["name"];
    ```

11. Press *F5* and run the application. Click on the `Parse` button. The values will be displayed as shown:

Chapter 1

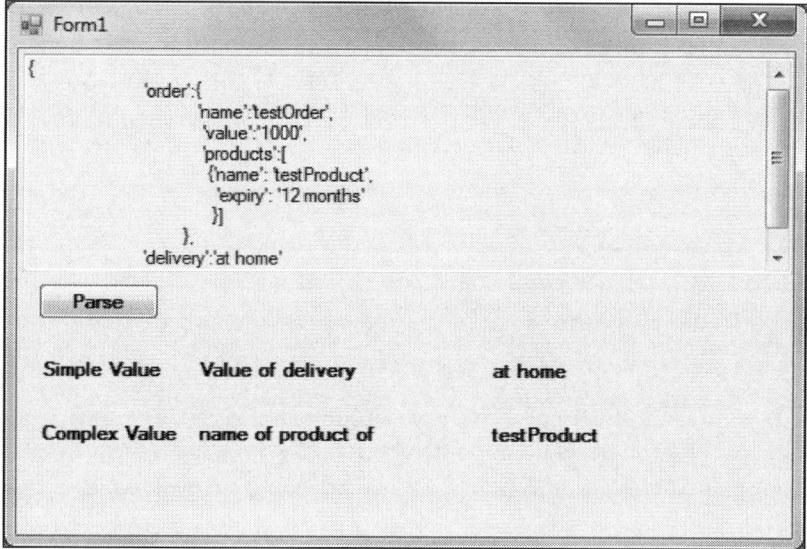

How it works...

The core work of accessing JSON happens in the event handler for the Parse button. We had assigned a string containing JSON. The data within the JSON string is about a particular order. The product contained in the order and the type of delivery is as shown:

```
{
    'order':{
            'name':'testOrder',
            'value':'1000',
            'products':[
                            {'name': 'testProduct',
                             'expiry': '12 months'
                            }]
            },
    'delivery':'at home'
}
```

In the JSON above, delivery is a normal data element. However, the name of a product is a complex data element since `name` is a part of the `products` array (note the square bracket), which itself is part of order element. For data of this type, if we go for the traditional approach to access the values, we will have to either create multiple classes or perform complex string manipulations. That is where having `dynamic` helps.

In the event handler for the `Parse` button, we first parsed the JSON using `JavaScriptSerializer` as shown:

```
var serializer = new JavaScriptSerializer();
var dictionary = serializer.Deserialize<Dictionary<string,
                                     dynamic>>(txtJson.Text);
```

The JSON data is deserialized or parsed into a dictionary having a `string` value as key and a `dynamic` object as value. If we look at the dictionary as a table of Key and Value, it will look something like the following:

Key	Value
delivery	at home

order	{
	     'name':'testOrder',
	     'value':'1000',
	     'products':[
	         {'name':'testProduct',
	         'expiry': '12 months'
	     }]
	 }

From the preceding table it is clear that the value for delivery is at home. So the following statement is nothing special, just a simple way of getting the value via the key:

```
lblValue.Text = dictionary["delivery"];
```

However, if we have to find the name of the product, simply using the key won't work. If we pass the order as the key, we will get a complete piece of complex JSON data. However, this data is of type `dynamic`. So, if we write statements like the ones written as follows, the compiler won't complain, and will leave it to the runtime check to assign the values:

```
dynamic order = dictionary["order"];
dynamic products = order["products"];
dynamic product = products[0];
dynamic name = product["name"];
```

The first statement assigns the value of the order to the `order` variable. The `order` variable will now contain an array of products. The first element of the `product` array is assigned to the `product` variable. Then, from the `product` variable, the name key is used to access the product name. On combining all four steps, we get:

```
lblComplexValue.Text = dictionary["order"]["products"][0]["name"];
```

So, by using dynamic programming, we were able to access the parsed JSON data without having to create the class hierarchies and without having to use string manipulation.

One point to keep in mind is that dynamic methods and statements are not compiled. This, errors will only be caught at runtime when the statements are compiled and executed.

2
Application Events and Windows Forms

In this chapter, we will cover:

- Creating an event that can have generic values as payload
- Creating a table layout that can dynamically add or remove rows based on the size of the collection
- Creating DataGridView dynamically
- Creating a video player using DirectX and Windows forms

Introduction

The focus of this chapter will be a **Windows Forms Application** project that will include event handling and dynamically generating controls and layouts. We will start with developing events that may have custom classes as their payloads. Then we will look at how to add and remove rows from a table layout container at runtime. Next, we will develop a control that can create and host DataGridView based on the values passed to it. To achieve this we will use the custom attribute, among others. The best is saved for last: we are going to develop a video player using DirectX controls and libraries.

Application Events and Windows Forms

Creating an event that can have generic values as payload

In a **Windows Forms Application** project, you can make communication happen among forms by using events. To raise custom events, you can make use of `EventHandler` delegates with `EventArgs` as argument. However, built-in `EventArgs` does not allow you to pass data as payload. So, by default, if you want to pass data among the forms, you will have to make use of both events (to indicate that the data has changed) and properties (to access the changed data). But there is another way – to extend `EventArgs` and add the capability to accept payloads. This recipe will tell you how to do it.

During the process of implementing the custom `EventArgs` by extending `EventArgs`, one point to keep in mind is that you can make it a part of the project that requires it or you can make it a part of a different project or class library. The second option is the recommended one since the need for custom event arguments can come up at the least expected time. Also, it will make your implementation modular and reusable.

How to do it...

Since the `EventArgs` class we are going to develop will have its own namespace, we will keep the name `EventArgs`. So, without further delay, the following are the steps for developing and using it:

1. Open Visual Studio 2012 and add a project of type **Class Library**. Name it `CookBook.Recipes.Winforms.Events`.
2. Add a reference to `System.Windows.Form`.
3. Rename `Class1.cs` to `EventArgs`.
4. Change the signature of the class as shown below to indicate that it is Generic type:

   ```
   public class EventArgs<T>
   ```

5. Add the following import:

   ```
   using System.ComponentModel;
   ```

6. Derive our `EventArgs` class from `System.ComponentModel.EventArgs`:

   ```
   public class EventArgs<T>: EventArgs
   {

   }
   ```

7. Add a public property of type T and name it Data:

   ```
   public T Data {get; set;}
   ```

8. Add a constructor that accepts an argument of type T. Assign the value of the parameter to the Data property:

   ```
   public EventArgs(T value)
   {
       Data = value;
   }
   ```

   To see how our custom class will work, we will require multiple forms. Hence, the project that we are going to create will have two forms.

9. Create a project of type **Windows Forms Application** and name it CustomEventArgsApp.
10. Add a reference to the CookBook.Recipes.Winforms.Events project.
11. Add a form to the project and name it Contacts.
12. Open the Contacts form in the design mode. Design the form so that it resembles the following screenshot:

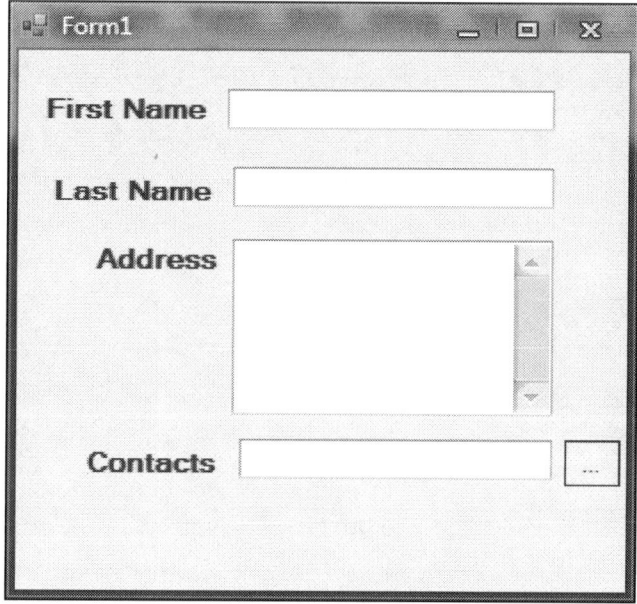

Application Events and Windows Forms

13. Name the controls as detailed in the following table:

Control	Description	Name
Textbox	To enter the first name of the contact	txtFname
Textbox	To enter the last name of the contact	txtLname
Textbox	To enter the phone number of the contact	txtPhone
Button	To raise an event indicating that the details have been filled, and to close the form	btnOK
Button	To close the form and discard entered values	btnCancel

14. Switch to the view code mode. Add the following import:

    ```
    using CookBook.Recipes.Winforms.Events;
    ```

15. Add an event to the class and name it `ContactDetailsAdded`. In code, it will be as follows:

    ```
    public event EventHandler<EventArgs<string>> ContactDetailsAdded = delegate { };
    ```

    Switch to the design view mode. Double-click on `btnOk` to add an event handler for `Click`.

16. Add the following statements to the handler:

    ```
    string data = String.Format("{0}-{1};{2}", txtLname.Text, txtFname.Text, txtPhone.Text);
    ContactDetailsAdded(this, new EventArgs<string>(data));
    this.Close();
    ```

17. Switch back to the design mode. Double-click on `btnCancel` to add an event handler for `Click`.

18. Add the code to close the form:

    ```
    this.Close();
    ```

Next, rename `Form1.cs` to `AddUserDetails.cs`. Design it so that it looks like the following screenshot:

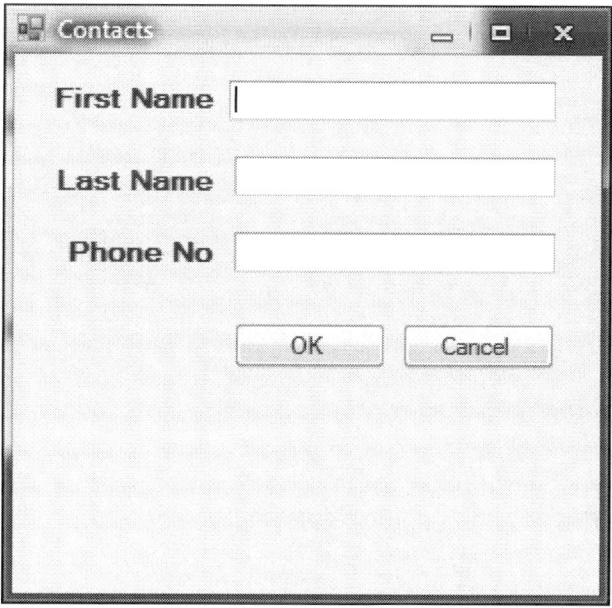

19. Name the controls as detailed in the following table:

Control	Description	Name
Textbox	To enter the user's first name	`txtFname`
Textbox	To enter the user's last name	`txtLname`
Textbox	To enter the user's address	`txtAddress`
Textbox	To hold the user's contact details	`txtContacts`
Button	To open the contacts form	`btnAdd` (Label is "...")

20. Double-click on `btnAdd` to add a handler for its `Click` event. In the handler, add the following statement:

```
var contacts = new Contacts();

contacts.ContactDetailsAdded += new
EventHandler<CookBook.Recipes.Winforms.Events.
EventArgs<string>>(contacts_ContactDetailsAdded);

contacts.Show();
```

Application Events and Windows Forms

21. In the event handler for `ContactDetailsAdded`, add the statement to append the contact details passed from the `Contact` form to the `txtContacts` textbox.

    ```
    void contacts_ContactDetailsAdded(object sender,
                        CookBook.Recipes.Winforms.Events.
    EventArgs<string>e)
    {
       txtContacts.Text += e.Data;
    }
    ```

22. Run the application. Click on the button with **...** as text to open the `Contacts` form. Enter the values for first name, last name, and phone number.

23. Click on **OK**. Observe the textbox for contacts.

Next, let us see how the application that we have developed works.

How it works...

There are two parts to our application: the library containing the custom `EventArgs` class and the **Windows Forms Application** project that makes use of it. Let us understand them one-by-one, starting with the custom `EventArgs` class.

There are three main aspects of the custom `EventArgs` class. First, it is a generic class. The following declaration of the class ensures that it can handle data of any type:

```
public class EventArgs<T>: EventArgs
{
}
```

When you add the suffix `<T>` to any class name, .NET treats it as a generic type. The second important aspect is that we have inherited it from the `EventArgs` class. Just by inheriting it from the `EventArgs` class, we have enabled it to be used with `EventHandler`.

The third one is that it will accept data as payload. To accept data, we first add a property of type `T`:

```
public T Data {get; set;}
```

`Data` is an automatic property. That means it does not require a private variable to store the values it gets and sets. It is also of type `T`. The `T` type indicates that data of any type can be assigned to it. One point to keep in mind is that the type `T` of `Data` is directly linked to the type `T` in the declaration of the class. To elaborate, you cannot assign a value of any other type except `string` to the `Data` property, if you instantiate `EventArgs` as follows:

```
EventArgs<string> e = new EventArgs<string>();
```

Now that that is out of the way, let us move on to the constructor. The constructor has only one parameter and it is of type T. We assigned the value of the parameter to the Data property:

```
public EventArgs(T value)
{
   Data = value;
}
```

We could have done without the constructor. However, without a constructor, passing the payload to the EventArgs class will take more lines of code. First we will have to instantiate EventArgs, then assign a value using the Data property. Only then can we pass the EventArgs object to the event. So it is better using the constructor. Next, let us understand how this class has been used.

In CustomEventArgsApp, it is the Contacts form that makes use of the custom EventArgs class. So let us start with the Contacts form. In the form, we have first declared our custom event and assigned an empty delegate to it:

```
public event EventHandler<EventArgs<string>> ContactDetailsAdded = delegate { };
```

The EventArgs class used in the EventHandler delegate for the ContactDetailsAdded event is our custom EventArgs class. Since the custom EventArgs class is of type Generic, we declared it to be of type string. Next, we assigned an empty delegate to it. By doing this we don't have to check whether anyone has subscribed to ContactDetailsAdded every time we want to raise it. If neither assignment nor null check is done, there is a chance of an exception being raised when the application is running.

We raised the ContactDetailsAdded event in the event handler for the Click event of btnOK. In raising it, we instantiated EventArgs and passed the string data to it. The string contained the contact details we want to pass to the AddUserDetails form:

```
string data = String.Format("{0}-{1};{2}", txtLname.Text, txtFname.Text, txtPhone.Text);
ContactDetailsAdded(this, new EventArgs<string>(data));
```

In the event handler for btnAdd, we instantiated the Contacts form and subscribed to the ContactDetailsAdded event by adding a handler to it:

```
var contacts = new Contacts();
contacts.ContactDetailsAdded += new EventHandler<CookBook.Recipes.Winforms.Events.EventArgs<string>>(contacts_ContactDetailsAdded);
```

Application Events and Windows Forms

In `contacts_ContactDetailsAdded`, we retrieved the data passed by the `Contacts` form by using the `Data` property of the custom `EventArgs`:

```
void contacts_ContactDetailsAdded(object sender, CookBook.Recipes.
Winforms.Events.EventArgs<string> e)
{
         txtContacts.Text += e.Data;
}
```

Since `EventArgs` is passed from the form that raises the event to the form that handles it, `EventArgs` is the simplest and most efficient way to carry payloads. That is what we have achieved in this recipe.

Creating a table layout that can dynamically add or remove rows based on the size of the collection

`TableLayoutPanel` is to Windows Forms as the table tag is to HTML. It is used to present elements in the UI in a tabular format. It is more flexible than other layouts as it provides good options to set up the rows and columns. For example, if one of the rows has control that needs two columns instead of one, you can use the `ColumnSpan` property to make the control span two columns. However, the ease of use exposed by the panel at design time is not evident when you try to do the same at runtime. A good example is adding rows. To add them at design time is easy. But when you want to do so at runtime, you will need to know various steps that result in adding a new row. This recipe will tell you how to wrap those steps into a helper class so that you can add or remove rows at runtime. So let us get started.

How to do it...

We will be using a **Class Library** project for the first step and a Windows Forms project for the second.

Though we are working with a UI element, the Helper will only modify the `TableLayoutPanel` element. It will not become a part of the UI. Hence, we will be implementing it as a library. The steps are as follows:

1. Launch Visual Studio 11 (2012). Create a project of type **Class Library** and name it `CookBook.Recipes.Winforms.Layouts`.
2. Add a reference to `System.Windows.Forms`.
3. Add a folder to the project and name it `Entities`.
4. To the `Entities` folder, add a C# Code file and name it `RowEnum`.

5. Open RowEnum and add the following statements:

```
public enum RowEnum
{
    Add,
    Delete
}
```

6. Add a class to the Entities folder and name it RowEntity.
7. Open the RowEntity class and add the following attributes:

Name	Type
List	ArrayList
Operation	RowEnum

After adding the properties, the class will look similar to the following code:

```
public class RowEntity
{
  public ArrayList List { get; set; }
  public RowEnum Operation { get; set; }
}
```

8. Rename Class1.cs, which was added to the project when we created the project, to DynamicTableHelper.cs. Make it public.

9. Open DynamicTableHelper and add a private variable of type TableLayoutPanel. Name it _layout:

```
private TableLayoutPanel _layout;
```

10. Add a parameterized constructor that will take TableLayoutPanel as an argument. Assign the parameter to _layout:

```
public DynamicTableHelper(TableLayoutPanel panel)
{
  _layout = panel;
}
```

11. Next, add a private method that will add rows to _layout. It takes int as its argument. Name it AddRows. Its signature will be as follows:

```
private void RemoveRows(int rowsToRemove)
{
}
```

Application Events and Windows Forms

12. Add the following statements to the `AddRows` method:

    ```
    for (int i = 0; i < rowsToAdd; i++)
    {
      _layout.RowCount++;
        RowStyle style = new RowStyle(SizeType.AutoSize,50);
        _layout.RowStyles.Add(style);
    }
    ```

13. Add another private method. It will remove rows from `_layout`. Its parameter will be of type `int`. Name it `RemoveRows`. Its signature will be as follows:

    ```
    private void RemoveRows(int rowsToRemove)
    {
    }
    ```

14. Add the following code to the `RemoveRows` method.

    ```
    for (int i = 0; i < rowsToRemove; i++)
    {
      _layout.RowCount = _layout.RowCount - 1;
      _layout.RowStyles.RemoveAt(_layout.RowStyles.Count - 1);

    }
    ```

15. Next, add a `public` method to the class. It will take `RowEntity` as its parameter and will return `TablePanelLayout`. Name it `AddOrRemoveRows`. Its signature will be as follows:

    ```
    public TableLayoutPanel AddOrRemoveRows(RowEntity entity)
    {
    }
    ```

16. Add the following statements to the `AddOrRemoveRows` method:

    ```
    int listSize = entity.List.Count;
    int rowCount = _layout.RowCount;
    if (entity.Operation == RowEnum.Add &&listSize>rowCount)
    {
            AddRow( listSize-rowCount);
      }
     else if (entity.Operation == RowEnum.Delete && listSize < rowCount)
      {
            RemoveRows(rowCount - listSize);
     }
    _layout.AutoScroll = true
    return _layout;
    ```

    We will now be creating a Windows Forms Application project to make use of the Helper.

17. Create a project of type **Windows Forms application** and name it `DynamicTableLayoutApp`.
18. Add a reference to `CookBook.Recipes.Winforms.Layouts`.
19. Rename `Form1.cs` to `TablelayoutTest.cs`.
20. Design the form so that it looks similar to the following screenshot:

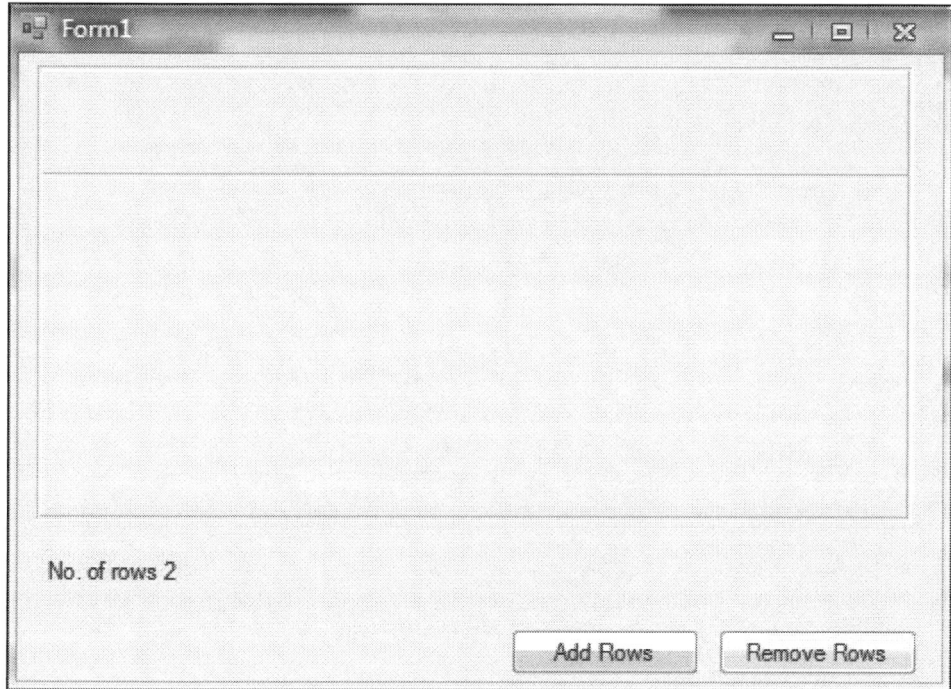

21. Name the controls of the form as detailed in the following table:

Control	Description	Name
Panel	To hold `TableLayoutPanel`	`pnlTableHolder`
Label	To display the number of rows in `TableLayoutPanel`	`lblRowCount`
Button	To add rows	`btnAdd`
Button	To remove rows	`btnRemove`

22. Switch to the view code mode. Add a private variable of type `ArrayList` and name it `_list`.

```
private ArrayList _list;
```

Application Events and Windows Forms

23. To the constructor, add the following statements after calling the `InitializeComponent` method:

    ```
    _list = new ArrayList();
    _list.Add("row 1");
    _list.Add("row 2");
    //since rows of the table are equal to the size of the list
    //we can display the row count based on list size
    lblRowCount.Text ="No. of rows "+_list.Count.ToString();
    ```

24. Switch to the design mode. Double-click on `btnAdd` to add the `Click` event handler. Add the following code to the handler:

    ```
    _list.Add("row "+_list.Count);
    RowEntity row = new RowEntity();
    row.List = _list;
    row.Operation = RowEnum.Add;
    TableLayoutPanel temp = (TableLayoutPanel)pnlTableHolder.Controls[0];
    DynamicTableHelper control = new DynamicTableHelper(temp);
    temp = control.AddOrRemoveRows(row);
    pnlTableHolder.Controls.Remove(tblMain);
    pnlTableHolder.Controls.Add(temp);
    //we will get the no. of rows directly from the table
    //to ascertain that rows have been added correctly
    lblRowCount.Text = "No. of rows " + temp.RowCount;
    ```

25. Switch to the design mode. Double-click on `btnRemove` to add the `Click` event handler. Add the following code to the handler:

    ```
    if (_list.Count>0)
    {
      _list.RemoveAt(_list.Count - 1);

      RowEntity row = new RowEntity();
      row.List = _list;
      row.Operation = RowEnum.Delete;
      TableLayoutPanel temp = (TableLayoutPanel)pnlTableHolder.Controls[0];
      DynamicTableHelper control = new DynamicTableHelper(temp);
      temp = control.AddOrRemoveRows(row);
      pnlTableHolder.Controls.Remove(tblMain);
      pnlTableHolder.Controls.Add(temp);
      //we will get the no. of rows directly from the table
      //to ascertain that rows have been added correctly
      lblRowCount.Text = "No. of rows " + temp.RowCount;
    }
    ```

Chapter 2

26. Run the application. Click on the **Add** button. Observe the rows being added. Click on the **Remove** button. Observe the rows being removed.

With that we come to the end of how to implement the Helper and use it. Next, let us see how it works.

How it works...

Before we go into the details of the code, I would like to clarify the term "helper". We implemented the logic to add or remove the rows as a helper and not a utility. Now, when we say **utility**, from the perspective of implementation, it is a collection of static methods that may be related or may not be related to each other. A utility that works with a file is the former and a utility containing commonly used methods such as conversions come is latter.

However, when you develop a helper, neither is it static nor is the functionality of the methods within it unrelated. Also, the helper itself will be geared towards providing extra functionality to a particular component such as `DataGrid` (UI) or sending e-mails (service).

With the difference between utilities and helpers clear, let us understand the code. First is the class containing the `enum` object. Its purpose is straightforward – to define the functionalities that we will be using to support the Helper. In our case there are only two, that is, add and remove. So the `enum` object also contains only two values:

```
public enum RowEnum
{
    Add,
    Delete
}
```

Next, we have the class `RowEntity` that has two attributes – one to hold an `ArrayList` object and another to hold the operation/functionality that the developer wants to use for the layout. Their names will be `List` and `Operation`, respectively, as shown in the following snippet:

```
public class RowEntity
{
    public ArrayList List { get; set; }
    public RowEnum Operation { get; set; }
}
```

Application Events and Windows Forms

We created this class instead of passing the list and the operation directly to the Helper because this helps in preventing a change in the signature of the method in the Helper. For example, if we want to add one more functionality, say custom height and weight for rows, we will not be changing the signature of the helper method. We will add it in `RowEntity` and change the logic of the helper method. We used `ArrayList` instead of generic `List<T>` because we do not know the type of object being added to the `List` attribute. `ArrayList` accepts variables of type `Object`. So we need not worry about the type.

Now, let us look at the helper class, that is, `DynamicTableHelper`. The core of the logic is in three methods – `AddOrRemoveRows`, `AddRow`, and `RemoveRow`. All three of them make use of the private variable `_layout`. It holds a reference to the instance of `TableLayoutPanel` that is being used by all three aforementioned methods. `_layout` is initialized in the parameterized constructor with the `TableLayoutPanel` instance passed by the code that will use the helper:

```
public DynamicTableHelper(TableLayoutPanel panel)
{
    _layout = panel;
}
```

Next is the `AddOrRemoveRows` method. In the method, the first thing we did was to use the instance of `RowEntity` to find the operation (add or remove), and the size of the list. It was passed as a parameter. We also assigned the current number of rows of `_layout` to the variable `rowCount`, as shown in the following statements:

```
int listSize = entity.List.Count;
int rowCount = _layout.RowCount;
```

Then we checked whether the operation is to add or remove. If it is to add, we checked if the size of the list is greater than the current row count of the table. If it is greater, we found the number of rows to be added and called the `AddRows` method with the number of rows to be added. This is what we did in the following statements:

```
int listSize = entity.List.Count;
int rowCount = _layout.RowCount;
if (entity.Operation == RowEnum.Add &&listSize>rowCount)
{
 AddRow( listSize-rowCount);
}
```

Similarly, if the operation is to remove, we checked whether the current row count is greater than the size of the list. If it is, we called the `RemoveRow` method with the number of rows to be removed, as shown in the following code snippet:

```
else if (entity.Operation == RowEnum.Delete && listSize < rowCount)
{
    RemoveRows(rowCount - listSize);
}
```

Once the operations are done, we set the `AutoScroll` value of `_layout` to true. We did this so that if the rows exceed the height of `TableLayoutPanel`, a scroll bar is displayed. After that is done we return the `_layout` value, as is evident from the following code:

```
_layout.AutoScroll = true;
return _layout;
```

To add a new row, first we have to increment the `RowCount` property. Then create a new instance of `RowStyle`. It takes two arguments depending on whether the row can grow to accommodate the size of the control within the row and the height of the row. After that, add the `RowStyle` instance to the `RowStyle` collection of `TableLayoutPanel`. Those are the steps we coded in the `AddRow` method. The additional step we did was to run the steps in a loop, as you can see in the following statements:

```
for (int i = 0; i < rowsToAdd; i++)
{
_layout.RowCount++;
RowStyle style = new RowStyle(SizeType.AutoSize,50);
_layout.RowStyles.Add(style);

}
```

To remove a row, first we have to remove the `RowStyle` instance corresponding to the row from the `RowStyle` collection. In our case it is the last row. We did all of the aforementioned steps in a loop. In code, the steps we implemented in the `RemoveRow` method are as follows:

```
for (int i = 0; i < rowsToRemove; i++)
{
 _layout.RowCount = _layout.RowCount - 1;
 _layout.RowStyles.RemoveAt(_layout.RowStyles.Count - 1);

}
```

Now let us look at how we used `DynamicTableHelper` in `DynamicTableLayoutApp` to add and remove rows based on the size of `_list`. `_list` is of type `ArrayList` initialized and populated in the constructor as shown in the following code snippet:

```
_list = new ArrayList();
_list.Add("row 1");
_list.Add("row 2");
```

Application Events and Windows Forms

We added only two items because during the designing of the form we added only two rows to `TableLayoutPanel`. The logic to add rows is implemented in the handler for `btnAdd`. In the handler, we added one more item, `_list`. So whenever the **Add** button is clicked, a new item will be added. Then we initialized `RowEntity` and set the `List` property to `_list` and the `Operation` property to `Add`, as shown in the following statements:

```
_list.Add("row "+_list.Count);
RowEntity row = new RowEntity();
row.List = _list;
row.Operation = RowEnum.Add;
```

Next, we need to get an instance of `TableLayoutPanel` whose rows we want to add. We know that it is placed inside `Panel` and it is the only item within the panel. So, `TableLayoutPanel` will be the item at index zero of the `Controls` property of `Panel`. The `Controls` property is a collection of all the controls within the `Panel` element. Once we get the instance of `TableLayoutPanel`, we instantiate `DynamicTableHelper`. The instance of `TableLayoutPanel` is passed to the constructor of `DynamicTableHelper`. Then, we call the `AddOrRemove` method of the helper. These steps are shown in the following code:

```
TableLayoutPanel temp = (TableLayoutPanel)pnlTableHolder.Controls[0];
DynamicTableHelper control = new DynamicTableHelper(temp);
temp = control.AddOrRemoveRows(row);
```

The next step is to remove the existing instance of `TableLayoutPanel` from `Panel`. This needs to be done because if we add the `TableLayoutPanel` instance returned by the Helper without removing the existing one, we will have two tables and we will not be able to see the rows being added. The last two steps are to add `temp` (which contains the `TableLayoutPanel` instance returned by the Helper) to `Panel` and set the text of `lblRowCount` to the current row count of `TableLayoutPanel`. The following statements in the process achieved what we discussed just now:

```
pnlTableHolder.Controls.Remove(tblMain);
pnlTableHolder.Controls.Add(temp);
//we will get the no. of rows directly from  the table
//to ascertain that rows have been added correctly
lblRowCount.Text = "No. of rows " + temp.RowCount;
```

The logic to remove rows is implemented in the handler for `btnRemove`. There are only two changes from the logic to add rows. First, the size of `_list` is checked. This is done so that if its size is zero then no more elements are removed from the list. Second, the `Operation` property of `RowEntity` is set to `Delete`. Those are the only changes that are evident from the following statements:

```
if (_list.Count>0)
{
  _list.RemoveAt(_list.Count - 1);
```

```
    RowEntity row = new RowEntity();
    row.List = _list;
    row.Operation = RowEnum.Delete;
    TableLayoutPanel temp = (TableLayoutPanel)pnlTableHolder.
Controls[0];
    DynamicTableHelper control = new DynamicTableHelper(temp);
    temp = control.AddOrRemoveRows(row);
    pnlTableHolder.Controls.Remove(tblMain);
    pnlTableHolder.Controls.Add(temp);
    //we will get the no. of rows directly from  the table
    //to ascertain that rows have been added correctly
    lblRowCount.Text = "No. of rows " + temp.RowCount;
}
```

With that we come to the end of this section as well as the recipe.

Creating DataGridView dynamically

`DataGridView` is a good control to display data in a tabular form. However, creating it without using the designer is difficult. In this recipe we will look at how to create `DataGridView` dynamically and assign a data source to it.

How to do it...

Implementation of `DynamicDataGrid` and its usage can be performed using the following steps:

1. Launch Visual Studio 2012. Create a project of type **Class Library** and name it `CookBook.Recipes.WindowForms.DataGrid`. Name the solution `DynamicDataGrid`.

2. Add a new folder to the project and name it `Entities`.

3. Add a new class to the `Entities` folder and name the class `DataGridEntity`.

4. Make the `DataGridEntity` class public, as shown in the following code snippet:

   ```
   public class DataGridEntity
   {
   }
   ```

5. To the class, add the following properties:

Name	Data type
Header	String
ColumnType	String
ColumnWidth	Int
DataMember	String

Once the properties are added, the class will look as shown in the following code snippet:

```
public class DataGridEntity
{
  public string Header {get; set;}
  public string ColumnType {get; set;}
  public int ColumnWidth {get; set;}
  public string DataMemeber {get; set;}
}
```

6. Next, add a control to the project and name it `DynamicDataGrid`.
7. Add `DataGridView` to the control and name it `dvgGrid`.
8. Set the `Dock` property of `dvgGrid` to `Fill`.
9. Switch to the view code mode. Add a private variable of type `List<DataGridEntity>` and name it `_details`.
10. Add another private variable of type `Object` and name it `_dataSource`.
11. Modify the constructor so that it takes two parameters, a list of `DataGridEntity` and an `Object` parameter. After the modification, the code will look as follows:

```
public DynamicDataGrid(List<DataGridEntity> details, Object dataSource)
{
   InitializeComponent();
}
```

12. Add the following code to the constructor below the call to the `InitializeComponent` method:

```
_entities = details;
_dataSource = dataSource;
```

13. Add a new `private` method of type `DataGridViewColumn` that takes a parameter of type `string` and returns `void`. Name it `GetColumn`.
    Its signature will be as follows:
    ```
    private DataGridViewColumn GetColumn(string columnType)
    {
    }
    ```

14. Add the following statements to the method:
    ```
    DataGridViewColumn temp = new DataGridViewTextBoxColumn();
    switch (columnType)
    {
     case "Text":
            temp = new DataGridViewTextBoxColumn();
            break;
     case "Combo":
            temp = new DataGridViewComboBoxColumn();
            break;
     case "Checkbox":
            temp = new DataGridViewCheckBoxColumn();
            break;
     default:
            break;
    }
    return temp;
    ```

15. Add another method of type `void` and name it `GenerateColumns`.

16. Add the following code to the method:
    ```
    private void GenerateColumns()
    {
     if (_entities != null && _entities.Count > 0)
     {
       foreach (var item in _entities)
       {
          DataGridViewColumn column = GetColumn(item.ColumnType);
          column.HeaderText = item.Header;
          column.Width = item.ColumnWidth;
          column.DataPropertyName = item.DataMemeber;
          dgvGrid.Columns.Add(column);
       }
       dgvGrid.DataSource = _dataSource;
     }
    }
    ```

17. Next, call the `GenerateColumns` method from the constructor as shown in the following highlighted code:

    ```
    public DynamicDataGrid(List<DataGridEntity> details, Object
    dataSource)
    {
      InitializeComponent();
      _entities = details;
      _dataSource = dataSource;
      GenerateColumns();
    }
    ```

With that we come to the end of the steps for creating/developing `DynamicDataGrid`. We will be using a regular Windows Forms Application project to test `DynamicDataGrid`. The following are the steps:

1. Create a new project of type **Windows Forms Application**, and name it `DynamicGridApp`.
2. Add a reference to `CookBook.Recipes.WindowForms.DataGrid`.
3. Rename `Form1.cs` to `DynamicGrid`.
4. Open the form in the design view mode. Design the form so that it matches the following screenshot:

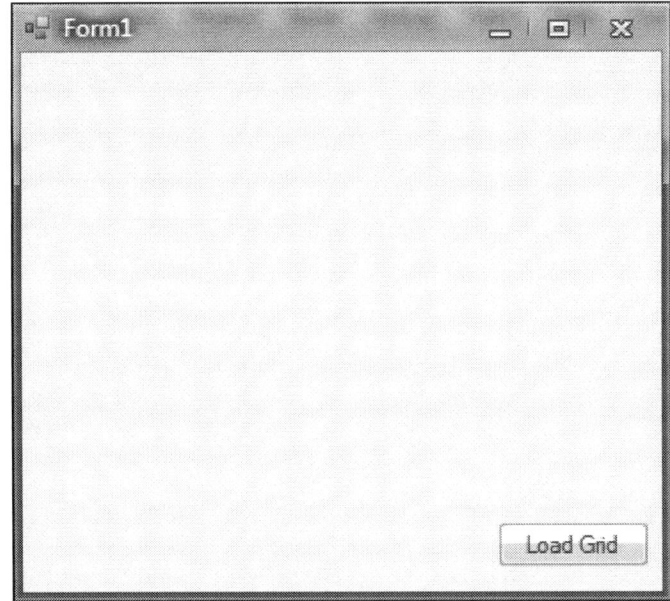

5. Name the controls as detailed in the following table:

Control	Description	Name
Panel	To hold the generated grid	`pnlGrid`
Button	To generate the grid	`btnLoad`

6. Add a new folder to the project and name it `Entities`.
7. Add a new class to the `Entities` folder and name it `User`.
8. Add the following properties to the `User` class.

Name	Data type
UserID	String
FirstName	String
LastName	String

After adding the properties, the class will look similar to the following code:

```csharp
public class User
{
    public string UserID { get; set; }
    public string FirstName { get; set; }
    public string LastName { get; set; }
}
```

9. Open the `DynamicGrid` class in the code view mode. Add a private method that takes a `Type` object and a dictionary having a `String` literal as a key and value. It will return a list of `DataGridEntity`. The signature of the method would be as follows:

```csharp
private List<DataGridEntity> GetColumnDetails(Type type,
                                Dictionary<string,string> headers)
```

10. We will use reflection to populate the list of `DataGridEntity`. Add the following code to the `GetColumnDetails` method:

```csharp
PropertyInfo[] info = type.GetProperties();
List<DataGridEntity> details = new List<DataGridEntity>();
foreach (var item in info)
{
    DataGridEntity temp = new DataGridEntity();
    temp.ColumnType = "Text";
    temp.ColumnWidth = 100;
```

Application Events and Windows Forms

```
        temp.Header = headers[item.Name];
        temp.DataMemeber = item.Name;
        details.Add(temp);
    }
    return details;
```

11. Switch to the design mode. Double-click on `btnLoad` to add the Click event handler.

12. In the event handler, add the following code:

```
List<User> users = new List<User>();
users.Add(new User() {
UserID = "1", FirstName = "John", LastName = "Wayne"
});
users.Add(new User() {
UserID = "2", FirstName = "John", LastName = "Carter"
});

Dictionary<string, string> headerMap = new Dictionary<string, string>();
headerMap.Add("UserID", "User ID");
headerMap.Add("FirstName", "First Name");
headerMap.Add("LastName", "Last Name");

if (pnlGrid.Controls.Count > 0)
{
   pnlGrid.Controls.Clear();
}
Control grid = new DynamicDataGrid(GetColumnDetails(typeof(User), headerMap), users);
grid.Dock = DockStyle.Fill;
pnlGrid.Controls.Add(grid);
```

13. Run the application. Click on the **Load Grid** button. The grid for the user list will be displayed as shown in the following screenshot:

Chapter 2

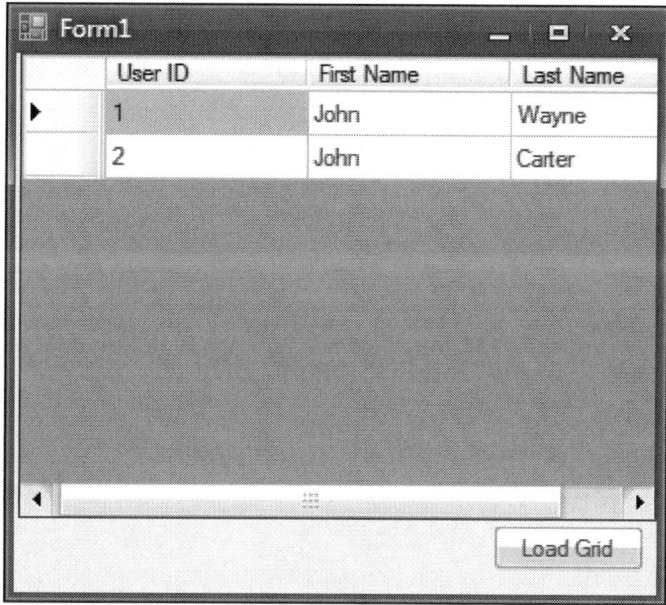

How it works...

In the last section we saw how to implement and use `DynamicDataGrid`. Now, let us understand how the code works. We will start with the implementation of `DynamicDataGrid`.

Columns are the core of `DataGridView`. To generate a `DataGridView` control at runtime, we need to know about the columns it will contain. That is where `DataGridEntity` comes into the picture. Through its properties, we can get details of the column to be generated. Each instance of the `DataGridEntity` class represents a column to be added to `DataGridView`. Each property of `DataGridEntity` tells us about the column we need to add. Let us have a look at each property of `DataGridEntity`:

- `ColumnType`: Its value tells us whether we want a column to hold a textbox, combobox, or checkbox
- `Header`: This is the header of the column
- `ColumnWidth`: This is the width of the column
- `DataMember`: This is the name of the property of the entity, which will be bound to the `DataGridView` control

Application Events and Windows Forms

We will discuss more about these properties when we will discuss populating `DataGridEntity`. We used this entity in the `GenerateColumns` method of `DynamicDataGrid` to add columns to `dgvGrid`. We first looped over the collection of `DataGridEntity` instances. After that, for each instance of `DataGridEntity`, we created an instance of `DataGridViewColumn` named `column`, so that `DynamicDataGrid` can know the type of column required for each instance of `DataGridEntity`. Then we set the properties of `temp` using the values of the current instance of `DataGridEntity`. This is shown in the following statements:

```
foreach (var item in _entities)
{
 DataGridViewColumn column = GetColumn(item.ColumnType);
 column.HeaderText = item.Header;
 column.Width = item.ColumnWidth;
 column.DataPropertyName = item.DataMemeber;
 dgvGrid.Columns.Add(column);
}
```

In the preceding code, we created a column based on the value of the `ColumnType` property of the `DataGridEntity` class. We passed the value of `ColumnType` to the `GetColumn` method. In the `GetColumn` method, we checked the value being passed and based on that created a new instance of the corresponding column. For example, if the parameter contained a value as `Text`, we created a `DataGridViewTextBoxColumn` class. That is what we have done in the following block:

```
private DataGridViewColumn GetColumn(string columnType)
{
    DataGridViewColumn temp = new DataGridViewTextBoxColumn();
    switch (columnType)
        {
          case "Text":
          temp = new DataGridViewTextBoxColumn();
          break;
          case "Combo":
          temp = new DataGridViewComboBoxColumn();
          break;
          case "Checkbox":
          temp = new DataGridViewCheckBoxColumn();
          break;
          default:
          break;
        }
            return temp;
}
```

Coming back to the `GenerateColumns` method, once we added all the required columns, we assigned `_dataSource` to the `DataSource` property of `dgvGrid`. The `_dataSource` object contained the value passed to `DynamicDataGrid` through the `dataSource` parameter of the constructor. The following highlighted code is the statement that performs the data source assignment:

```
foreach (var item in _entities)
{
  DataGridViewColumn column = GetColumn(item.ColumnType);
  column.HeaderText = item.Header;
  column.Width = item.ColumnWidth;
  column.DataPropertyName = item.DataMemeber;
  dgvGrid.Columns.Add(column);
}
dgvGrid.DataSource = _dataSource;
```

We have called the `GenerateColumns` method from the constructor so that once the constructor is called, the generation of columns takes place without further assistance from the user of `DynamicDataGrid`. That is all there is to `DynamicDataGrid`. Now let us look at how it is used, in detail.

In `DynamicGrid`, we have implemented the `Click` handler for the `Load` button. We have implemented the logic to call `DynamicDataGrid` in this method. To display the grid, we created a list of user entities and populated it with test data in the following statements:

```
List<User> users = new List<User>();
users.Add(new User() {
UserID = "1", FirstName = "John", LastName = "Wayne"
});
users.Add(new User() {
UserID = "2", FirstName = "John", LastName = "Carter"
});
```

We don't want to show the header as `UserID`. Instead, we want to display it as `User ID`. So, we have to map the property name to the display name. This mapping is being done using `Dictionary`, as shown in the following statements:

```
Dictionary<string, string> headerMap = new Dictionary<string, string>();
headerMap.Add("UserID", "User ID");
headerMap.Add("FirstName", "First Name");
headerMap.Add("LastName", "Last Name");
```

Application Events and Windows Forms

Next, we have to make sure that `pnlGrid` does not contain any previous instance of `DynamicDataGrid`. So we removed all the controls from it if we find that the size of its `Controls` collection is greater than zero, as shown in the following snippet:

```
if (pnlGrid.Controls.Count > 0)
{
  pnlGrid.Controls.Clear();
}
```

The next step is to instantiate `DynamicDataGrid` with a list of `DataGridEntity` and the data source, that is, the list of user entities. In the following statement we have done the same:

```
Control grid = new DynamicDataGrid(GetColumnDetails(typeof(User),
headerMap), users);
```

In the preceding statement, we populated the list of `DataGridEntity` using the `GetColumnDetails` method. We passed the `Type` instance corresponding to the `User` class. In `GetColumnDetails`, we retrieved the information of all the properties of the `User` class as an array of `PropertyInfo`. Each item of the `PropertyInfo` array contains details of a specific property of the `User` class. We iterated over the array and populated the collection of `DataGridEntity` using the details provided by `PropertyInfo`, as shown in the following code snippet:

```
PropertyInfo[] info = type.GetProperties();
List<DataGridEntity> details = new List<DataGridEntity>();
foreach (var item in info)
{
  DataGridEntity temp = new DataGridEntity();
  temp.ColumnType = "Text";
  temp.ColumnWidth = 100;
  temp.Header = headers[item.Name];
  temp.DataMemeber = item.Name;
  details.Add(temp);
}
```

In the preceding code, we have assigned the value of the `Header` property by using the header name mapping dictionary. In the dictionary, the name of the property was the key and the value of the header to be displayed was the value. Coming back to the event handler of the `Load` button, we assigned the grid instance to a `Control` variable named `temp`. The `Dock` style of `temp` is set to `Fill` so that it covers the entire `pnlGrid`. As shown in the following code, `temp` is then added to the `Controls` collection of `pnlGrid`:

```
grid.Dock = DockStyle.Fill;
pnlGrid.Controls.Add(grid);
```

With that we come to the end of this section as well as the recipe.

See also

See *Chapter 1, Core .NET Recipes*, for more details on using reflection, and the following section of MSDN for an overall idea about how to use reflection:

http://msdn.microsoft.com/en-us/library/ms173183%28v=vs.110%29.aspx

Creating a video player using DirectX and Windows Forms

Before **Windows Presentation Framework** (**WPF**) was introduced, if you wanted to add 3D graphics, animation, or audio/video to your application, Managed DirectX was the only option. At present, Managed DirectX has been deprecated in favor of WPF. However, if you want to embed a video in your application and do not want to use the non-trivial approach of hosting WPF, Managed DirectX is a good approach. In this recipe we will look at how to use Managed DirectX to develop a video player. So, let's get started.

 You will require the DirectX 9 SDK for this recipe.

How to do it...

The steps to implement the video player are as follows:

1. Launch Visual Studio .NET 11 and create a project of type **Windows Forms Application**. Name it `MediaPlayer`.
2. Right-click on **References** of the project. Select **Add Reference**.
3. In the dialog box, click on the **Browse** button. Navigate to `<WinDir>\Microsoft.NET\DirectX for Managed Code\`.

   `<WinDir>` is the path to the Windows folder. Select `Microsoft.DirectX.AudioVideoPlayback.dll` and click on **OK**.

4. Open `App.config` and modify the `startup` tag so that it looks like the following snippet:

   ```
   <startup useLegacyV2RuntimeActivationPolicy="true">
   <supportedRuntime version="v4.0"
                   sku=".NETFramework,Version=v4.5,Profile=Client" />
   </startup>
   ```

   We set `useLegacyV2RuntimeActivationPolicy` to `true` so that we can use Managed DirectX along with .NET Version 4.5 libraries.

Application Events and Windows Forms

5. Next, go to **Debug | Exceptions**. Uncheck **LoaderLock** under **Managed Debugging Assistant**. If it is not unchecked, Visual Studios will always report the Loader Lock exception when we try to run the application.
6. Rename `Form1.cs` to `Player.cs`.
7. Design the form so that it looks similar to the following screenshot:

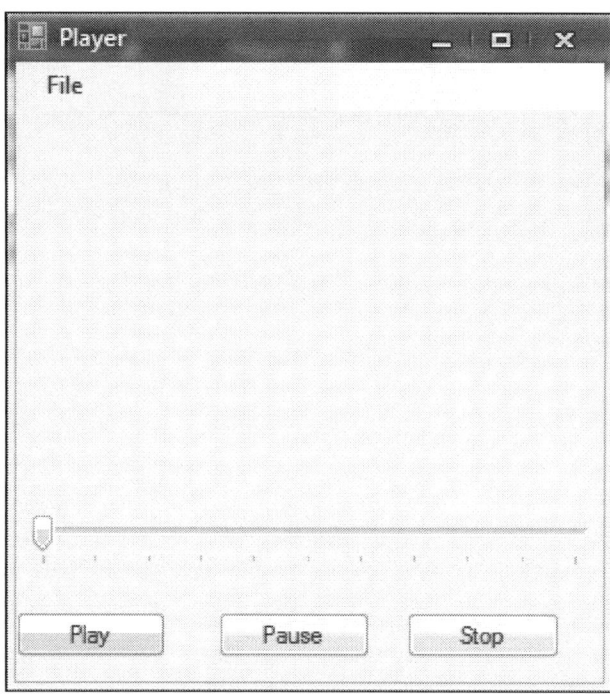

8. Name the controls as detailed in the following table:

Control	Description	Name
TabStripMenuItem	To display an open file dialog box	`tsmiOpen`
Panel	To display the video	`pnlVideo`
TrackBar	To play the video to a certain position	`tbSeek`
Button	To play the video	`btnPlay`
Button	To pause the video	`btnPause`
Button	To stop the video	`btnStop`

9. Switch to the view code mode. Add the following import:

    `using Microsoft.DirectX.AudioVideoPlayback;`

Chapter 2

10. To the Player class, add the following private variables:
    ```
    private string _fileName;
    private Video _video;
    ```

11. Switch back to the design mode. Double-click on tsmiOpen to add a Click event handler.

12. To the handler, add the following code:
    ```
    OpenFileDialog diagOpen = new OpenFileDialog();
    diagOpen.DefaultExt = "*.avi,*.wmv";
    if (diagOpen.ShowDialog() == System.Windows.Forms.DialogResult.OK)
       {
         _fileName = diagOpen.FileName;
         if (_video != null)
           {
             _video.Dispose();
           }
        _video = new Video(_fileName);

          int height = pnlVideo.Height;
          int width = pnlVideo.Width;

          _video.Owner = pnlVideo;
          pnlVideo.Width = width;
          pnlVideo.Height = height;
          _video.Play();
          _video.Pause();
    }
    ```

13. Switch to the design mode. Double-click on btnPlay to add a Click event handler.

14. To the handler, add the following code:
    ```
    if (_video != null && !_video.Playing)
     {
       _video.Play();
     }
    ```

15. Similarly, add Click event handlers for btnPause and btnStop.

16. To the event handler of btnPause, add the following code:
    ```
    if (_video != null && _video.Playing)
    {
      _video.Pause();
    }
    ```

73

Application Events and Windows Forms

17. To the event handler of `btnStop`, add the following code:

    ```
    if (_video != null && _video.Playing)
    {
        _video.Stop();
    }
    ```

18. Switch to the design mode. Add a handler for the `ValueChanged` event of `tbSeek`.

19. To the handler, add the following code:

    ```
    if (_video != null)
    {
      _video.SeekCurrentPosition((tbSeek.Value * 5000000000D),
    SeekPositionFlags.RelativePositioning);
    }
    ```

20. Run the application and test out the various controls.

With that we come to the end of how to make a video player (albeit a basic one) using Managed DirectX. Next, let us see how the player works.

How it works...

The core of the Player is the `_video` variable, which is of type `Video`. The `Video` class resides in the `Microsoft.DirectX.AudioVideoPlayback` namespace. To play a video using the `Video` class, the first step is to instantiate it by passing it the path of the video that we want to play. That is what we are doing in the `Click` handler of `tsmiOpen`.

When the user clicks the `Open` menu item, we will have to provide the user with a file open dialog so that he/she can choose the video file. To achieve the same, we created an instance of `OpenFileDialog` and assigned it to the `diagOpen` variable. Then we called the `ShowDialog` method of `diagOpen`. If the user selected a file and clicked on **OK**, the returned value of `ShowDialog` will contain `OK`. If that is the case, we get the filename and assign it to the `_fileName` variable. Those were the steps we implemented in the following code:

```
OpenFileDialog diagOpen = new OpenFileDialog();
diagOpen.DefaultExt = "*.avi,*.wmv";
if (diagOpen.ShowDialog() == System.Windows.Forms.DialogResult.OK)
{
    _fileName = diagOpen.FileName;
}
```

Once we obtain the filename, we can use it to instantiate and initialize the `Video` class. However, before doing so, we will have to check whether `_video` was initialized to some other video. If yes, we will have to dispose it so that we can use `_video` to play a new file. The code highlighted in the following statements accomplishes the same:

```
if (diagOpen.ShowDialog() == System.Windows.Forms.DialogResult.OK)
{
   _fileName = diagOpen.FileName;
   if (_video != null)
   {
      _video.Dispose();
   }
}
```

After disposing the existing `Video` instance, we created a new instance of the `Video` class by passing the file path in `_fileName` to the constructor of the `Video` class. Then we saved the current height and width of `pnlVideo`. `_video` needs a drawable surface to display the video it contains. We provided it one by assigning the `Owner` property of `Video` to `pnlVideo`.

A slight catch with the `Owner` property is that it sets the height and width of the control, in our case `pnlVideo`, to the height and width of the video file to be played. So, after assigning the `Owner` property, we have to restore the original height and width of the control, that is `pnlVideo`. Then, we play and pause the video so that the user can know that the video can be played. In the following statements we have implemented the aforementioned steps:

```
_video = new Video(_fileName);

int height = pnlVideo.Height;
int width = pnlVideo.Width;

_video.Owner = pnlVideo;
pnlVideo.Width = width;
pnlVideo.Height = height;
_video.Play();
_video.Pause();
```

Now let us see how the **Play** button works. To play a video, we can use the `Play` method of the `Video` class. However, before playing a video, it is better to check whether it is already playing. We will not call the `Play` method if the `Playing` property of `_video` is false. That is what the code in the event handler of the `Play` button did:

```
if (_video != null && !_video.Playing)
{
  _video.Play();
}
```

Application Events and Windows Forms

Similarly, for the `Pause` button we check if the video is playing. If yes, we pause it using the `Pause` method, as shown here:

```
if (_video != null && _video.Playing)
{
  _video.Pause();
}
```

In the event handler for the `Stop` button, we first checked whether the video is playing, and if it is we stopped it by calling the `Stop` method:

```
if (_video != null && _video.Playing)
{
  _video.Stop();
}
```

Last is the seek functionality. To implement the seek functionality, we have to use the `SeekToCurrentPosition` method of the `Video` class. To the method, we have to pass the amount of position to move/seek and also pass whether the seek is relative or absolute to the previous seek movement. We have tied the amount of seek to the track bar. So whenever the slider of the track bar moves, we will have to call the `SeekToCurrentPosition` method with the amount calculated based on the current value of the track bar. That is what we have done in the following statements, which are part of the `ValueChanged` event handler:

```
if (_video != null)
{
  _video.SeekCurrentPosition((tbSeek.Value * 5000000000D),
  SeekPositionFlags.RelativePositioning);
}
```

The multiplier for the seek value was arrived at using an equation related to video time and frame rate. Explaining the equation is beyond the scope of this book.

3
Threading and Parallel Programming

In this chapter, we will cover:

- Handling Producer-Consumer race condition using locking
- How to handle background threads in Windows Forms
- Points to keep in mind when threading
- Parallelizing image processing
- Chaining two parallelized bulk image processing operations

Introduction

The focus of this chapter will be on threading and parallel programming. We will start with using the `Monitor` class to implement locking in order to avoid race conditions. Race conditions are common occurrences in Producer-Consumer scenarios. This recipe will use console-based applications and not Windows Forms since we will see how to handle user/background threads along with UI threads in Windows Forms in the third recipe. Then we will move on to main points that one should keep in mind while developing threaded applications. The last two recipes will discuss the concept of parallel programming. Between them, the fifth will introduce you to the concepts of parallel programming and the sixth one will tell you how to chain operations in parallel programming. That is the agenda for this chapter. So, let's get started.

Creating a shared resource

In a multi-threaded environment, resources are shared between multiple threads. So, it is critical that such resources should be capable of handling access by multiple threads. In this recipe, we will see how to create a shared resource that provides an in-built functionality that handles access by multiple threads using lock and monitors. .NET provides an implementation of monitor for threading in the form of Monitor class. In this recipe, we will see how to use the `Monitor` class to create a `SharedBuffer` class.

How to do it...

1. Launch Visual Studio 2012. Create a new **Console Application** and name it `ProducerConsumerModel`.
2. Add a new class to the project and name it `SharedBuffer`.
3. Add a private variable of type `int` and name it `_contents`.
4. Add another private variable of type `bool` and name it `_reading`. Initialize it to `false`.
5. Add a public method that returns the `int` value and name it `Read` as shown in the following code snippet:

   ```
   public int Read()
   {
   }
   ```

6. Add the following code to the `Read` method:

   ```
   lock (this)
   {
      if (!_reading)
        {
          try
            {
              Monitor.Wait(this);
            }
          catch (SynchronizationLockException e)
            {
                Console.WriteLine(e);
            }
          catch (ThreadInterruptedException e)
            {
               Console.WriteLine(e);
            }
        }
   ```

```
                Console.WriteLine("Reading: {0}", _contents);
                _reading = false;
                Monitor.Pulse(this);
            }
        return _contents;
```

7. Add another public method of type `void` with a parameter of type `int`. Name it `Write`:

```
public void Write(int value)
{
}
```

8. Add the following code to the `Write` method:

```
lock (this)
{
   if (_reading)
     {
       try
          {
             Monitor.Wait(this);
          }
          catch (SynchronizationLockException e)
          {
             Console.WriteLine(e);
          }
          catch (ThreadInterruptedException e)
          {
             Console.WriteLine(e);
          }
     }
     _contents = value;
     Console.WriteLine("Writing: {0}", _contents);
     _reading = true;
     Monitor.Pulse(this);
}
```

9. Save the solution as `ConsumerProducerModel.sln`.

Now let's understand how it works.

Threading and Parallel Programming

How it works...

All of the action in `SharedBuffer` happens in the `Read` and `Write` methods that make use of the `lock` statement and the `Monitor` class. Before we go into details of these methods, let us have a closer look at the `lock` statement. Whenever you want to tell the framework that a specific set of statements can be treated as a critical section, you wrap those statements in a `lock` statement. One main point to remember about `lock` is that it is a convenience method for `Monitor.Enter` and `Monitor.Exit`. For example, .NET transforms the following statements:

```
lock (this)
{
//critical section statements
}
```

The transformation results in the following code that makes use of the `Monitor.Enter` and `Monitor.Exit` methods:

```
Monitor.Enter(this)
{
   // critical section statements
}
finally
{
   Monitor.Exit(this);
}
```

In short, the `lock` statement tells the framework which statements form the critical section. So, obtaining a lock means the `Monitor` class would not allow any other threads to execute statements in the critical section except `Wait`, until the current thread is done with the critical section. So, it is good practice to check for `Wait` conditions first.

Coming back to the `Read` and `Write` methods, let us start with the `Write` method. A thread that wants to write to the buffer calls the `Write` method to write into the *buffer*. Before writing into the buffer, we have to tell the framework which statements are part of the critical section. So we first used a `lock` statement. The object the `lock` statement used was the class itself, as shown in the following code snippet:

```
lock (this)
{
}
```

Next we have to be sure that any other thread is not reading from the buffer. So we check the status of _reading. If it is true, we will have to wait till all the threads are done reading from the buffer. We did that by using the Wait method of Monitor, as shown in the following code:

```
lock (this)
{
if (_reading)
{
   try
   {
     Monitor.Wait(this);
   }
   catch (SynchronizationLockException e)
   {
    Console.WriteLine(e);
   }
   catch (ThreadInterruptedException e)
   {
    Console.WriteLine(e);
   }
 }
}
```

Since we tried to obtain a lock on the class itself, we had to pass an instance of the class to the Wait method. Next, we added the statements to write to the buffer. In our case, the buffer is _contents. Then we wrote the value of the buffer to the console as shown in the following line of code:

```
_contents = value;
Console.WriteLine("Writing: {0}", _contents);
```

Once the contents are written, we set the reading to true, indicating that the thread can now start reading the value. If it is already waiting, we have to tell it to come out of the wait state. For that we used Monitor.Pulse on the instance of the class as shown in the following code snippet:

```
_reading = true;
Monitor.Pulse(this);
```

The Read method works in a similar way. First it sets up the critical section using the `lock` statement. Next, it checks whether `_reading` is false. If it is false, it waits for `Monitor.Pulse` from the Write method. Once it receives the *go ahead* signal from Monitor, it reads from `_content`, which is our buffer, and then sends its own *work done* signal using `Monitor.Pulse`. That's what we have done in the following statements:

```
lock (this)
{
 if (!_reading)
 {
   try
   {
    Monitor.Wait(this);
   }
   catch (SynchronizationLockException e)
   {
    Console.WriteLine(e);
   }
   catch (ThreadInterruptedException e)
   {
    Console.WriteLine(e);
   }
 }
   Console.WriteLine("Reading: {0}", _contents);
   _reading = false;
   Monitor.Pulse(this);
}
return _contents;
```

Handling Producer-Consumer race conditions

The Producer-Consumer problem is one of the classic thread-related problems. Simply put, it can be described as follows:

Two threads, one that writes to the shared resource (Producer) and one that reads from the shared resource (Consumer), should be synchronized so that the Consumer does not consume more than what the Producer has produced.

The approach to handling this problem involves use of semaphores or monitors. We have seen how monitors are used to create a shared resource. We will now use `SharedBuffer` created in the previous recipe to avoid a race condition in a Producer-Consumer scenario. We will also create a `Producer` class to write into it and a `Consumer` class to read from it, and use threads to run them simultaneously.

Chapter 3

How to do it...

1. Launch Visual Studios 2012. Open `ProducerConsumerModel.sln`.
2. Add a new class to the project and name it `Producer`.
3. Add a `private` variable of the type `SharedBuffer` and name it `_buffer`.
4. Add another variable of type `int` and name it `_maxCount`.
5. Next add a parameterized constructor that takes an `int` type and an instance of `SharedBuffer` as a parameter. The signature of the constructor is as shown in the following line of code:

   ```
   public Producer(SharedBuffer buffer, int count)
   ```

6. Now, add the following statements to the constructor:

   ```
   _buffer = buffer;
   _maxCount = count;
   ```

7. Next, add a method of type `void` that takes no parameter and name it `Start`. The signature will be as follows:

   ```
   public void Start()
   ```

8. Add the following code to the `Start` method:

   ```
   for (int i = 0; i < _maxCount; i++)
   {
     _buffer.Write(i);
   }
   ```

9. Add a new class and name it `Consumer`.
10. Add a `private` variable of the type `SharedBuffer` to the `Consumer` class. Name it `_buffer`.
11. Add another variable of type `int` and name it `_maxCount`.
12. Next add a parameterized constructor that takes an `int` type and an instance of `SharedBuffer` as a parameter. The signature of the constructor is as shown in the following line of code:

    ```
    public Consumer(SharedBuffer buffer, int count)
    ```

13. Add the following code to the constructor:

    ```
    _buffer = buffer;
    _maxCount = count;
    ```

14. Add a method of type `void` and name it `Start`. The signature of the method will be as follows:

    ```
    public void Start()
    ```

Threading and Parallel Programming

15. Add the following code to the `Start` method:

    ```
    int temp;
    for (int i = 0; i < _maxCount; i++)
    {
      temp = _buffer.Read();
    }
    ```

16. Open `Program.cs`. In the `Main` method, first add a variable of type `int`. Name it `result` and initialize it to zero.

17. Next, instantiate `SharedBuffer`, `Consumer`, and `Producer` classes. After the additions, the `Main` method will look like the following code:

    ```
    int result = 0;
    SharedBuffer buffer = new SharedBuffer();
    Producer producer = new Producer(buffer, 10);
    Consumer consumer = new Consumer(buffer, 10);
    ```

18. Now add two variables of type `Thread`. Name them `producerThread` and `consumerThread`.

19. Instantiate `producerThread` with the `Start` method of `Producer`.

20. Similarly, instantiate `consumerThread` with the `Start` method of `Consumer`. After the instantiation, the `Main` method will look similar to the following code. The highlighted code contains instantiation of the `Thread` variables:

    ```
    int result = 0;
    SharedBuffer buffer = new SharedBuffer();
    Producer producer = new Producer(buffer, 10);
    Consumer consumer = new Consumer(buffer, 10);

    Thread producerThread = new Thread(new ThreadStart(producer.Start));
    Thread consumerThread = new Thread(new ThreadStart(consumer.Start));
    ```

21. Now add the following code for controlling the thread:

    ```
    try
    {
      producerThread.Start();
      consumerThread.Start();

      producerThread.Join();
      consumerThread.Join();

      Console.ReadLine();
    }
    ```

```
      catch (ThreadStateException e)
      {
        Console.WriteLine(e);
        result = 1;
      }
      catch (ThreadInterruptedException e)
      {
        Console.WriteLine(e);

        result = 1;
      }
```

22. Now add the statement to return `result` back to the calling process:

    ```
    // Even though Main returns void, this provides a return code to
    // the parent process.
    Environment.ExitCode = result;
    ```

23. Run the application. The output will look similar to the following screenshot:

Threading and Parallel Programming

How it works...

Let us start with `Producer`. The `Producer` class used the `Write` method of `_buffer`, which is a variable of type `SharedBuffer`, to write to the buffer. How many values are written to the buffer is determined by the `_maxCount` variable. The instance of `SharedBuffer` and the value of `_maxCount` are passed to the class through the parameters of the constructor as shown in the following line of code:

```
public Producer(SharedBuffer buffer, int count)
{
  _buffer = buffer;
  _maxCount = count;
}
```

Then, in the `Start` method a loop is run from zero to the value in `_maxCount`, and the current value is stored in variable `i`. Within the loop, the `Write` method of `_buffer` is called with `i` to write to the shared buffer. That is what we have done in the `Start` method:

```
public void Start()
{
  for (int i = 0; i < _maxCount; i++)
  {
      _buffer.Write(i);
  }
}
```

The `Consumer` class is similar to the `Producer` class except that it uses the `Read` method of `SharedBuffer` to read from the shared buffer. Similar to the `Producer` class, `Consumer` has a `_buffer` variable to hold instance of `SharedBuffer`, and `_maxCount` to hold the maximum number of values to be read from the shared buffer. We set the values of these variables using the parameters of the constructor as shown in the following line of code:

```
public Consumer(SharedBuffer buffer, int count)
{
  _buffer = buffer;
  _maxCount = count;
}
```

In the `Start` method we used `_maxCount` and a *for* loop to read values from the shared buffer. We started from zero and continued up to `_maxCount`. For each value of `i`, the loop counter, we called the `Read` method of `_buffer`, as is evident from the following code:

```
public void Start()
{
  int temp;
  for (int i = 0; i < _maxCount; i++)
```

```
    {
        temp = _buffer.Read();
    }
}
```

The threads are created and run in the `Main` method of the `Program` class. In the `Main` method, we created instances of `SharedBuffer`, `Producer`, and `Consumer` classes. While instantiating the `Producer` and `Consumer` classes, we passed the instance of `SharedBuffer` and the maximum number of values to be written to and read from the buffer. That is what the following statements accomplished:

```
SharedBuffer buffer = new SharedBuffer();

Producer producer = new Producer(buffer, 10);

Consumer consumer = new Consumer(buffer, 10);
```

In the preceding code, we have passed the same number as the maximum number of values to be written and read. It is required because if that number is greater in `Producer`, then it will write more items to the buffer than the number of items that can be read by `Consumer`. Such a scenario is called **buffer overflow**. In the reverse case, if the maximum number of the items to be read is greater than the maximum number of items being written, `Consumer` will try to read/consume more than `Producer` can produce. Such a scenario is called **buffer underflow**.

Next, we created the instances of two `Thread` variables. To instantiate a `Thread` variable we will have to create an instance of the `ThreadStart` class. To instantiate the `ThreadStart` class, we will have to pass the name of the method we want to run in a separate thread. That's what we have done for running the `Start` method of both `Producer` and `Consumer` in the following statements:

```
Thread producerThread = new Thread(new ThreadStart(producer.Start));
Thread consumerThread = new Thread(new ThreadStart(consumer.Start));
```

Then we start the threads by calling the `Start` method of the `Thread` variables:

```
producerThread.Start();
consumerThread.Start();
```

Next we wait for the threads to complete their tasks by calling their `Join` method. The `Join` method tells the main thread (the thread on which the application is running) to wait till the thread has completed its execution. We used the following statements to tell the main thread to wait till `producerThread` and `consumerThread` have finished running.

```
producerThread.Join();
consumerThread.Join();
```

All of the preceding statements have been wrapped in a `try/catch` statement because both the `Start` method and the `Join` method can throw exceptions. In the `catch` block we have set the value of the `result` variable to 1 to indicate that the application did not run successfully. That's what we have done in these statements:

```
try
{
  producerThread.Start();
  consumerThread.Start();

  producerThread.Join();
  consumerThread.Join();

  Console.ReadLine();
}
catch (ThreadStateException e)
{
  Console.WriteLine(e);
  result = 1;
}
catch (ThreadInterruptedException e)
{
    Console.WriteLine(e);

    result = 1;
}
```

In the end we pass the value of the result to the `Exit` property of the `Environment` class so that if this application (child) is run by another application (parent), the parent application can know whether the execution of the child has been successful or not.

```
// Even though Main returns windows forms void, this provides a return code to
// the parent process.
Environment.ExitCode = result;
```

Handling background threads in Windows Forms

In Windows Forms, any thread except the UI thread is considered a background thread. If you want to perform any long operation in a separate thread, then you will have to understand how to handle the background thread. The main aspect of handling a background thread is passing data from the background thread to the UI thread. If you don't handle the data passing in the right way, the controls will not be updated with the correct values. In the worst case, your application will stop responding.

How to do it...

The following recipe will tell you how to handle the background thread in the right way:

1. Launch Visual Studios 2012. Create a new project of type **Windows Forms Application** and name it `UIThreadHandlingWinForms`.
2. Rename `Form1.cs` to `DirectoryLister.cs`.
3. Switch to the design mode. Design the form so that it looks similar to the following screenshot:

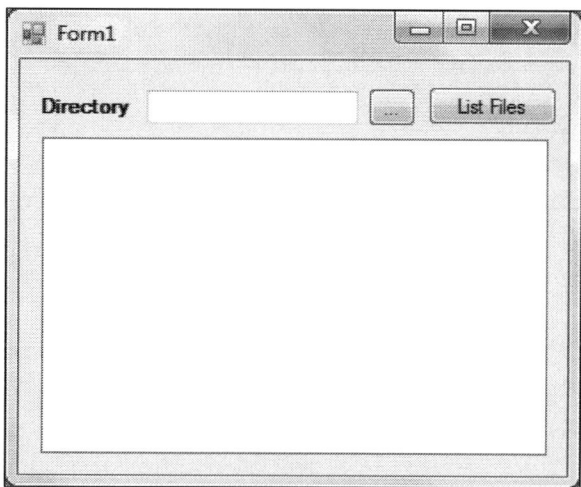

4. Name the controls as detailed in the following table:

Control	Description	Name
Textbox	To hold the path of selected folder	txtDirectory
Button	To display the dialog of the selected folder. Its text will be "..."	btnSelectDir
Button	To start listing the files in the selected directory	btnListFiles
ListBox	To display the file list	lstFiles

5. Switch to the view code mode. Add a private variable of type `Thread`. Name it `_thread` as shown in the following line of code:

```
private Thread _thread;
```

Threading and Parallel Programming

6. Declare a delegate of type `void` and taking parameter of type `string` array. Name it `FileList`. In the code it will look similar to the following statement:

    ```
    private delegate void FileList(string[] fileNames);
    ```

7. Declare a variable of type `FileList delegate` as shown in the following line of code:

    ```
    private FileList fileList;
    ```

8. Add a method of type `void` taking a string array as parameter. Name it `DisplayFiles`. Its signature will be as follows:

    ```
    private void DisplayFiles(string[] files)
    {
    }
    ```

9. Add the following statement to the `DisplayFiles` method:

    ```
    lstFiles.DataSource = files;
    ```

10. Add another method of type `void` and name it `ListFiles`. It will look as shown in the following code:

    ```
    private void ListFiles()
    {
    }
    ```

11. Add the following statements to the `ListFiles` method:

    ```
    string directoryPath = txtDirectory.Text;
    if (!String.IsNullOrEmpty(directoryPath))
    {
      string[] files;

      try
      {
        files = Directory.GetFiles(directoryPath);
      }
      catch (Exception e)
      {
        return;
      }
      IAsyncResult result = BeginInvoke(fileList, new object[] { files });
    ```

12. Switch to the design mode. Double-click on `btnSelectDir` to add the Click event handler.

13. In the event handler for `btnSelectDir`, add the following code:

    ```
    FolderBrowserDialog diagFolder = new FolderBrowserDialog();
    if (diagFolder.ShowDialog() == System.Windows.Forms.DialogResult.
    OK)
    {
     txtDirectory.Text = diagFolder.SelectedPath;
    }
    ```

14. Switch to the design mode. Double-click on `btnListFiles` to add the Click event handler.

15. In the event handler for `btnListFiles`, add the following code:

    ```
    if (!String.IsNullOrEmpty(txtDirectory.Text))
    {
    _thread = new Thread(new ThreadStart(ListFiles));
    _thread.Start();
    _thread.Join();
    }
    ```

16. In the constructor, add the following code below the call to the `IntializeComponents` method:

    ```
    fileList = new FileList(DisplayFiles);
    ```

17. Run the application. Click on the **...** button to select a folder.
18. Click on the **List Files** button. Observe the listbox.

Next, let us look at how the application works.

How it works...

Use of `delegate` forms the core of handling background threads correctly, along with passing data to the UI thread. To use `delegate`, we have to perform three steps. First, we need to declare a new delegate type. We can declare a new delegate type by providing a name, the return type, the number of parameters, and the type of each parameter. That is what we have done in the following statement by declaring a `FileList` delegate type:

```
private delegate void FileList(string[] fileNames);
```

The second step is to declare a variable of the newly declared `delegate` type. We did the same in the following statement:

```
private FileList fileList;
```

Threading and Parallel Programming

In the last step, we have to instantiate the `delegate` type by passing a method of the same signature. That is what we did in the constructor, as shown in the statement highlighted in the following code:

```
public DirectoryLister()
{
 InitializeComponent();
 fileList = new FileList(DisplayFiles);
}
```

The `DisplayFiles` method passed to the `FileList` delegate did only one thing and that was to update the UI, as shown in the following code:

```
private void DisplayFiles(string[] files)
{
   lstFiles.DataSource = files;
}
```

Next, let us look at the background thread and how it made use of `fileList`. Along with the delegate type, we had also declared a variable of type `Thread`:

```
private Thread _thread;
```

We have instantiated `_thread` in the `Click` event handler for the `List Files` button. To instantiate it, we passed a new instance of `ThreadStarter`, to which we passed the `ListFiles` method. Then we started the thread by calling the `Start` method and waited for it to complete by calling the `Join` method. That is what we achieved in the following statements:

```
_thread = new Thread(new ThreadStart(ListFiles));
_thread.Start();
_thread.Join();
```

In the preceding statements, we have passed `ListFiles` to the constructor of `ThreadStart`. The reason is that we want to run the logic implemented in the `ListFiles` method in a separate thread, which is represented by `_thread`. Now, in the `ListFiles` method we retrieved the list of files within a directory chosen by the user, as shown in the following code:

```
string directoryPath = txtDirectory.Text;
if (!String.IsNullOrEmpty(directoryPath))
{
 string[] files;
 try
```

```
{
  files = Directory.GetFiles(directoryPath);
}
catch (Exception e)
{
  return;
}
```

In the previous code, the `Directory.GetFiles` statement is surrounded with `try/catch`. The reason is that if any IO exception occurs, we don't want it to stop the execution of our application.

Next, we have to pass the list of files to the UI thread. The recommended way to do so is by using an asynchronous approach. To make use of the asynchronous communication/approach, .NET has provided us with the `BeginInvoke` method. We need to pass the `delegate` type that we want to invoke and the argument for the delegate, if any. The arguments will be passed as an array of objects. In our case, the delegate we want to invoke is `fileList` and the argument for `fileList` is `files`. That's what we have done in the following statement:

```
IAsyncResult result = BeginInvoke(fileList, new object[] { files });
```

`BeginInvoke` returns an object of type `IAsyncResult` that can later be used to determine whether the invocation has been successful or not. We have saved the result of the invocation in the result variable as previously shown. However, we are not using it. It has been shown so that you can use `IAsyncResult` if you require it in the future.

Handling threads in WPF

In the previous recipe, we looked at the best way to run operations in non-UI/background threads in Windows Forms. The concerns that we addressed for Windows Forms exist for WPF as well. You cannot access any control on the UI thread from the background thread. In such a case, how do you pass data to a UI thread? In this recipe, we are going to discuss the best approach to doing this.

Threading and Parallel Programming

How to do it...

1. Launch Visual Studio 2012. Create a project of type **WPF Application** and name it `ThreadHandlingWPF`.

2. Open `MainWindow.xml` in the design mode. Design the UI so that it looks similar to the following screenshot:

3. Name the controls as detailed in the following table:

Control	Description	Name
Textblock	To hold the path of the selected folder.	`txtDirectory`
Button	To display the select folder dialog. Its text will be "..."	`btnSelectDir`
Button	To start listing the files in the selected directory.	`btnListFiles`
ListBox	To display the file list.	`lstFiles`

4. Open `MainWindow.xaml.cs`. Create a new delegate type that accepts an array of strings as a parameter. Its return type will be `void`. Name it `ListDelegate`. In code it will look as follows:

```
private delegate void ListDelegate(string[] files);
```

5. Next create a variable of type `ListDelegate`, as shown in the following line of code:

```
private ListDelegate listFiles;
```

6. Next add two variables, one of type `string` and another of type `Thread`. They will look similar to the following statements:

   ```
   Thread _thread;
   string _path;
   ```

7. Then add a method that accepts an array of strings. Name it `DisplayFiles`. Its signature will be as follows:

   ```
   private void DisplayFiles(string[] files)
   {
   }
   ```

8. Add the following statement to the `DisplayFiles` method:

   ```
   lstFileList.ItemsSource = files;
   ```

9. Next, add another method and name it `ListFiles`. It will look similar to the following code:

   ```
   private void ListFiles()
   {
     if (!String.IsNullOrEmpty(_path))
     {
       string[] files;

       try
       {
         files = Directory.GetFiles(_path);
       }
       catch (Exception)
       {
         return;
       }
       lstFileList.Dispatcher.BeginInvoke(listFiles, new object[] { files });
     }
   }
   ```

10. In the constructor, add the following statement below the call to `InitializeComponent`:

    ```
    listFiles = new ListDelegate(DisplayFiles);
    ```

11. Open `MainWindow.xaml`. Add Click event handlers for `btnSelectDir` and `btnListFiles` by double-clicking on them.

Threading and Parallel Programming

12. In the event handler for `btnSelectDir`, add the following statements:

    ```
    FolderBrowserDialog diagFolder = new FolderBrowserDialog();
    if (diagFolder.ShowDialog() == System.Windows.Forms.DialogResult.OK)
    {
      txtPath.Text = diagFolder.SelectedPath;
      _path = txtPath.Text;
    }
    ```

13. In the event handler for `btnListFiles`, add the following statements:

    ```
    ThreadStart start = new ThreadStart(ListFiles);
    _thread = new Thread(start);
    _thread.Start();
    _thread.Join();
    ```

14. Run the application. Click on the button with **...** on it and select a folder. Click on **List Files**. Observe the listbox for the list of files from the selected folder.

Next, let us see how it works.

How it works...

The main aspect of a UI thread and a non-UI/background thread communication is passing data between them. To pass data between the threads, we have used a delegate. To use a delegate, we have to create a `delegate` type and create a variable of that type. We did that in the following statements:

```
private delegate void ListDelegate(string[] files);
private ListDelegate listFiles;
```

Then we initialized the `listFiles` delegate to the `DisplayFiles` method in the constructor, as shown by the highlighted statement in the following code:

```
public MainWindow()
{
  InitializeComponent();
  listFiles = new ListDelegate(DisplayFiles);
}
```

In the `DisplayFiles` method, we assigned the string array as `ItemSource` of `ListBox`.

```
private void DisplayFiles(string[] files)
{
 lstFileList.ItemsSource = files;
}
```

WPF is very strict regarding the ownership of controls. That's why we can't directly access `txtSelectedDir` from the background thread. Hence, we assigned its text to a string variable, as shown in the highlighted statement of the following code:

```
private void btnSelectDir_Click(object sender, RoutedEventArgs e)
{
  FolderBrowserDialog diagFolder = new FolderBrowserDialog();
  if (diagFolder.ShowDialog() == System.Windows.Forms.DialogResult.OK)
  {
    txtPath.Text = diagFolder.SelectedPath;
    _path = txtPath.Text;
  }
}
```

Next, in the event handler for `btnListFiles`, we instantiated a thread that runs the logic implemented in the `ListFiles` method, as shown in the following code:

```
private void btnListFiles_Click(object sender, RoutedEventArgs e)
{
   ThreadStart start = new ThreadStart(ListFiles);
   _thread = new Thread(start);
   _thread.Start();
   _thread.Join();
}
```

The core of the thread communication is in the `ListFiles` method, especially in the following statement:

```
lstFileList.Dispatcher.BeginInvoke(listFiles, new object[] { files });
```

Each WPF UI control has a `Dispatcher` object that can be used to pass data to the particular control. The `Dispatcher` object has a `BeginInvoke` method, which accepts the `delegate` to be called and the values to be passed to it. In the preceding statement, we passed the list to be displayed by calling `BeginInvoke` of the `Dispatcher` object of `ListBox`. The `BeginInvoke` method would call the `listFile` delegate with an array of strings as the argument. `listFile`, in turn, would call `DisplayFiles` to display the file list.

> Background/non-UI thread handling in Silverlight also makes use of the `Dispatcher` object of the UI controls to pass data from the thread to the control.

Threading and Parallel Programming

Using parallel programming to make bulk image processing faster

.NET 4.0 introduced the concept of parallel programming. In parallel programming, the concept of threading is taken to the next level. A multi-threaded application generally targets a single processor core. Parallel programming targets processors with multiple cores. What it essentially does is distribute the logic of your application across multiple cores of your processors. This distribution of logic makes use of all the available processor power to make the execution of the application faster. One of the areas where parallelization provides massive gains in execution speed is image processing. In this recipe, we will use parallel programming to make bulk image processing tasks faster. The task we will handle in this recipe is rotating all the images in a folder by 180 degrees and saving them as new images at a different location.

How to do it...

1. Launch Visual Studio 2012. Create an application of type **WPF Application** and name it `ParallelImageRotate`.

2. Open `MainWindow.xaml`. Design the UI so that it resembles the following screenshot:

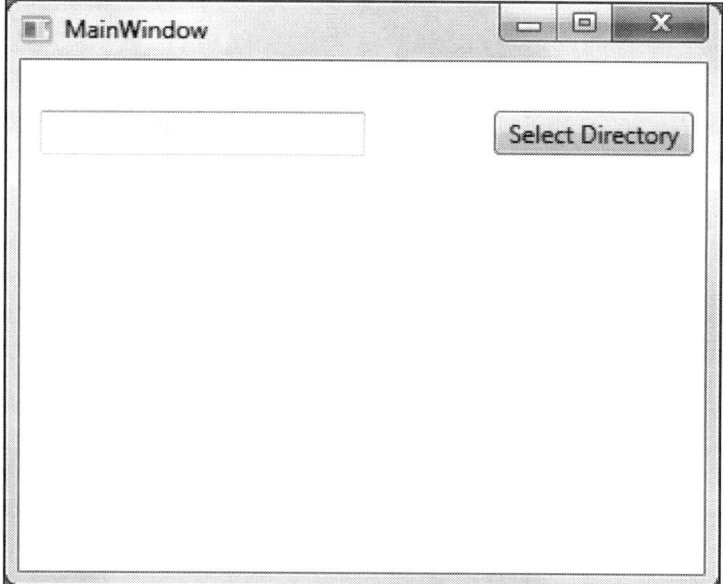

3. Name the controls as detailed in the following table:

Control	Description	Name
Textbox	To display the path of the selected directory	txtPath
Button	To display the folder selection dialog and call the function to process images in the selected folder	btnSelectedDir
Label	To display the names of images processed	lblImagesProcessed

4. Open `MainWindow.xaml.cs`. Add a method that accepts a `string` parameter. The signature will be as follows:

```
private void DoRotate(string path)
{
}
```

5. Add the following code to the `DoRotate` method:

```
string[] files = System.IO.Directory.GetFiles(path, "*.jpg");
string newDir = @"C:\Users\Public\Pictures\Sample Pictures\Modified";
System.IO.Directory.CreateDirectory(newDir);

//  Method signature: Parallel.ForEach(IEnumerable<TSource> source,
//Action<TSource> body)
Parallel.ForEach(files, currentFile =>
{
  // The more computational work you do here, the greater
  // the speedup compared to a sequential foreach loop.
  string filename = System.IO.Path.GetFileName(currentFile);
  System.Drawing.Bitmap bitmap = new System.Drawing.Bitmap(currentFile);

                 bitmap.RotateFlip(System.Drawing.RotateFlipType.Rotate180FlipNone);
   bitmap.Save(System.IO.Path.Combine(newDir, filename));
lblImagesProcessed.Dispatcher.BeginInvoke((Action)delegate() {
   lblImagesProcessed.Content += filename + Environment.NewLine;
});
  } //close lambda expression
         ); //close method invocation
```

6. Switch to `MainWindow.xaml`. Add a `Click` event handler for `btnSelectDir`. In the event handler add the following statements:

   ```
   FolderBrowserDialog diagFolder = new FolderBrowserDialog();
   if (diagFolder.ShowDialog() == System.Windows.Forms.DialogResult.OK)
   {
      DoRotate(diagFolder.SelectedPath);
   }
   ```

7. Run the application. Select a directory containing images and observe the speed with which the images are being rotated and saved.

How it works...

There are two ways to achieve parallelism: **data parallelism** and **task parallelism**. In this recipe, we have used data parallelism. In data parallelism, the collection on which the operation needs to be performed is partitioned so that multiple threads, each containing the logic of the operation, can work on different segments concurrently. In our case, the collection contains image files in a directory and the operation rotates each image and saves it at a new location. To achieve data parallelism, we need to use `Parallel.ForEach`. It takes the collection to iterate over and the action to be performed on individual items of the collection. The action parameter can be a lambda expression, which is a code block without any name.

In the following code, we have passed the list of files in the directory, selected by a user as the collection parameter. The lambda expression takes the file passed to it, rotates it, and then saves the file in a new location:

```
//  Method signature: Parallel.ForEach(IEnumerable<TSource> source,
//Action<TSource> body)
Parallel.ForEach(files, currentFile =>
{
 // The more computational work you do here, the greater
 // the speedup compared to a sequential foreach loop.
  string filename = System.IO.Path.GetFileName(currentFile);
  System.Drawing.Bitmap bitmap = new System.Drawing.Bitmap(currentFile);


bitmap.RotateFlip(System.Drawing.RotateFlipType.Rotate180FlipNone);
  bitmap.Save(System.IO.Path.Combine(newDir, filename));

lblImagesProcessed.Dispatcher.BeginInvoke((Action)delegate() {
   lblImagesProcessed.Content += filename + Environment.NewLine; });
          } //close lambda expression
              ); //close method invocation.
```

Since the parallelization works similar to threads, the rule for passing data to a UI is the same as that for threads. We have used WPF. So, to pass the name of the processed file to the label control, we have used the `Dispatcher` object of the `Label` control. By typecasting a delegate into an `Action` object, we were able to provide the logic to set content of the `Label` control inline. To know more about the `Dispatcher` object refer to the *Handling threads in WPF* recipe in this chapter.

Chaining two parallelized bulk image processing operations

In the previous recipe, we saw how to parallelize a bulk image processing operation. However, what should be done if you wanted to do another parallelized operation just after the completion of the first one in continuation? The answer is chaining of operations. .NET provides you an option to chain multiple parallelized operations so that once an operation is complete, the next can be started without waiting for input or a command. In this recipe we will chain two operations, first, rotating all the images in a directory and saving them to a new location, and second, saving the rotated images under a new name after adding transparency to them.

How to do it...

1. Launch Visual Studio 2012. Create an application of type **WPF Application** and name it `ParallelImageRotate`.
2. Open `MainWindow.xaml`. Design the UI so that it resembles the following screenshot:

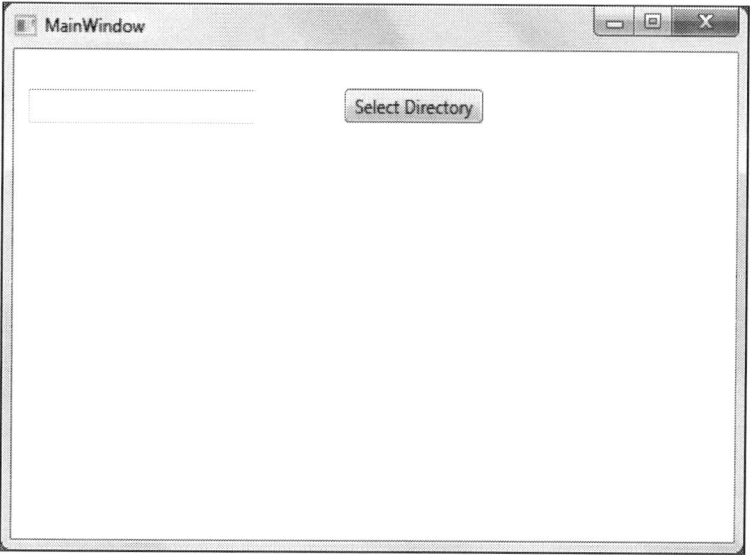

Threading and Parallel Programming

3. Name the controls as detailed in the following table:

Control	Description	Name
Textbox	To display the path of the selected directory	`txtPath`
Button	To display the folder selection dialog and call the function to process images in the selected folder	`btnSelectedDir`
Label	To display the names of images processed	`lblImagesProcessed`

4. Open `MainWindow.xaml.cs`. Add a method that accepts an array of strings containing filenames and a second string containing the path to save the files as parameters. The signature will be as follows:

   ```
   private void DoRotate(string[] files, string newDir)
   {
   }
   ```

5. Add the following code to the `DoRotate` method:

   ```
   Parallel.ForEach(files, currentFile =>
   {
     // The more computational work you do here, the greater
     // the speedup compared to a sequential foreach loop.
     string filename = System.IO.Path.GetFileName(currentFile);
     System.Drawing.Bitmap bitmap = new System.Drawing.Bitmap(currentFile);
     bitmap.RotateFlip(System.Drawing.RotateFlipType.Rotate180FlipNone);
     bitmap.Save(System.IO.Path.Combine(newDir, filename));

   } //close lambda expression
           ); //close method invocation
   ```

6. Add another method that accepts parameters similar to the `DoRotate` method and name it `MakeTransparent`. Its signature will be as follows:

   ```
   private void MakeTransparent(string[] files, string newDir)
   {
   }
   ```

7. To the `MakeTransparent` method, add the following code:

   ```
   Parallel.ForEach(files, currentFile =>
   {
     // The more computational work you do here, the greater
     // the speedup compared to a sequential foreach loop.
     string filename = System.IO.Path.GetFileName(currentFile);
   ```

Chapter 3

```
   System.Drawing.Bitmap bitmap = new System.Drawing.
Bitmap(currentFile);
   string newFile = "trans_" + filename;
   bitmap.MakeTransparent(System.Drawing.Color.Blue);
   bitmap.Save(System.IO.Path.Combine(newDir, newFile));

   lblImagesProcessed.Dispatcher.BeginInvoke((Action)delegate() {
   lblImagesProcessed.Content += filename + Environment.NewLine; });
   } //close lambda expression
             ); //close method invocation
```

8. Next, let us add a method that will set up the chaining of operations implemented in `DoRotate` and `MakeTransparent`. It will accept a `string` parameter. Its signature will be as follows:

    ```
    private void StartBulkProcessing(string path)
    {
    }
    ```

9. Add the following code to `StartBulkProcessing`:

    ```
    string[] files = System.IO.Directory.GetFiles(path, "*.jpg");
    string newDir = @"C:\Users\Public\Pictures\Sample Pictures\
    Modified";

    System.IO.Directory.CreateDirectory(newDir);
    try
    {
      var firstTask = new Task(() => DoRotate(files,newDir));
      var secondTask = firstTask.ContinueWith((t) =>
    MakeTransparent(files, newDir));
      firstTask.Start();
    }
    catch (AggregateException e)
    {
      Console.WriteLine(e.Message);
    }
    ```

10. Open `MainWindow.xaml`. Add the Click event handler for `btnSelectDir`.

11. Add the following code to the Click event handler for `btnSelectDir`:

    ```
    FolderBrowserDialog diagFolder = new FolderBrowserDialog();
    if (diagFolder.ShowDialog() == System.Windows.Forms.DialogResult.
    OK)
    {
      StartBulkProcessing(diagFolder.SelectedPath);
    }
    ```

12. Run the application. Click on the **Select Directory** button. Observe the output.

Threading and Parallel Programming

How it works...

The methods `DoRotate` and `MakeTransparent` make use of `Parallel.ForEach` to set up the parallel operations. We have seen the working of `Parallel.ForEach` in the previous recipe. The core of this recipe is in the `StartBulkProcessing` method. We set up the chaining of operations in it. First, we created an instance of `Task` by passing `DoRotate` to its constructor as anonymous `delegate`:

```
var firstTask = new Task(() => DoRotate(files,newDir));
```

Then we called `ContinueWith` on `firstTask`. The `ContinueWith` method takes instance of `Action` as its parameter. We used a lambda functionality to pass the `MakeTransparent` method as the `Action` instance to the `ContinueWith` method:

```
var secondTask = firstTask.ContinueWith((t) => MakeTransparent(files, newDir));
```

After that we called the `Start` method on `firstTask` to start it:

```
firstTask.Start();
```

Since multiple exceptions may occur during execution, we have wrapped the previously mentioned statements in a `try/catch` block:

```
try
{
 var firstTask = new.Task(() => DoRotate(files,newDir));
   var secondTask = firstTask.ContinueWith((t) =>
MakeTransparent(files, newDir));
   firstTask.Start();
 }
 catch (AggregateException e)
 {

 }
```

We used an Aggregate exception because many exceptions can be mapped to `AggregateException` and we can handle it as required.

4
ASP.NET Recipes – I

In this chapter, we will cover:

- Creating a user registration page using HTML5 controls
- Saving a draft of a user registration page using HTML5 client storage
- Binding objects to controls using strongly-typed data controls
- Implementing communication between an ASPX page and a Silverlight application

Introduction

ASP.NET is the core of web application development in .NET. In this chapter we will discuss the UI related features provided by ASP.NET 4.5 along with passing data between Silverlight and an ASPX page. The first recipe will focus on using HTML5-based input controls. Then we will look at using client storage in HTML5 to implement the **draft** functionality. A new feature of ASP.NET 4.5 is binding objects directly to controls. In the third recipe, we will focus on how to use this functionality to edit a user's details. In the last recipe the focus will be on passing a user's data between a Silverlight application and an ASPX page.

Creating a user registration page using HTML5 controls

HTML5 has introduced many new input controls. They include (but are not limited to) input controls for e-mail, date, date and time, number, phone number, and range. ASP.NET 4.5 incorporates all of the previously mentioned controls. So, if you are working with .NET 4.5, you would not have to create a separate HTML page to develop an HTML5-based page. In this recipe we will see how to develop a user registration page using HTML5-based ASP.NET controls.

How to do it...

1. Launch Visual Studio 2012.
2. Create a project of type **ASP.NET Web Forms Application** and name it `RegistrationFormHtml5`.
3. Save the solution as `RegistrationFormHtml5`.
4. Remove `Default.aspx` and `AboutUs.aspx`, as we will not be using them.
5. Add a new ASPX page and name it `Default.aspx`.
6. Open `Default.aspx` and switch to the **Source** tab.
7. Add a table to the form:

```
<form id="form1" runat="server">
  <div>
     <table style="width:59%;">
     </table>

  </div>
</form>
```

8. Next, add a row with two columns.
9. Set the text of the first column to `UserName`.
10. In the second column, add a textbox. Set its `ID` attribute to `txtUserName`. The markup for the first row will be as follows:

```
<tr>
  <td class="auto-style1">Username</td>
  <td>
    <asp:TextBox ID="txtUserName" runat="server"
                 Width="186px"></asp:TextBox>
  </td>
</tr>
```

11. Add another row for a user to enter his/her e-mail address. Set the text of the first column to e-mail.
12. Add a textbox control to the second column. Set its `ID` attribute to `txtEmail`. Set its `TextMode` attribute to `Email`. The markup will be as follows:

```
    <tr>
       <td class="auto-style1">Email</td>
       <td>
       <asp:TextBox ID="txtEmail" runat="server" TextMode="Email"
                    Width="184px"></asp:TextBox>
       </td>

</tr>
```

13. Add a row for date of birth. Set the text of the first column to `Date of Birth`.
14. Add a textbox to the second column. Set its `ID` attribute to `txtDob`. Set its `TextMode` attribute to `Date`. The markup will be as follows:

```
<tr>
    <td class="auto-style1">Date of Birth</td>
    <td>
    <asp:TextBox ID="txtDob" runat="server" TextMode="Date"
                Width="184px"></asp:TextBox>
    </td>
</tr>
```

15. Next, add a row for age. Set the text of the first column to `Age In Years`.
16. Add a textbox to the second column. Set its `ID` attribute to `txtAge`. Set its `TextMode` attribute to `Number`. The markup will be as follows:

```
<tr>
    <td class="auto-style1">Age In Years</td>
    <td>
    <asp:TextBox ID="txtAge" runat="server" TextMode="Number"
                Width="184px"></asp:TextBox>
    </td>
</tr>
```

17. Next, add a row for phone number. This row will contain a control for the user to enter a phone number. Set the text of the first column to `Phone`.
18. Add a textbox to the second column. Set its `ID` attribute to `txtPhone`. Set its `TextMode` to `Phone`. The markup will be:

```
<tr>
    <td class="auto-style1">Phone</td>
    <td>
    <asp:TextBox ID="txtPhone" runat="server" TextMode="Phone"
                Width="184px"></asp:TextBox>
    </td>
</tr>
```

19. Now add a row for blog URL. A user can enter the URL of his/her blog using the controls in this row. Set the text of the first column to `Blog address`.
20. Add a textbox to the second column. Set its `ID` attribute to `txtBlog`. Set its `TextMode` attribute to `Url`. The markup will be as follows:

```
<tr>
    <td class="auto-style1">Blog address</td>
    <td>
    <asp:TextBox ID="txtBlog" runat="server" TextMode="Url"
                Width="184px"></asp:TextBox>
    </td>
</tr>
```

ASP.NET Recipes - I

21. The last row will contain a **Submit** button. The markup for that row will be as follows:

    ```
    <tr>
      <td> </td><td><input type="submit"/></td>
    </tr>
    ```

22. Now run the application. In the **Email** field, enter `user`. Click on **Submit Query**. You will see the following message:

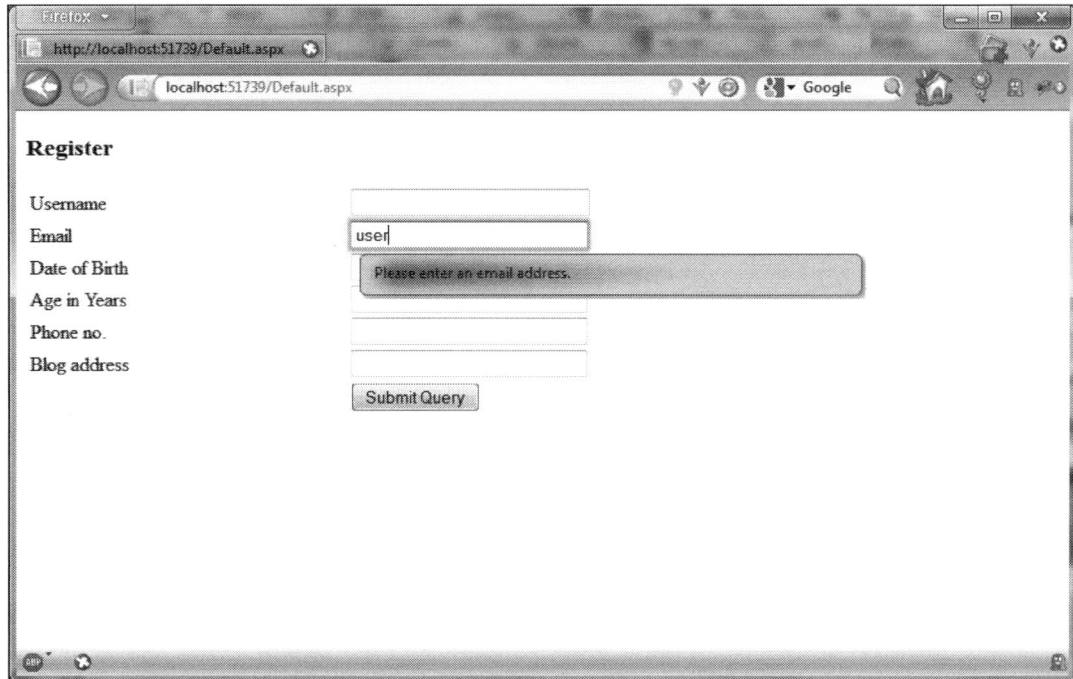

23. Try adding invalid values to the other fields and check by clicking on **Submit Query**. You will find error messages corresponding to the field's input type.

How it works...

HTML5 has introduced new input types that cover number, range, date, e-mail, and so on. ASP.NET has incorporated all of these input types into a Textbox control or a `<asp:textbox>` tag. The control has a property named `TextMode`. All the text input types have been mapped to `TextMode`. In case of the `<asp:textbox>` tag, `TextMode` is its attribute. We have used `<asp:textbox>` and its `TextMode` property to construct our registration form. The following table details the `TextMode` values we have used along with their corresponding HTML5 input types:

Chapter 4

Control ID	TextMode	What it does	HTML5 input type
txtEmail	Email	User can enter only a valid e-mail ID. If an invalid e-mail ID is entered, the user will be shown a message.	`<input type ="email"/>`
txtDob	Date	Only a valid date can be entered. If the user enters anything else, a message will be presented stating that input is invalid.	`<input type = "date"/>`
txtAge	Number	A user can enter only numbers. If anything else is entered, the user will be shown a message.	`<input type = "number"/>`
txtPhone	Phone	Only a valid phone number can be entered. If the user enters anything else, a message will be presented stating that input is invalid.	`<input type = "tel"/>`
txtBlog	Url	Only a valid URL can be entered. If the user enters anything else, a message will be presented stating that input is invalid.	`<input type = "url"/>`

The point to keep in mind is that the validations are done implicitly. You don't have to add validators to implement the functionality. It is built-in even if you are using plain HTML5 input types.

You will need an HTML5 compatible web browser to run this application. Even in a supported browser, the results may vary. Of the existing browsers, Opera supports most of the input types.

Saving a draft of a user registration page using HTML5 client storage

HTML5 has introduced the concept of client storage. A HTML5 enabled browser can save up to 10 MB of data on the client side. The data will be stored in the form of name-value pairs. This storage is accessible via JavaScript. Even though ASP.NET 4.5 does not include controls that take advantage of this functionality, we can make use of JavaScript within an ASPX page to access the local storage.

ASP.NET Recipes – I

In this recipe we will enhance the registration form by adding a *save as draft* functionality. Save as draft functionality will make use of HTML5 client storage and JavaScript to save the data entered by the user on his/her machine itself, which can be loaded later whenever required.

How to do it...

1. Launch Visual Studio 2012. Open the solution named `RegistrationFormHtml5`.
2. Open `Default.aspx`. Switch to the **Source** tab.
3. Go to the row containing the `Submit` button. Add another column next to the `Submit` button.
4. Add a Button control to the column. Set its `ID` attribute to `btnReset`. Set its `Text` to `Reset`.
5. Add an `onClick` handler to `btnReset`. The markup will be as follows:

   ```
   <td class="auto-style2">
      <asp:Button ID="btnReset" OnClick="btnReset_Click" runat="server" Text="Reset" />
   </td>
   ```

6. Open `Default.aspx.cs`. In the handler for `btnReset`, add the following code:

   ```
   txtAge.Text = string.Empty;
   txtBlog.Text = string.Empty;
   txtDob.Text = string.Empty;
   txtEmail.Text = string.Empty;
   txtPhone.Text = string.Empty;
   txtUserName.Text = string.Empty;
   ```

7. Open `Default.aspx`. Switch to the **Source** tab. Add another column next to the `Reset` button. Add an HTML button to the column. Set its `id` attribute to `draft`. Add an `onClick` handler. Let the name of the handler be `saveDraft`. The markup will be as follows:

   ```
   <td class="auto-style1">
      <button id="draft" onclick="saveDraft()">Save Draft</button>
   </td>
   ```

8. In the `<head>` section of the page, add a `<script>` section:

   ```
   <head runat="server">
     <script>
     </script>
   </head>
   ```

9. In the `<script>` section, add the following code:

   ```
   function saveDraft() {
     window.localStorage.username =
   ```

```
    document.getElementById("txtUserName").value;

  window.localStorage.email = document.getElementById("txtEmail").
value;
  window.localStorage.dob = document.getElementById("txtDob").
value;

  window.localStorage.age = document.getElementById("txtAge").
value;
  window.localStorage.phone = document.getElementById("txtPhone").
value;

  window.localStorage.blog = document.getElementById("txtBlog").
value;
}
```

10. Now, add one more column to the row containing the buttons.

11. Add an HTML button to the column. Set its `id` attribute to `load`. Add an `onClick` handler. Let the name of the handler be `loadDraft`. The markup will be as follows:

```
<td class="auto-style1">
  <button id="load" onclick="loadDraft()">Load Draft</button>
</td>
```

12. In the `<script>` section, add the following function:

```
function loadDraft() {
  document.getElementById("txtUserName").value = window.
localStorage.username;

  document.getElementById("txtEmail").value = window.localStorage.
email;

  document.getElementById("txtDob").value = window.localStorage.
dob;

  document.getElementById("txtAge").value = window.localStorage.
age;

  document.getElementById("txtPhone").value = window.localStorage.
phone;

  document.getElementById("txtBlog").value = window.localStorage.
blog;
}
```

13. Run the application.

14. Enter valid values for all the fields. Click on **Save Draft**:

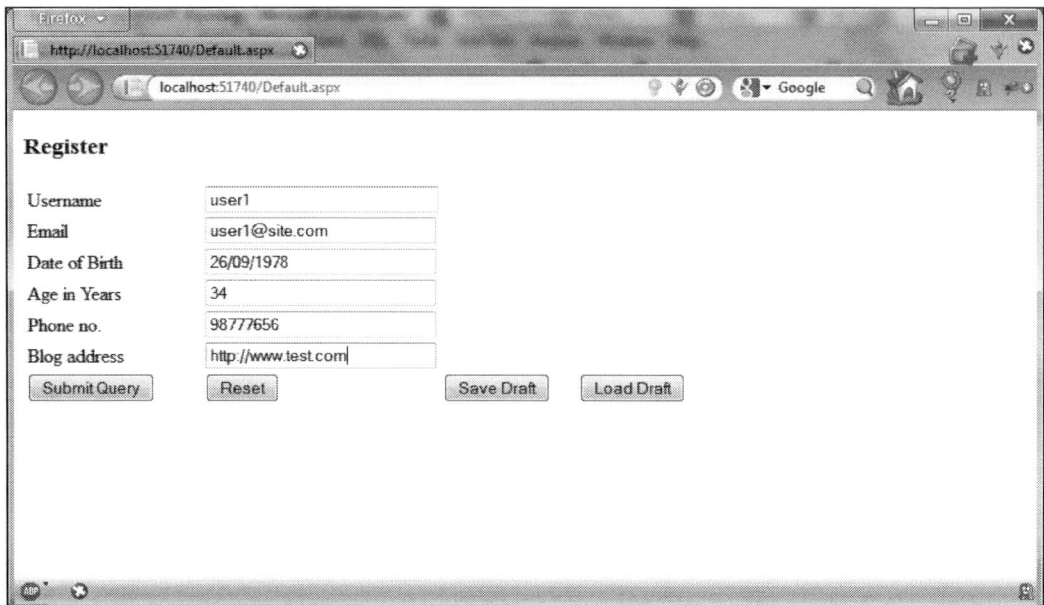

15. Next, click on **Reset**. All the values will be cleared as shown in following screenshot:

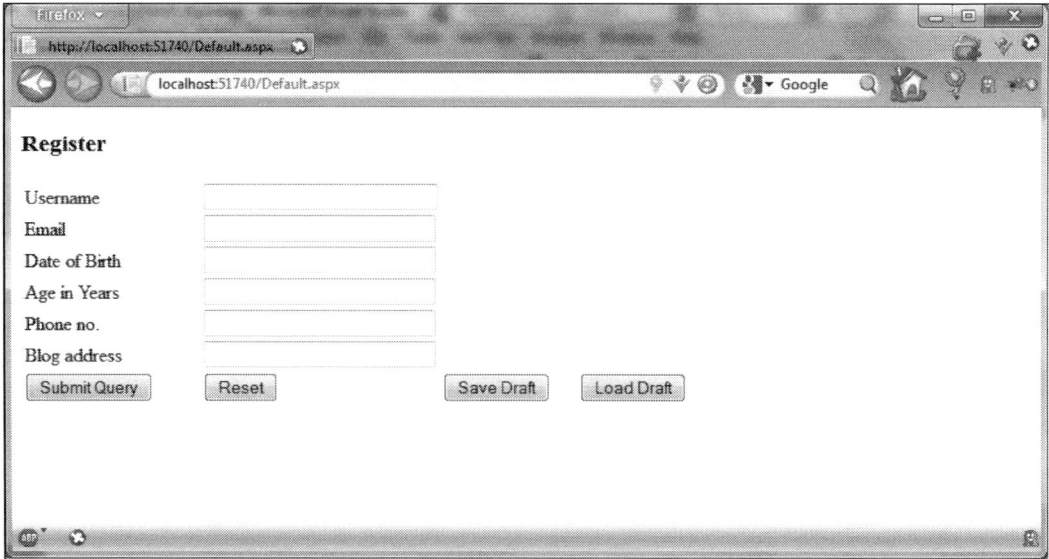

16. Click on **Load Draft**. The controls will be filled with values previously entered:

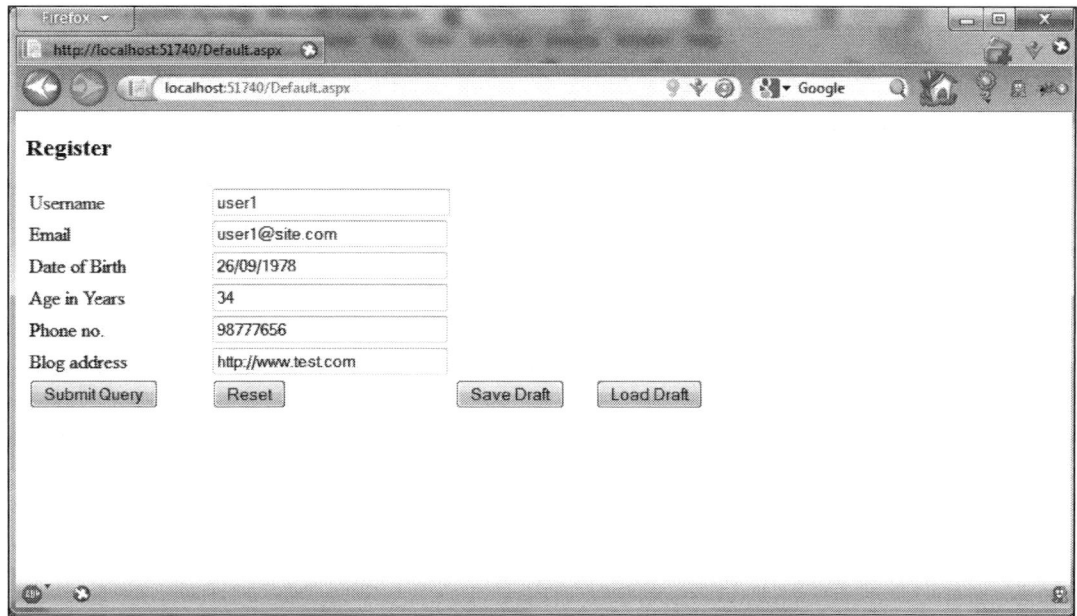

How it works...

The core of the implementation for local storage is done in two of the JavaScript functions, `saveDraft()` and `loadDraft()`. Both of them used the HTML5 related object and the DOM functionality to save to and retrieve from the local storage. Let us start with `saveDraft`.

In `saveDraft` we used the `localStorage` property of the `window` object. The `localStorage` property provided us with the `LocalStorage` object that wraps the local storage functionality provided by the browser. We can save data into the local storage as key-value pairs. In JavaScript, this can be achieved either by using the `setItem` method of the `localStorage` object, or by using key as a property of the `localStorage` object. We have used the second approach in the following code snippet:

```
window.localStorage.email = document.getElementById("txtEmail").value;
```

In the preceding statement, we used `email` as a property of `window.localStorage` and assigned the value present in the **Email** field. This is equivalent to the following code snippet:

```
window.localStorage.setItem("email", document.
getElementById("txtEmail").value);
```

In the `loadDraft` method we did the reverse of what we have done in `saveDraft`. By using key as the property of the `localStorage` object, we retrieved the corresponding value and assigned it to the required field. For example, in the following statement, we retrieve the saved value of the **Email** field and assign it back to the **Email** field:

```
document.getElementById("txtEmail").value = window.localStorage.email;
```

One point to keep in mind is that the preceding statement is equivalent to:

```
document.getElementById("txtEmail").value = window.localStorage.getItem("email");
```

Binding objects to controls using strongly-typed data controls

In the previous versions of ASP.NET, to bind a property of an object to a control we needed to use `Eval`. `Eval` makes use of reflection to check whether the property is present in the data bound to the control or not. If the property is present, the value of the property is retrieved and displayed. The main problem with `Eval` is that checking for the property name is not done at compile time.

ASP.NET 4.5 introduces strongly-typed controls. The main property of these controls is that we can declare the data type of the object that the controls are bound to. In this recipe we will use some of these strongly-typed data controls to display the data entered by the user in the registration page.

How to do it...

1. Launch Visual Studio 2012. Open the solution named `RegistrationFormHtml5`.
2. Add a folder and name it `Entities`.
3. Add a new class to the `Entities` folder and name it `User`.
4. Add properties to the class as detailed in the following table:

Property name	Data type
ID	Int
UserName	String
Email	String
Dob	DateTime
Age	Int
Phone	String
Blog	String

5. Once the properties have been added, the class will be similar to the following:
   ```
   public class User
   {
        public int ID { get; set; }
        public string UserName { get; set; }
        public string Email { get; set; }
        public DateTime Dob { get; set; }
        public int Age { get; set; }
        public string Phone { get; set; }
        public string Blog { get; set; }
   }
   ```

6. Open `Default.aspx`. Switch to the **Source** tab.
7. Go to the row containing the `Submit` button.
8. Replace the `Submit` button with a Button control.
9. Name the Button control as `btnSubmit`. Set its `Text` property to `Submit`.
10. Add the `onClick` handler to `btnSubmit`. The markup will be as follows:
    ```
    <td class="auto-style1">
    <asp:Button ID="btnSubmit" runat="server" Text="Submit"
    OnClick="btnSubmit_Click"/>
    </td>
    ```

11. Open `Default.aspx.cs`. Add the following code to the event handler for `btnSubmit`:
    ```
    User user = new User();
    user.UserName = txtUserName.Text;
    user.Age = Convert.ToInt32( txtAge.Text);
    user.Blog = txtBlog.Text;
    user.Email = txtEmail.Text;
    List<User> users = new List<Entities.User>();
    users.Add(user);
    Session.Add("users", users);
    Server.Transfer("~/Display.aspx");
    ```

12. Add a new `Web Form` and name it `Display`.
13. Open `Display.aspx`. Switch to the **Source** tab. Add the following markup to the `<div>` element within the `<form>` tag:
    ```
    <asp:FormView ID="UserDetails" ItemType="RegistrationFormHtml5.
    Entities.User"
                  runat="server" CssClass="auto-style1">
    <ItemTemplate>
        <div>
    ```

```
        <asp:Label ID="Label1" runat="server"
AssociatedControlID="UserName" CssClass="auto-style1">
        User Name:</asp:Label>
    <asp:Label ID="UserName" runat="server"
            Text='<%#BindItem.UserName %>'  />
    </div>
    <div>
        <asp:Label ID="Label4" runat="server"
AssociatedControlID="email" CssClass="auto-style1">
        Email:</asp:Label>
        <asp:Label ID="email" runat="server"
            Text='<%#BindItem.Email %>'  />
    </div>
    <div>
        <asp:Label ID="Label2" runat="server"
AssociatedControlID="age">
            Age:</asp:Label>
        <asp:Label ID="age" runat="server"
            Text='<%#BindItem.Age %>' />
    </div>
    <div>
        <asp:Label ID="Label3" runat="server"
AssociatedControlID="blog">
            Blog Address:</asp:Label>
        <asp:Label ID="blog" runat="server"
            Text='<%#BindItem.Blog %>' />
    </div>
 </ItemTemplate>
</asp:FormView>
```

14. Open `Display.aspx.cs`. In the `Page_Load` method, add the following code:

    ```
    List<RegistrationFormHtml5.Entities.User> users =
    (List<RegistrationFormHtml5.Entities.User>)Session["users"];
    UserDetails.DataSource = users;
    UserDetails.DataBind();
    ```

15. Open `Default.aspx` and run the application. In the page displayed in the browser, enter the values as shown in the following screenshot:

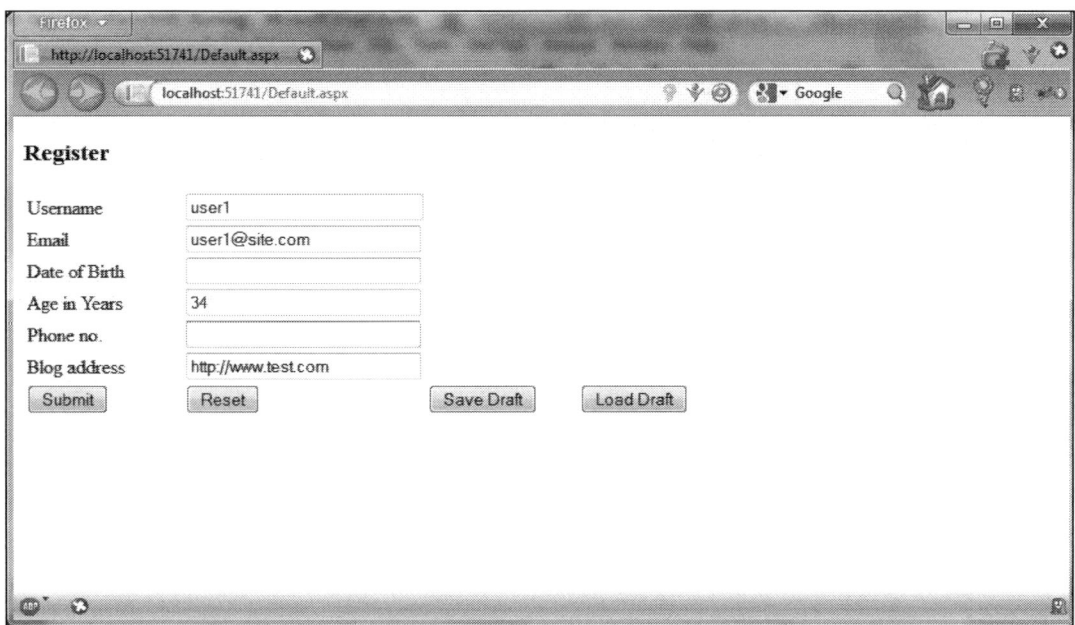

16. Click on **Submit**. You will get a page similar to the following screenshot:

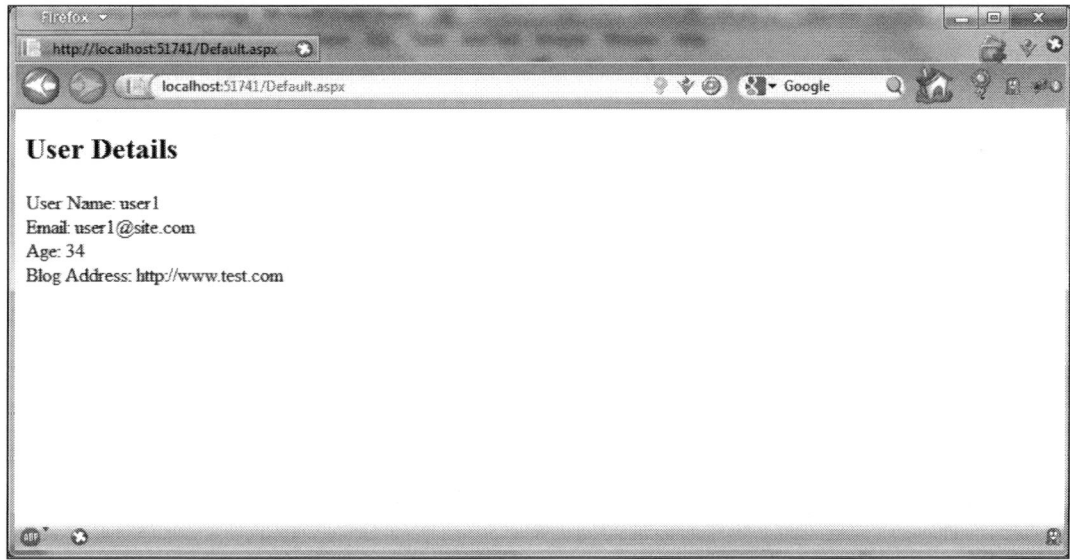

ASP.NET Recipes – I

How it works...

We have used strongly-typed data controls in `Display.aspx`. However, we populated the data for the controls in `Default.aspx`. So, let us start from there. In `Default.aspx`, we changed the HTML button to an ASP Button control. We did this so that we can create a `User` object and populate it with the values entered by the user. We populated the data and set it in the session object in the click handler of `btnSubmit` as shown in the following code:

```
User user = new User();
user.UserName = txtUserName.Text;
user.Age = Convert.ToInt32(txtAge.Text);
user.Blog = txtBlog.Text;
user.Email = txtEmail.Text;
List<User> users = new List<Entities.User>();
users.Add(user);
Session.Add("users", users);
Server.Transfer("~/Display.aspx");
```

In the preceding code, we added the instance of the `User` class to `List` because the data control in `Display.aspx` binds only to classes implementing `IEnumerable`. Once we set the instance of `List` in the session, we transfer the execution to `Display.aspx` using `Server.Transfer`.

In `Page_Load` of `Display.aspx`, we retrieved `List` from the session and bound it to the data control:

```
List<RegistrationFormHtml5.Entities.User> users =
(List<RegistrationFormHtml5.Entities.User>)Session["users"];
UserDetails.DataSource = users;
UserDetails.DataBind();
```

`UserDetails` is an instance of the `FormView` control. It is the data control that we have used to display the user data. It is a strongly-typed data control. The attribute/property that makes `FormView` a strongly-typed control is `ItemType`. We set its value to `RegistrationFormHtml5.Entities.User`, which tells the `FormView` control that its child controls will be bound to the properties of the `User` class. In the following markup we have bound the child controls of `FormView` to the properties of the `User` class:

```
<asp:FormView ID="UserDetails" ItemType="RegistrationFormHtml5.
Entities.User"
            runat="server" CssClass="auto-style1">
        <ItemTemplate>
            <div>
            <asp:Label ID="Label1" runat="server"
AssociatedControlID="UserName" CssClass="auto-style1">
                User Name:</asp:Label>
```

```
                <asp:Label ID="UserName" runat="server"
                    Text='<%#BindItem.UserName %>' />
            </div>
            <div>
                <asp:Label ID="Label4" runat="server"
    AssociatedControlID="email" CssClass="auto-style1">
                    Email:</asp:Label>
                <asp:Label ID="email" runat="server"
                    Text='<%#BindItem.Email %>' />
            </div>
            <div>
                <asp:Label ID="Label2" runat="server"
    AssociatedControlID="age">
                    Age:</asp:Label>
                <asp:Label ID="age" runat="server"
                    Text='<%#BindItem.Age %>' />
            </div>
            <div>
                <asp:Label ID="Label3" runat="server"
    AssociatedControlID="blog">
                    Blog Address:</asp:Label>
                <asp:Label ID="blog" runat="server"
                    Text='<%#BindItem.Blog %>' />
            </div>
        </ItemTemplate>
    </asp:FormView>
```

In the preceding markup, `Label` with `ID` set to `UserName` is bound to the `UserName` property of the `User` class. Since we set `ItemType` to the `User` class, we can access the properties of the `User` class in the `FormView` control's child controls using `BindItem`. In short, to use strongly-typed data controls, we need to use `ItemType` and `BindItem` together.

Implementing communication between an ASPX page and a Silverlight application

Silverlight applications are hosted in the ASPX pages through the Silverlight plugin. The plugin is embedded using the `<object>` tag, due to which we can pass data between an ASPX page and the application using JavaScript. To make Silverlight applications JavaScript-aware, some extra steps are required at the development stage. In this recipe we will see what those steps are, and how to enable ASPX pages to communicate with Silverlight using those steps.

How to do it...

1. Launch Visual Studio 2012. Create an application of type **Silverlight Application** and name it `SLAspxCommunication`.

2. Open `MainPage.xaml`. Add a `DataGrid` control to the `Grid` control. Name it `dgUsers`. The markup will be as follows:

   ```
   <Grid x:Name="LayoutRoot" Background="White">
   <sdk:DataGrid x:Name="dgUsers" HorizontalAlignment="Left"
   Height="100" Margin="10,50,0,0" VerticalAlignment="Top"
   Width="380"/>
   </Grid>
   ```

3. Next, add a folder to `SLAspxCommunication`. Name it `Entities`.

4. Add a class to the `Entities` folder and name it `User`.

5. Add properties to the `User` class as detailed in the following table:

Property name	Data type
ID	Int
UserName	String
Email	String
Dob	DateTime
Age	Int
Phone	String
Blog	String

6. Once the properties are added, the class will be as follows:

   ```
   public class User
   {
       public int ID { get; set; }
       public string UserName { get; set; }
       public string Email { get; set; }
       public DateTime Dob { get; set; }
       public int Age { get; set; }
       public string Phone { get; set; }
       public string Blog { get; set; }
   }
   ```

7. Next, open `MainPage.xaml.cs`. Add a private instance variable of type `ObservableCollection<User>`. Name it `_users`:

   ```
   private ObservableCollection<User> _users;
   ```

8. Add another private instance variable of type string and name it _userName:

    ```
    private string _userName;
    ```

9. Add a method that returns ObservableCollection<User>. Name it GenerateList. Its signature will be as follows:

    ```
    private ObservableCollection<User> GenerateList()
    {
    }
    ```

10. Add the following code to GenerateList:

    ```
    _users = new ObservableCollection<User>();
    _users.Add(new User()
      {
        UserName = "User1",
        Age = 19,
        Email = "user1@user.com"
      });
     _users.Add(new User()
      {
        UserName = "User2",
        Age = 19,
        Email = "user2@user.com"
      });

     _users.Add(new User()
      {
        UserName = "User3",
        Age = 19,
        Email = "user3@user.com"
      });
     _users.Add(new User()
      {
        UserName = "User4",
        Age = 19,
        Email = "user4@user.com"
      });
    return _users;
    ```

11. Add the following statement in the constructor, below the call to InitializeComponent:

    ```
    _users = GenerateList();
    ```

12. Next, add the following statement in the constructor, below the call to `GenerateList`:

    ```
    HtmlPage.RegisterScriptableObject("Page", this);
    ```

13. After adding the statements, the constructor will be as follows:

    ```
    public MainPage()
    {
     InitializeComponent();
     _users = GenerateList();
     HtmlPage.RegisterScriptableObject("Page", this);
    }
    ```

14. Add a method that returns `ObservableCollection<User>`. Name it `SearchUserName`. The signature will be as follows:

    ```
    private ObservableCollection<User> SearchUserName()
    {
    }
    ```

15. Add the following code in `SearchUserName`:

    ```
    User user = _users.First<User>(e => e.UserName == _userName);
    ObservableCollection<User> temp = new ObservableCollection<User>();
    temp.Add(user);
    return temp;
    ```

16. Add another method of type `void` and with `string` as parameter. Name it `SetUser`. The signature will be as follows:

    ```
    public void SetUser(string user)
    {
    }
    ```

17. Add the following statements to the `SetUser` method:

    ```
    _userName = user;
    try
    {
     dgUsers.ItemsSource = SearchUserName();
     HtmlPage.Window.Invoke("setResult", "User found");
    }
    catch (Exception)
    {
     HtmlPage.Window.Invoke("setResult", "User not found");
    }
    ```

18. Decorate `SetUser` with the `ScriptableMember` attribute. After it is done, the method will be displayed as given in the following code block:

    ```
    [ScriptableMember]
    public void SetUser(string user)
    {
      _userName = user;
      try
      {
        dgUsers.ItemsSource = SearchUserName();
        HtmlPage.Window.Invoke("setResult", "User found");
      }
      catch (Exception)
      {
        HtmlPage.Window.Invoke("setResult", "User not found");
      }
    }
    ```

19. Open `SLAspxCommunicationTestPage.aspx`, which is present in the `SLAspxCommunication.Web` project.

20. Remove the `<form>` tag.

21. Add a `<div>` tag after the `<body>` tag. Within the `<div>` tag add the text `User name to search`.

22. Next, place an `<input>` tag after the text. Set its `ID` attribute to `txtUser`.

23. Now, add a `<button>` tag. Set its `ID` attribute to `search`. Add an `onclick` handler. Name it `search`. The markup will be as follows:

    ```
    <div>
      User Name to search:
      <input id="txtUser" /> <button id="search"
    onclick="search()">Search</button>
    </div>
    ```

24. Add a `<br/>` tag after the `<div>` tag.

25. Add another `<div>` tag. Set its `ID` attribute to `result`.

26. Next, add a `<script>` tag to the `<head>` tag. Add a function to the `<script>` tag. Name it `search`. The markup will be as follows:

    ```
    <script type="text/javascript">
      function search() {

      }
    </script>
    ```

ASP.NET Recipes – I

27. Add the following code to the `search` function:

    ```
    try {
         var control = document.getElementById("silverlightControl");
    control.Content.Page.SetUser(document.getElementById("txtUser").
    value);
         } catch (e) {
            alert(e.description);
       }
    ```

28. Add another JavaScript method. Name it `setResult`. It will be accepting an argument. The method will be as follows:

    ```
    function setResult(result) {
       document.getElementById("result").innerHTML = "<b>" + result +
    "</b>";
    }
    ```

29. Run the application. The web page will be similar to the following screenshot:

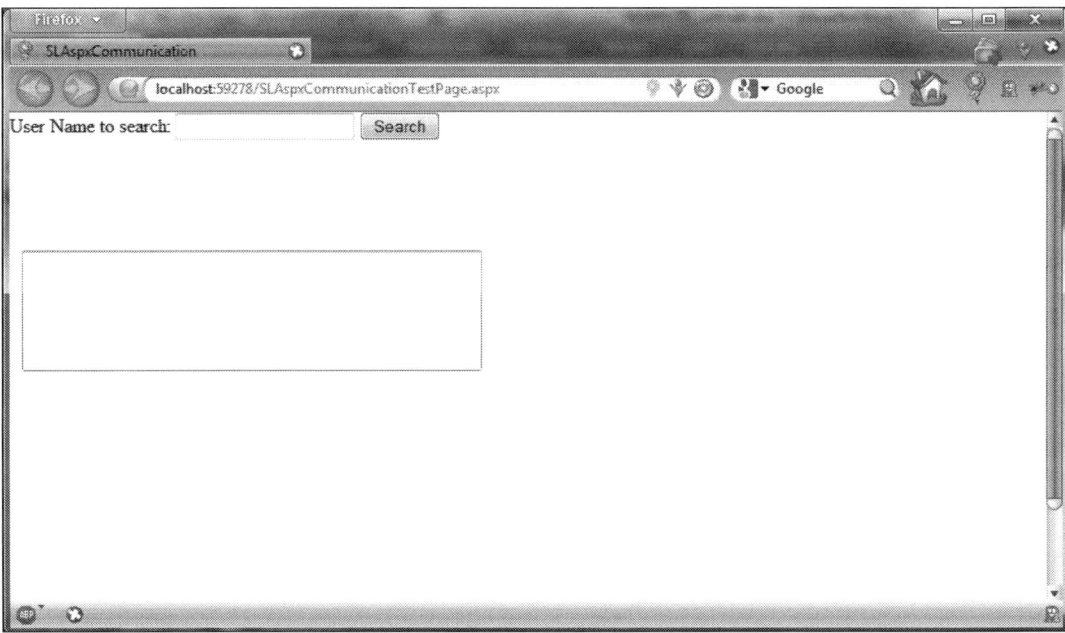

30. Enter an invalid username. The web page will show a message similar to the one displayed in the following screenshot:

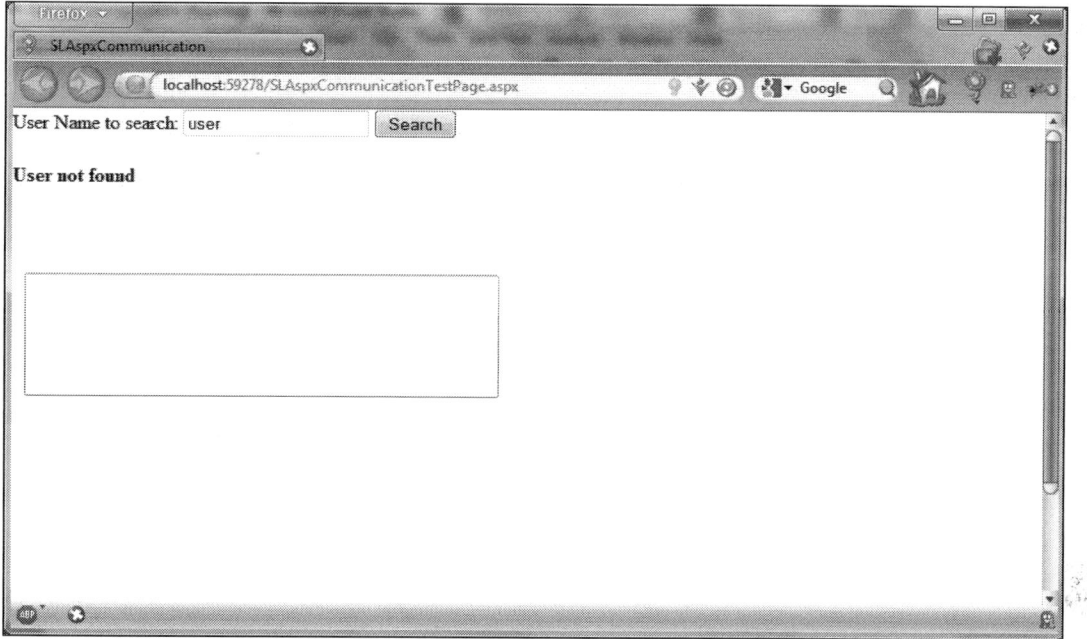

31. Enter a valid username. The web page will be similar to the following screenshot:

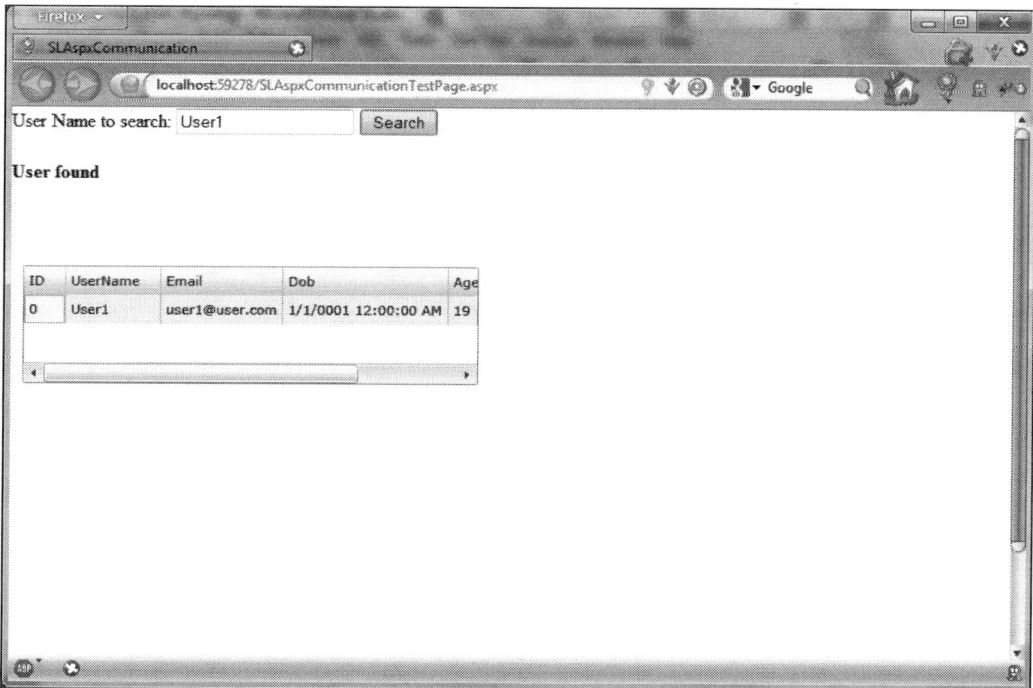

How it works...

To make the `MainPage.xaml` file interact with JavaScript, we carried out two main tasks. First, we registered our page as a scriptable object in the constructor using the following statement:

```
HtmlPage.RegisterScriptableObject("Page", this);
```

The `RegisterScriptableObject` method of `HtmlPage` registers the `MainPage` class with the script manager as an object that can interact with a client-side script (JavaScript, JScript, and so on). Next, we made `SetUser` a method of the class that can be called from the client-side script. We did it by decorating it with the `ScriptableMember` attribute as shown in the following code snippet:

```
[ScriptableMember]
public void SetUser(string user)
{
  _userName = user;
  try
  {
    dgUsers.ItemsSource = SearchUserName();
    HtmlPage.Window.Invoke("setResult", "User found");
  }
  catch (Exception)
  {
    HtmlPage.Window.Invoke("setResult", "User not found");
  }
}
```

To send the value back to the ASPX page, we can use the `Invoke` method of the `Window` object, which we can get from the `HtmlPage` class. The `Invoke` method accepts two arguments – the client-side script function to be invoked and the data to be passed to the function. In our case, the function is `saveResult` and data is either `User found` or `User not found`. We have used it as shown in the following highlighted code:

```
[ScriptableMember]
public void SetUser(string user)
{
  _userName = user;
  try
  {
    dgUsers.ItemsSource = SearchUserName();
    HtmlPage.Window.Invoke("setResult", "User found");
  }
```

```
    catch (Exception)
    {
      HtmlPage.Window.Invoke("setResult", "User not found");
    }
}
```

In the ASPX page, we implemented two JavaScript functions – `setResult` and `setUser`. The `setResult` function is used by the Silverlight page to send data back to the ASPX page. We used the `setUser` function to pass the username to the Silverlight page by calling the `SetUser` method of the page as shown in the following code:

```
var control = document.getElementById("silverlightControl");
control.Content.Page.SetUser(document.getElementById("txtUser").
value);
```

First, we got the handle to the Silverlight container. Then we called the `SetUser` method on the `Page` object of the `Content` object. The `Content` object is a property of the Silverlight container. We had registered `MainPage` as `HtmlPage.RegisterScriptableObject` in the constructor of `MainPage`. That's why the following statement works:

```
control.Content.Page.SetUser(document.getElementById("txtUser").
value);
```

5
ADO.NET Recipes

In this chapter we will cover:

- Saving large files (BLOB) in MS SQL Server using ADO.NET
- Retrieving large files (BLOB) from MS SQL Server using ADO.NET
- Using transactions to maintain database consistency when saving multiple files
- Using DataSet to modify custom XML configuration files

Introduction

This chapter will focus on recipes that deal with ADO.NET, which is the basis for all database-based operations in .NET. We will start with saving files of large size in SQL Server. The next recipe will tell you how to retrieve the saved file. The third recipe will focus on implementing transactions. The last recipe will be about using `DataSet` to operate upon XML data.

Please keep in mind that the recipes in this chapter use MS SQL Server 2012.

Saving large files (BLOB) in MS SQL Server using ADO.NET

SQL Server allows you to save data in binary format. By making use of this feature, we can save files of large size (more than 2 GB). Data having a large size are known as **Binary Large Objects** or **BLOB**. This recipe will detail the steps to use this feature in a .NET application. The saving of files at database level will be handled through a stored procedure. The application will pass the required data to the stored procedure and execute it.

ADO.NET Recipes

We will be using image files for this recipe. Neither the application nor the stored procedure will check for uniqueness of the name of the file being saved. Checking for the uniqueness of the uploaded file is beyond the scope of this recipe.

How to do it...

The following steps will help you to save large files in SQL Server:

1. Launch SQL Server Management Studio 2012.
2. Add a new database and name it CookBook.
3. Add a new table to the CookBook database and name it tb_FileStorage.
4. Add columns to the tb_FileStorage table as detailed in the following table:

Name	Data type	Is Identity column
ID	Tinyint	Yes
File_name	Varchar	No
File_content	Varbinary	No

5. Next, add a stored procedure that will save the file to tb_FileStorage and name it SaveFile. The procedure will be as follows:

```sql
USE [CookBook]
GO

SET ANSI_NULLS ON
GO

SET QUOTED_IDENTIFIER ON
GO

CREATE PROCEDURE [dbo].[SaveFile]
    @vFileName varchar(50),
    @vFile varbinary(MAX)
AS
BEGIN
    -- SET NOCOUNT ON added to prevent extra result sets from
    -- interfering with SELECT statements.
    SET NOCOUNT ON;

    INSERT INTO [dbo].[tb_FileStorage]
            ([File_name]
            ,[File_content])
        VALUES
```

```
    (@vFileName,
    @vFile)



END

GO
```

6. Press *F5* to execute the procedure.
7. Launch Visual Studio 2012. Create an application of type **Windows Forms Application** and name it `SaveRetrieveFile`.
8. Save the solution as `SaveRetrieveFile.sln`.
9. Add reference to `Microsoft.SqlServer.ConnectionInfo.dll`.
10. Rename `Form1.cs` to `SaveRetrieveFileDB`.
11. Open `SaveRetrieveFileDB` in the design mode. Design the form so that it looks similar to the following screenshot:

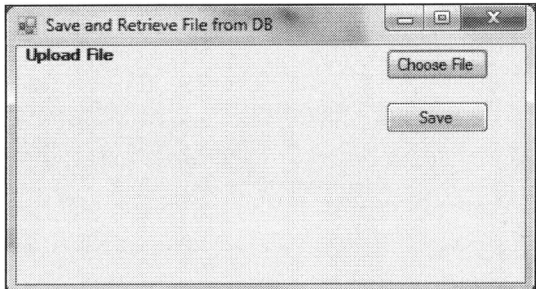

12. Name the controls as detailed in the following table:

Control	Name	Description
Label	lblFile	To hold and display the path of the selected file
Button	btnChoose	To display the file open dialog to the user
Button	btnSave	To save the file in the table

13. Switch to the view source mode. Add a method that accepts `string` as a parameter and returns an array of `byte`. Name it `ReadFile`. The signature will be as follows:

```
private byte[] ReadFile(string path)
{

}
```

ADO.NET Recipes

14. Add the following code to the `ReadFile` method:

    ```
    byte[] data = null;

    FileInfo info = new FileInfo(path);
    long numBytes = info.Length;

    FileStream stream = new FileStream(path, FileMode.Open,
    FileAccess.Read);

    BinaryReader reader = new BinaryReader(stream);
    data = reader.ReadBytes((int)numBytes);
    return data;
    ```

15. Switch to the design mode. Double-click on `btnChoose` to add a `Click` event handler.

16. In the `Click` event handler of `btnChoose`, add the following statements:

    ```
    OpenFileDialog diagFile = new OpenFileDialog();
    if (diagFile.ShowDialog() == DialogResult.OK)
    {
       lblFile.Text = diagFile.FileName;
    }
    ```

17. Switch to the design mode. Double-click on `btnSave` to add a Click event handler.

18. In the Click event handler of `btnSave`, add the following statements:

    ```
    try
    {
        byte[] imageData = ReadFile(lblFile.Text);

        SqlConnection connection = new SqlConnection(ConfigurationManager.
    ConnectionStrings["local"].ConnectionString);
        SqlCommand command = new SqlCommand();
        command.Connection = connection;
        command.CommandType = CommandType.StoredProcedure;
        command.CommandText = "SaveFile";

        command.Parameters.Add(new SqlParameter("@vFileName",
        (object)Path.GetFileNameWithoutExtension(lblFile.Text)));

        command.Parameters.Add(new SqlParameter("@vFile",
        (object)imageData));

        //Open connection and execute insert query.
        connection.Open();
    ```

Chapter 5

```
    command.ExecuteNonQuery();
    }
   catch (Exception)
   {
    MessageBox.Show("Could not save file", "Database Error",
   MessageBoxButtons.OK, MessageBoxIcon.Error);
   }finally{
   connection.Close();
   }
```

19. Open `app.config`. Add connection string for your MS SQL Server. It will be similar to the following entry:

    ```
    <connectionStrings>
        <add connectionString="Data Source=APRAJSHEKHAR-HP;Initial
    Catalog=CookBook;Integrated Security=True" name="local"/>
    </connectionStrings>
    ```

20. Run the application.

21. Choose a high quality image and click on **Save**:

How it works...

The core of the recipe lies in the `btnSave_Click` and `ReadFile` methods. Let us start with `ReadFile`. The table saves the file as binary data. In .NET, binary data is generally represented using the `byte` array. So before sending image files to the database, we have to convert it to a `byte` array. That is what we did in the following statements of the `ReadFile` method:

```
FileStream stream = new FileStream(path, FileMode.Open,
        FileAccess.Read);

BinaryReader reader = new BinaryReader(stream);
data = reader.ReadBytes((int)numBytes);
```

ADO.NET Recipes

In the preceding code, we used `BinaryReader` to get the bytes from the file using `FileStream` connected with the file. One point to keep in mind is that `ReadBytes` requires the number of bytes to be read. That is why we used the `Length` property of the `FileInfo` class to get the length of file in the following statements of `ReadFile`:

```
FileInfo info = new FileInfo(path);
long numBytes = info.Length;
```

Let us now look at `btnSave_Click`. We used the byte array returned from `ReadFile` as a parameter to the `Add` method of the `Parameters` property of the `SqlCommand` instance in the following code:

```
byte[] imageData = ReadFile(lblFile.Text);
command.Parameters.Add(new SqlParameter("@vFile", (object)imageData));
```

The `SaveFile` stored procedure accepts a file content as value of the `@vFile` parameter. So, we passed the `byte` array when we added the parameter to the command. By doing so, the `byte` array gets passed on to SQL Server when the command gets executed.

Retrieving large files (BLOB) from SQL Server using ADO.NET

In the last recipe, we saw how to save files of large size, or BLOB, into tables using ADO.NET. In this recipe we will focus on how to retrieve the saved files. Similar to the last recipe, we will work with high quality image files. We will be retrieving the data from the table and displaying it in a picture box. At the database side, we will use a stored procedure to retrieve the file data corresponding to the name. At the application level, we will make use of the `DataSet` class of ADO.NET to pass the filename to the stored procedure and get the data.

How to do it...

1. Launch SQL Server Management Studio 2012.
2. Open the database named `CookBook`.
3. Next, add a stored procedure that will retrieve data from `tb_FileStorage` and name it `ReadFile`. The procedure will be as follows:

```
USE [CookBook]
GO

SET ANSI_NULLS ON
GO

SET QUOTED_IDENTIFIER ON
GO
```

```
CREATE PROCEDURE [dbo].[ReadFile]
  -- Add the parameters for the stored procedure here
  @vFileName varchar(50)
AS
BEGIN
  -- SET NOCOUNT ON added to prevent extra result sets from
  -- interfering with SELECT statements.
  SET NOCOUNT ON;

  SELECT [ID]
      ,[File_name]
      ,[File_content]
    FROM [dbo].[tb_FileStorage]
    WHERE [File_name] = @vFileName


END

GO
```

4. Launch Visual Studio 2012. Open the solution named `SaveRetrieveFile.sln`.
5. Open `SaveRetrieveFileDB` in design mode.
6. Design the form so that it looks similar to the following screenshot:

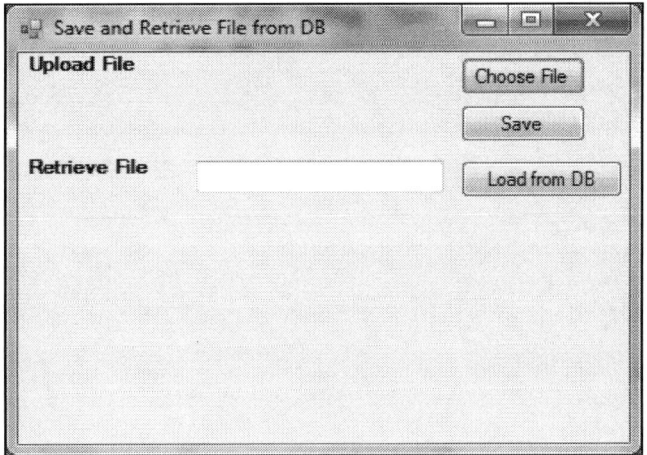

7. Name the controls as detailed in the following table:

Control	Control Name	Description
Textbox	`txtFile`	To enter the name of the file to be retrieved.
Button	`btnLoad`	To retrieve the file from the table and display it using the picture box control.
Picture Box	`pbImage`	To display the image retrieved from the table.

8. Double-click on `btnLoad` to add an event handler for the `Click` event.

9. In the event handler, add the following code:

   ```
   SqlConnection connection = new SqlConnection(ConfigurationManager.
   ConnectionStrings["local"].ConnectionString);
   SqlDataAdapter adapter = new SqlDataAdapter();
   adapter.SelectCommand = new SqlCommand();
   adapter.SelectCommand.CommandText = "ReadFile";
   adapter.SelectCommand.CommandType = CommandType.StoredProcedure;
   adapter.SelectCommand.Connection = connection;
   adapter.SelectCommand.Parameters.Add(new SqlParameter(
   "@vFileName", txtFile.Text));
   SqlCommandBuilder MyCB = new SqlCommandBuilder(adapter);
   DataSet ds = new DataSet("MyImages");

   byte[] data = new byte[0];

   adapter.Fill(ds, "MyImages");
   DataRow row;
   row = ds.Tables["MyImages"].Rows[0];

   data = (byte[])row["File_content"];
   MemoryStream imageStream = new MemoryStream(data);
   pbImage.Image = Image.FromStream(imageStream);
   ```

10. Run the application. Enter the name of a file previously saved. Click on the **Load from DB** button. The image will be loaded on to the picture box, as shown in the following screenshot:

Chapter 5

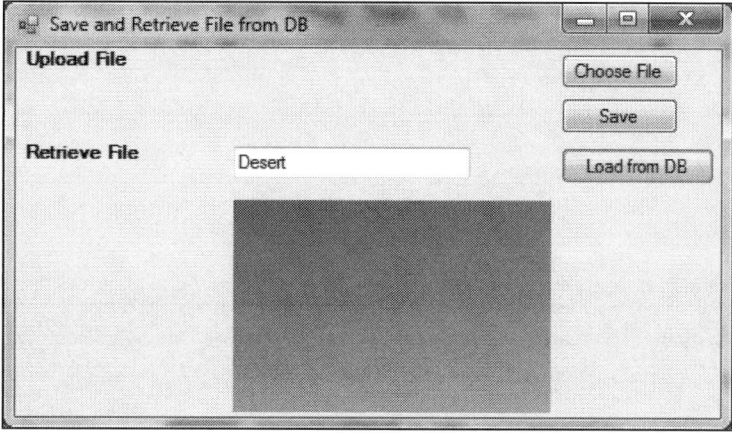

How it works...

The whole logic to retrieve data of the image file from the table and display it using the picture box control is in the event handler for the `Click` event of the **Load from DB** button. The code in the event handler up to execution of the stored procedure using `SqlDataAdapter` in the following statement is similar to any other code that uses `SqlDataAdapter` and ADO.NET library:

```
adapter.Fill(ds, "MyImages");
```

Once `SqlDataAdapter` fills the `DataSet` instance with the data and the structure from the result of the executed query/stored procedure, the steps change. First we accessed the very first row of the table within the `DataSet` instance:

```
row = ds.Tables["MyImages"].Rows[0];
```

We were confident that the data will be in the first row because of the `where` clause in the `Select` statement of the stored procedure. Then we extracted the binary data from the `File_content` column of the row and assigned it to the `byte` array:

```
data = (byte[])row["File_content"];
```

We typecasted the result of `row["File_content"]` because `row["File_content"]` returns an `object` type and to use the binary data we needed the `byte` array. Then we created an instance of `MemoryStream` from the `byte` array:

```
MemoryStream imageStream = new MemoryStream(data);
```

ADO.NET Recipes

The `MemoryStream` class is similar to the `FileStream` class except that `FileStream` works with files, while `MemoryStream` works with the in-memory data. If we were using `FileStream`, we would have to create a temporary file and save the `byte` array into it. Since we are using `MemoryStream`, we can directly work with the `byte` array. Next, we used the `ImageFromStream` method of the `Image` class to create an image from the `byte` array and set it to the `Image` property of the `ImageBox` control:

```
pbImage.Image = Image.FromStream(imageStream);
```

Using transactions to maintain database consistency when saving multiple files

When saving or updating a set of records in a table or across multiple tables, scenarios occur for which the set should be saved as a whole. In other words, if saving or updating of any record fails, then no further inserts or updates of any of the records within that set should happen. Also, the records saved till that point should be removed. For example, when trying to save seven images, if saving the fifth image fails, then the next two images should not be saved. And the first four saved images must be removed from the table. This is required to maintain consistency of the database. In such a scenario, **transactions** comes into the picture.

ADO.NET provides the functionality to execute select, insert, update, and delete tasks within transactions. In this recipe, we will see how to use the transaction functionality provided by ADO.NET by applying it to the save image task.

How to do it...

1. Launch Visual Studio 2012. Open the solution named `SaveRetrieveFile.sln`.
2. Open `SaveRetrieveFileDB` in the design mode.
3. Remove the `Label` control `lblFile`.
4. Add the `ListBox` control to the column from which we removed the `lblFile` label in the previous step.
5. Name `ListBox` as `lstFiles`.

6. The form would look similar to the following screenshot:

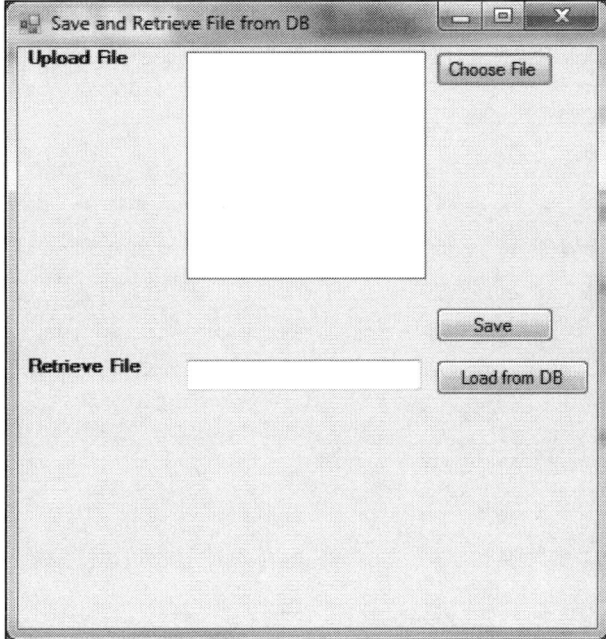

7. Double-click on btnChoose to open the Click event handler of btnChoose.
8. Modify the code within the handler so that it becomes similar to the following code:

```
lstFiles.DataSource = null;

OpenFileDialog diagFile = new OpenFileDialog();
diagFile.Multiselect = true;
if (diagFile.ShowDialog() == DialogResult.OK)
{
   lstFiles.DataSource = diagFile.FileNames;
}
```

9. Modify the Click event handler of btnLoad so that it resembles the following:

```
private void btnSave_Click(object sender, EventArgs e)
{
  SqlConnection connection = new  SqlConnection(ConfigurationManager.ConnectionStrings["local"].ConnectionString);
  connection.Open();
  using (SqlTransaction transaction=connection.BeginTransaction())
            {
```

```csharp
                    try
                    {
                        SqlCommand command = new SqlCommand();
                        command.Connection = connection;
                        command.CommandType = CommandType.StoredProcedure;
                        command.CommandText = "SaveFile";
                        command.Transaction = transaction;
                        foreach (String item in lstFiles.Items)
                        {
                            command.Parameters.Clear();
                            command.Parameters.Add(new SqlParameter(
"@vFileName", (object)Path.GetFileNameWithoutExtension(item)));

                            byte[] imageData = ReadFile(item);
                            command.Parameters.Add(new SqlParameter(
"@vFile", (object)imageData));

                            command.ExecuteNonQuery();
                        }
                        transaction.Commit();
                        MessageBox.Show("Files have been successfully saved");
                    }
                    catch (Exception)
                    {
                        transaction.Rollback();
                        MessageBox.Show("Could not save file",
"Database Error", MessageBoxButtons.OK, MessageBoxIcon.Error);
                    }
                    finally
                    {
                        connection.Close();
                    }
            }
    }
```

10. Run the application.

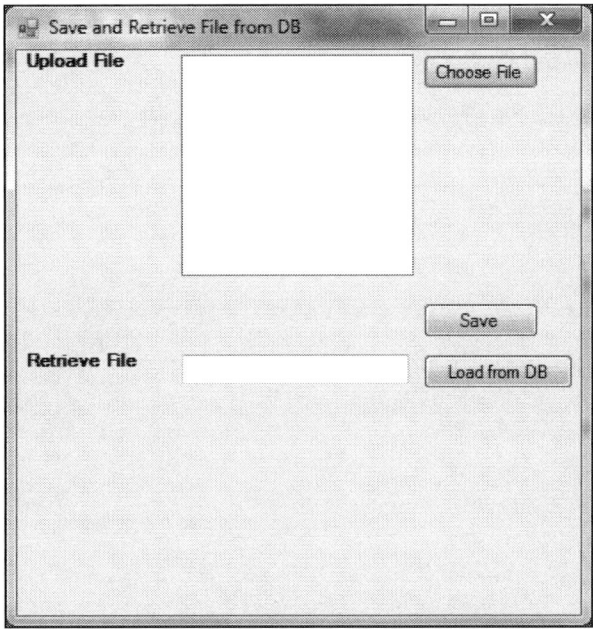

11. Choose multiple files by clicking the **Choose File** button. You will see the listbox filled with filenames, as shown in the following screenshot:

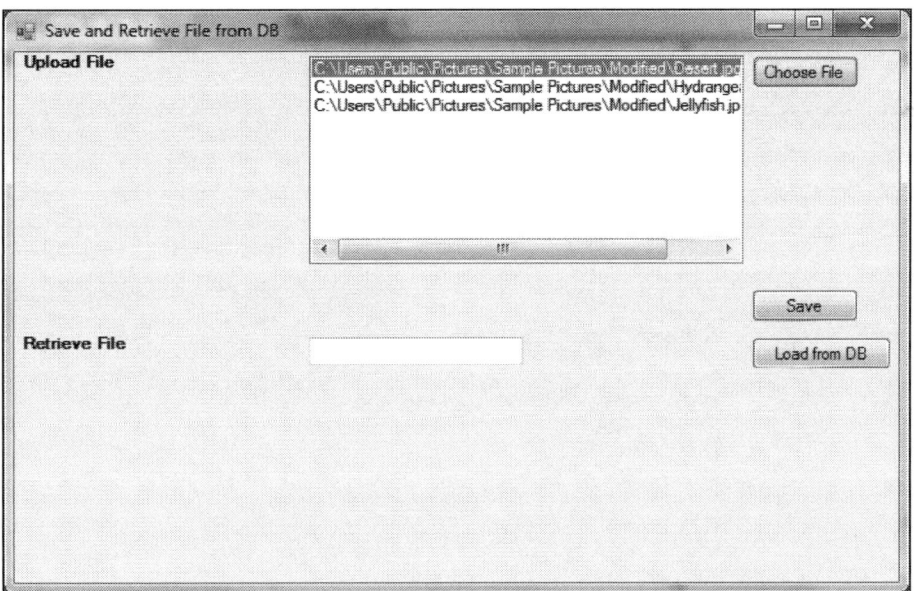

ADO.NET Recipes

12. Click on the **Save** button. You will see the following message if the images are saved successfully:

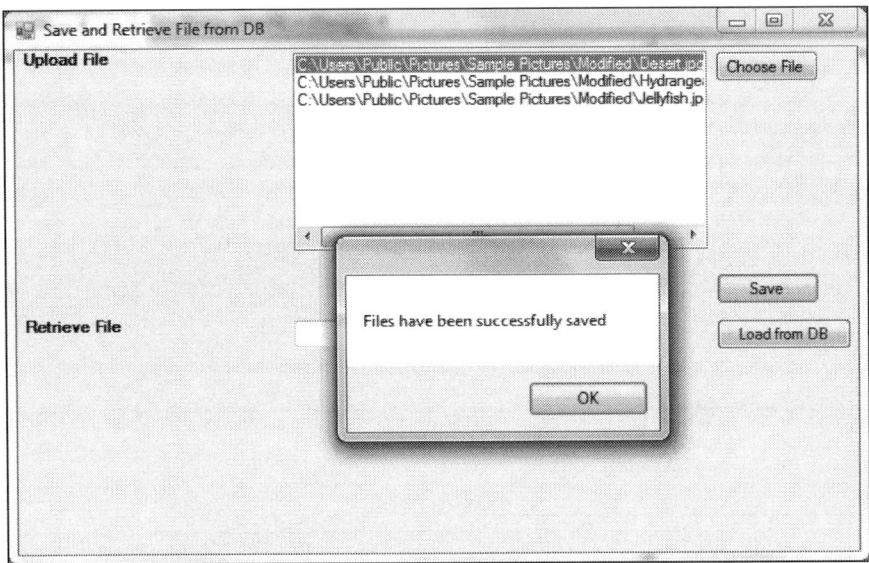

13. If the images are not saved successfully, you will see the following message:

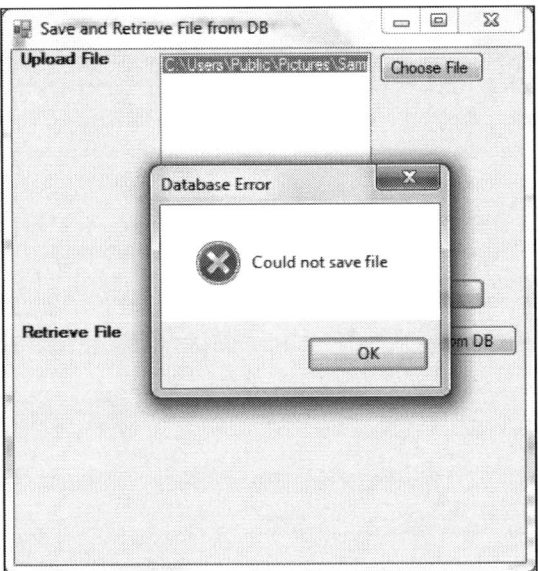

14. If the images are not saved successfully, check `tb_FileStorage`. You will find that none of the images were saved.

How it works...

A transaction is said to be complete if all the statements within the transaction are executed successfully, also known as a **commit**. In case of failure of any statement, the previous state of the table(s) would be restored. This is known as **rollback**. So, a transaction completes either with a commit or a rollback. In ADO.NET, a transaction is represented by an instance of the `SqlTransaction` class. You complete a transaction either by calling the `Commit` or `Rollback` method on the instance of the transaction class.

In our recipe, we have placed saving of the images within the transaction by wrapping the code that saves the file within the `using` block, as shown in the following highlighted code:

```
using (SqlTransaction transaction=connection.BeginTransaction())
            {
                try
                {
                    SqlCommand command = new SqlCommand();
                    command.Connection = connection;
                    command.CommandType = CommandType.StoredProcedure;
                    command.CommandText = "SaveFile";
                    command.Transaction = transaction;
                    foreach (String item in lstFiles.Items)
                    {
                        command.Parameters.Clear();
                        command.Parameters.Add(new SqlParameter(
"@vFileName", (object)Path.GetFileNameWithoutExtension(item)));

                        byte[] imageData = ReadFile(item);
                        command.Parameters.Add(new SqlParameter(
"@vFile", (object)imageData));

                        command.ExecuteNonQuery();
                    }
                    transaction.Commit();
                    MessageBox.Show("Files have been successfully
saved");
                }
                catch (Exception)
                {
                    transaction.Rollback();
                    MessageBox.Show("Could not save file", "Database
Error", MessageBoxButtons.OK, MessageBoxIcon.Error);
```

```
            }
            finally
            {
                connection.Close();
            }
    }
```

By making use of the `using` statement, we do not need to close the transaction explicitly. To get an instance of `SqlTransaction`, we called `BeginTransaction` of the `SqlConnection` instance:

```
using (SqlTransaction transaction=connection.BeginTransaction())
```

We set the `Transaction` property of the `SqlCommand` instance to the `SqlTransaction` instance to tell ADO.NET that the `SqlCommand` instance will be part of the transaction:

```
SqlCommand command = new SqlCommand();
command.Connection = connection;
command.CommandType = CommandType.StoredProcedure;
command.CommandText = "SaveFile";
command.Transaction = transaction;
```

Then we executed the save image statements in a loop:

```
foreach (String item in lstFiles.Items)
{
  command.Parameters.Clear();
  command.Parameters.Add(new SqlParameter("@vFileName",
        (object)Path.GetFileNameWithoutExtension(item)));

  byte[] imageData = ReadFile(item);
  command.Parameters.Add(new SqlParameter("@vFile",
                    (object)imageData));

    command.ExecuteNonQuery();
}
```

One point to keep in mind is that `command.ExecuteNonQuery()` only sends the data to the database server. The data is not saved permanently until we call commit on the instance of `SqlTransaction`. That is what we did in the following statement after the loop.

```
transaction.Commit();
```

If any exception occurs during the loop, we catch that in the `catch` block and rollback the transaction:

```
catch (Exception)
{
  transaction.Rollback();
  MessageBox.Show("Could not save file", "Database Error",
MessageBoxButtons.OK, MessageBoxIcon.Error);
}
```

At this point, none of the files sent to the database will be saved. And thus consistency of the database will be maintained, which is the whole point of transactions.

Using DataSet to modify custom XML configuration files

`DataSet` is the most versatile component of ADO.NET as it can load data from not only database objects but also XML, Excel worksheets, and so on. Its ability to load data from XML documents is really helpful if you want to keep configuration data such as Web Service host address and locale-based messages. In this recipe, we will make use of `DataSet` to load the configuration details from the XML document, modify the data, and save it back into the XML document.

We will also use `DataGridView` to display the loaded data and provide a UI to the user for modifying and saving the data. In this recipe you will also see how well `DataGridView` plays with `DataSet`.

How to do it...

1. Launch Visual Studio 2012. Create a new project of type Windows Forms Project and name it `XmlConfigUI`.
2. Save the solution as `XmlConfigUI.sln`.
3. Rename `Form1` to `XmlConfigUI`.
4. Add an XML file and name it `messages.xml`.
5. Open `messages.xml` and add the following:

   ```
   <messages>
     <message>
       <locale>en</locale>
       <text>User name is not unique</text>
     </message>
   </messages>
   ```

6. Open XmlConfigUI in the design mode. Design the form so that it looks similar to the following screenshot:

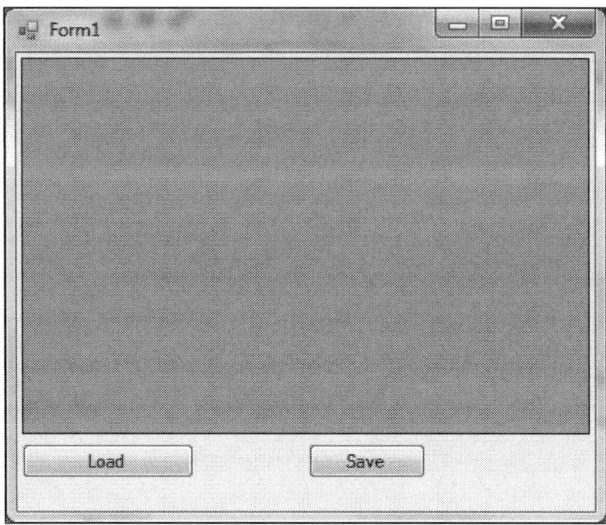

7. Name the controls as detailed in the following table:

Control	Control name	Description
DataGridView	dgvConfig	To display the data loaded from messages.xml
Button	btnLoad	To load data from messages.xml and display it on dgvConfig
Button	btnSave	To save data in the DataSet class back to messages.xml

8. Switch to the view source mode. Add a private instance variable of type DataSet:
   `private DataSet _dataSet;`
9. In the constructor, add the following code after the call to InitializeComponents:
   `_dataSet = new DataSet("Messages");`
10. Switch to the design mode. Double-click on btnLoad to add a Click event handler.
11. In the Click event handler of btnLoad, add the following code:

    ```
    _dataSet.ReadXml(Application.StartupPath + "\\messages.xml");
    dgvConfig.DataSource = _dataSet;
    dgvConfig.DataMember = "message";
    ```

12. Switch to the design mode. Double-click on btnSave to add a Click event handler.

13. In the Click event handler of `btnSave`, add the following code:

    `_dataSet.WriteXml(Application.StartupPath + "\\messages.xml");`

14. Run the application.

15. Next, click on the **Load** button. The screen will look similar to the following screenshot:

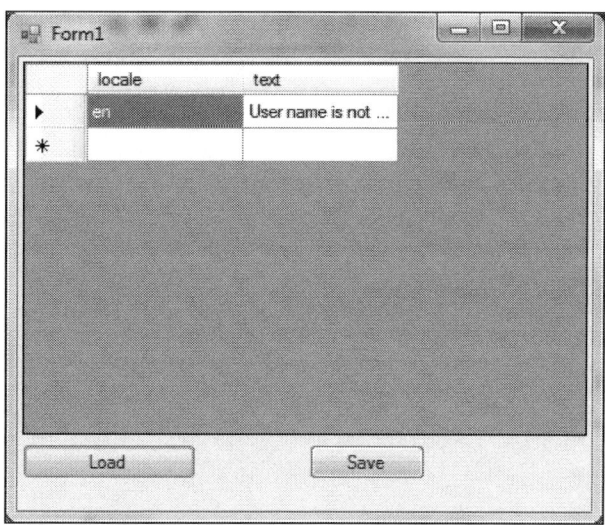

16. Add a new row. Click on **Save**:

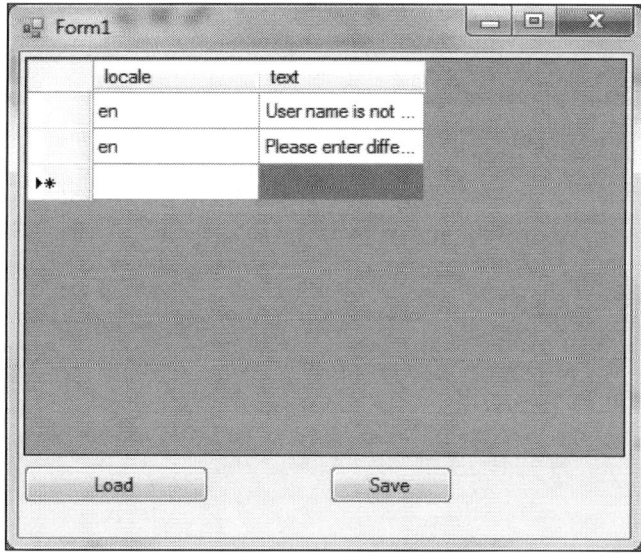

17. Close the application.

18. Run the application again. Click on the **Load** button. The added row will be visible, as shown in the following screenshot:

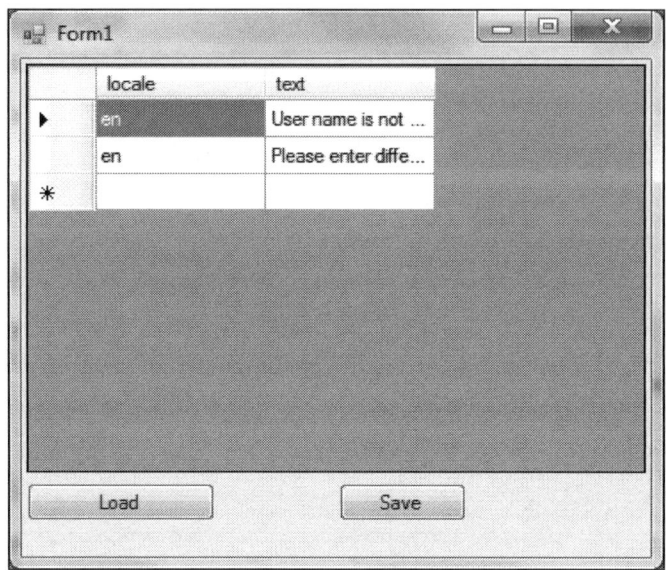

How it works...

The first step in loading XML into DataSet is to specify the path to the XML file, that is, messages.xml. Since we did not want it to be an embedded resource, we set the file's Copy to Output Directory to true. In our case (that is, debug), the output directory will be bin\debug. We did this so that the following statements would provide the path to messages.xml at runtime:

```
Application.StartupPath + "\\messages.xml"
```

In the Click event handler for the Load button, we used the preceding statement to load the data into DataSet:

```
_dataSet.ReadXml(Application.StartupPath + "\\messages.xml");
```

The ReadXml method of DataSet reads the data and creates tables and columns based on the schema. It then populates the table with the data present in XML. Next, we assigned _dataSet to the DataSource property of dgvConfig:

```
dgvConfig.DataSource = _dataSet;
```

Just assigning the data source will not be sufficient to display the data. We have to tell the data source which member will provide the column names. In `messages.xml`, we have the following structure:

```
<messages>
  <message>
    <locale>en</locale>
    <text>User name is not unique</text>
  </message>
</messages>
```

In the previous code, `<locale>` and `<text>` are under `<message>`. Since `<locale>` and `<text>` would become columns in a data set, `<message>` will be the member that will provide the column names. Hence, we added the following statement:

```
dgvConfig.DataMember = "message";
```

The way data that is in the `DataSet` instance is saved onto an XML file works in the opposite way from reading it from XML and populating the `DataSet` instance. By calling the `WriteXml` method of the `DataSet` instance, we essentially told `DataSet` to write out the data according to the schema of the XML data loaded earlier:

```
_dataSet.WriteXml(Application.StartupPath + "\\messages.xml");
```

Using `DataSet` to read and save XML data is easy. However, it can be used in many ways, one of them being handling of configuration data, as you have seen in this recipe.

6
WCF Recipes

In this chapter we will cover:

- Implementing custom binding in WCF
- Creating a WCF REST service
- Handling exceptions using FaultContract and FaultException
- Uploading files using Stream
- Securing a service using role-based security

Introduction

Windows Communication Framework (**WCF**) is the base of Service Oriented Architecture in .NET 3.5 and higher. The focus of this chapter will be on tasks such as uploading files and implementing a REST service, among others, using WCF. We will start with creating custom bindings for a ping service. Then we move on to implementing WCF REST service. The next recipe will tell you how to implement Inversion-of-Control using Dependency Injection. The last two recipes will deal with a service that can be used to upload a file and secure the ping WCF service.

Implementing custom binding in WCF

In WCF, binding dictates many aspects such as the protocol being used, the size of the data/payload, and so on. The default binding is based on HTTP and the default values provided will work well in most of the scenarios. However, there may be cases where the default HTTP binding may not work for you. The scenario can be anything from a need to use TCP instead of HTTP to a requirement that needs a specific Web Service Security version to be used. For such scenarios, custom binding comes in handy.

WCF Recipes

In this recipe, we will create a service that will check whether the SQL Server is up or not. The service will use custom binding to set up the protocol and the encoding to be used for communication between the service and client.

How to do it...

1. Launch Visual Studio 2012. Create a project of type **WCF Service Library**. Name it `WcfDbPingService`.
2. Rename the `IService` interface to `IPingService` and the `Service` class to `PingService`.
3. Add a reference to `Microsoft.SqlServer.ConnectionInfo.dll`.
4. Open the `IPingService` class and remove the existing code.
5. Add a method that accepts `string` as parameter and returns `bool` to the `IPingService` class. Name it `IsDbUp`. Its signature will be:

   ```
   bool IsDbUp(string connectionString);
   ```

6. Decorate the method with the `OperationContract` attribute:

   ```
   [OperationContract]
   bool IsDbUp(string connectionString);
   ```

7. After the modifications the `IPingService` class will look similar to the following code:

   ```
   [ServiceContract]
   public interface IPingService
   {
     [OperationContract]
     bool IsDbUp(string connectionString);
   }
   ```

8. Next, open the `PingService` class that implements `IPingService`. Remove the existing code from the class.
9. Implement the `IsDbUp` method from `IPingService`.
10. Add the following code to the `IsDbUp` method:

    ```
    bool isUp = true;
    try
    {
      SqlConnection connection = new SqlConnection(connectionString);
      connection.Open();
      connection.Close();
    }
    ```

```csharp
    catch (Exception)
    {
      isUp = false;
    }
      return isUp;
```

11. Open `App.config` and add the following code before the `<services>` section:

    ```xml
    <bindings>
      <customBinding>
        <binding name="CustomBinding_IPingService">
          <textMessageEncoding messageVersion="Soap11"/>
          <httpTransport />
        </binding>
      </customBinding>
    </bindings>
    ```

12. Next, modify the `<service>` section so that it is similar to the following code:

    ```xml
    <service name="WcfDbPingService.PingService">
    <endpoint address="" binding="customBinding"
    bindingConfiguration="CustomBinding_IPingService"
    contract="WcfDbPingService.IPingService">
      <identity>
        <dns value="localhost" />
      </identity>
    </endpoint>
    <endpoint address="mex" binding="mexHttpBinding"
    contract="IMetadataExchange" />
      <host>
        <baseAddresses>
          <add baseAddress="http://localhost:8735/Design_Time_Addresses/WcfDbPingService/Service1/" />
        </baseAddresses>
      </host>
    </service>
    ```

13. Add another project of type **Windows Forms Application** and name it `PingDbTestApp`.

14. Rename `Form1.cs` to `PingDbTestForm.cs`.

WCF Recipes

15. Open `PingDbTestForm` in Design mode. Design the form so that the UI resembles the following screenshot:

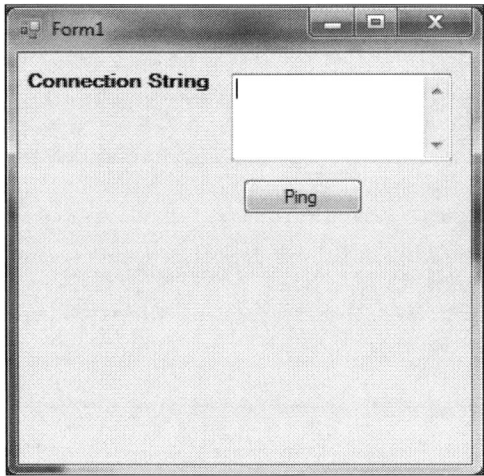

16. Name the controls as detailed in the following table:

Control	Name	Description
Textbox	`txtConnString`	To enter the connection string for the database that needs to be pinged
Button	`btnPing`	To call the ping service
Label	`lblResult`	To display the result of the service call

17. Add Service Reference to `PingService` and name it `PingDbServiceReference`.
18. Double-click on `btnPing` to add the Click event handler.
19. In the event handler, add the following code:

    ```
    PingDbServiceReference.PingServiceClient client = new
    PingDbServiceReference.PingServiceClient();
    bool result = client.IsDbUp(txtConnString.Text);
    lblResult.Text = "Database with connection string " +
    txtConnString.Text + " is up? " + result;
    ```

20. Run the application as a new instance.
21. Enter the connection string of the SQL Server to be pinged and then click on the **Ping** button.

22. If the server is up, you will get the following screen:

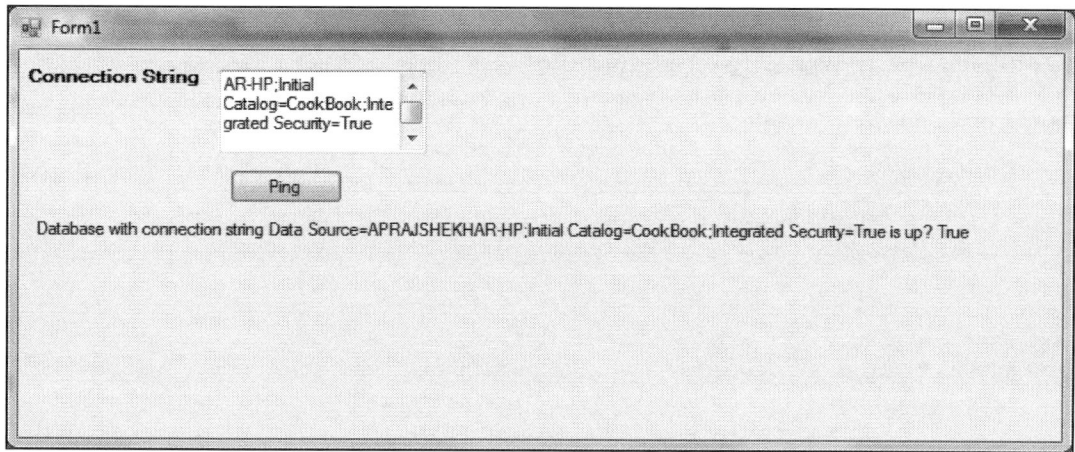

23. If the server is not up, you will get the following screen:

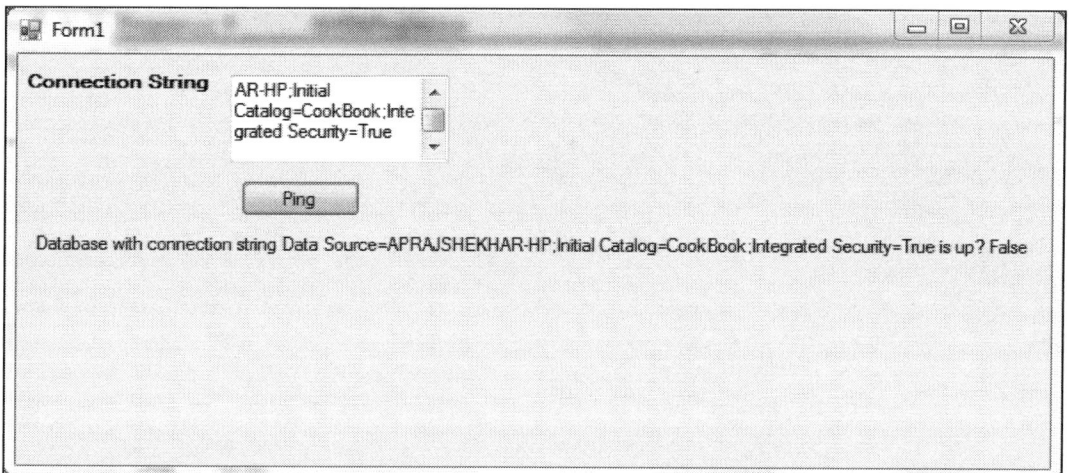

 The ping service is very basic in its implementation. The reason is that the focus of this recipe is on custom binding. Implementing a sophisticated ping service is out of the scope of this recipe.

How it works...

The core of the implementation is in the `<bindings>` section in `App.config`. The default binding provided by WCF is based on HTTP. We want to use HTTP itself. However, we want to ensure that Version 1.1 of SOAP is being used. So, we add the following custom binding:

```
<customBinding>
   <binding name="CustomBinding_IPingService">
   <textMessageEncoding messageVersion="Soap11"/>
   <httpTransport />
</binding>
```

In the preceding code, we named the `<binding>` section `CustomBinding_IPingService` so that we can use it later. Next, we have set the value of the `messageVersion` attribute of `<textMessageEncoding>` to `Soap11` so that SOAP Version 1.1 is used. Then by adding `<httpTransport/>`, we are ensuring that HTTP is used.

To make sure that .NET uses the custom binding, we add two attributes to `<endpoint>`: `binding` and `bindingConfiguration`. We set binding to `customBinding` so that our custom binding will be used. Then we set `bindingConfiguration` to the name of our custom binding, as shown in the following code:

```
<service name="WcfDbPingService.PingService">
   <endpoint address="" binding="customBinding"
bindingConfiguration="CustomBinding_IPingService"
contract="WcfDbPingService.IPingService">
      <identity>
         <dns value="localhost" />
      </identity>
   </endpoint>
   <endpoint address="mex" binding="mexHttpBinding"
contract="IMetadataExchange" />
   <host>
     <baseAddresses>
        <add baseAddress="http://localhost:8735/Design_Time_Addresses/
WcfDbPingService/Service1/" />
     </baseAddresses>
   </host>
</service>
```

If you look at `App.config` of `PingDbTestApp`, you will see the following code:

```
<system.serviceModel>
   <bindings>
     <basicHttpBinding>
        <binding name="CustomBinding_IPingService" />
     </basicHttpBinding>
```

```
    </bindings>
    <client>
      <endpoint address="http://localhost:8735/Design_Time_Addresses/
WcfDbPingService/Service1/"
        binding="basicHttpBinding"
        bindingConfiguration="CustomBinding_IPingService"
        contract="PingServiceReference.IPingService"
name="CustomBinding_IPingService" />
    </client>
</system.serviceModel>
```

Since we have used HTTP as transport for our service configuration in the previous code (taken from `App.config` of `PingDbTestApp`), `<basicHttpBinding>` is present. The point of significance is that the name of `<binding>` is `CustomBinding_IPingService`. Keep in mind that the port number will be different from what you see in the preceding code, since that will be generated based on your system's setup.

Creating a WCF REST service

In the previous recipe, we implemented a ping database service using WCF. Since we are using SOAP, we need to create a separate client to consume it. What if we want to check the status of a database by passing the connection string as a query parameter and view the result using a web browser? For such scenarios, we will have to implement a ping service as a REST service.

A **Representational State Transfer** (**REST**) service uses HTTP(S) along with XML, HTML, and JSON for communication. It does not require a WSDL to discover the functionality provided or an SOAP for sending and receiving data. It uses HTTP and the HTTP methods (GET, POST, PUT, DELETE, and OPTIONS) for **Create**, **Retrieve**, **Update**, and **Delete** (**CRUD**) operations. In this recipe, we will see how to implement a RESTful WCF service having the retrieve (GET) functionality.

You can find out more about REST from `http://www.ibm.com/developerworks/webservices/library/ws-restful/`.

How to do it...

1. Launch Visual Studio 2012. Create a project of type **WCF Service Library**. Name it `WcfRestService`.
2. Add a new class and name it `Result`.
3. Open the `Result` class and decorate the class with `[DataContract]`.

4. Add a property of type `bool` to the class and name it `IsUp`. Decorate it with `[DataMember]`.

5. After the modifications, the `Result` class will be similar to the following code:

    ```
    [DataContract]
      public class Result
      {
        [DataMember]
        public bool IsUp { get; set; }
      }
    ```

6. Rename `IService` to `IPingService` and `Service` to `PingService`.

7. Add a reference to `Microsoft.SqlServer.ConnectionInfo.dll`.

8. Open the `IPingService` class and remove the existing code.

9. Add a method that accepts `string` as a parameter and returns an instance of `Result` to the `IPingService` class. Name it `IsUp`. Its signature will be as follows:

    ```
    Result IsDbUp(string connectionString);
    ```

10. Decorate the method with the `OperationContract` and `WebGet` attributes, as shown in the following code snippet:

    ```
    [OperationContract]
    [WebGet(UriTemplate="IsUp?server={connectionString}",
    ResponseFormat=WebMessageFormat.Xml)]
    Result IsDbUp(string connectionString);
    ```

11. After the modifications the `IPingService` class will look similar to the following code:

    ```
    [ServiceContract]
    public interface IPingService
    {
      [OperationContract]
      [WebGet(UriTemplate="IsUp?server={connectionString}",
    ResponseFormat=WebMessageFormat.Xml)]
      Result IsDbUp(string connectionString);
    }
    ```

12. Next, open the `PingService` class that implements `IPingService` and remove the existing code from the class.

13. Implement the `IsDbUp` method from `IPingService`.

14. Add the following code to the `IsDbUp` method:

    ```
    Result isUp = new Result();
    isUp.IsUp = true;
    try
    {
    ```

```
      SqlConnection connection = new SqlConnection(connectionString);
      connection.Open();
      connection.Close();
  }
  catch (Exception)
  {
    isUp.IsUp = false;
  }
      return isUp;
```

15. Open `App.config` and modify the `<services>` section so that it looks similar to the following code:

```
<service name="WcfRestService.PingService">
  <endpoint address="" binding="webHttpBinding"
contract="WcfRestService.IPingService">
    <identity>
      <dns value="localhost" />
    </identity>
  </endpoint>
  <endpoint address="mex" binding="webHttpBinding"
contract="IMetadataExchange" />
  <host>
    <baseAddresses>
      <add baseAddress="http://localhost:8733/Design_Time_
Addresses/WcfRestService/Service1/" />
    </baseAddresses>
  </host>
</service>
```

16. Next, add the following code before the `<serviceBehaviors>` section:

```
<behaviors>
  <endpointBehaviors>
    <behavior>
      <webHttp/>
    </behavior>
  </endpointBehaviors>
```

17. Run the application.
18. Open the browser and enter the URL `http://localhost:8733/Design_Time_Addresses/WcfRestService/Service1/IsUp?server=server`.
19. The URL may be different. You can find the exact URL in `App.config`.

20. You will see a message similar to the one shown in the following screenshot:

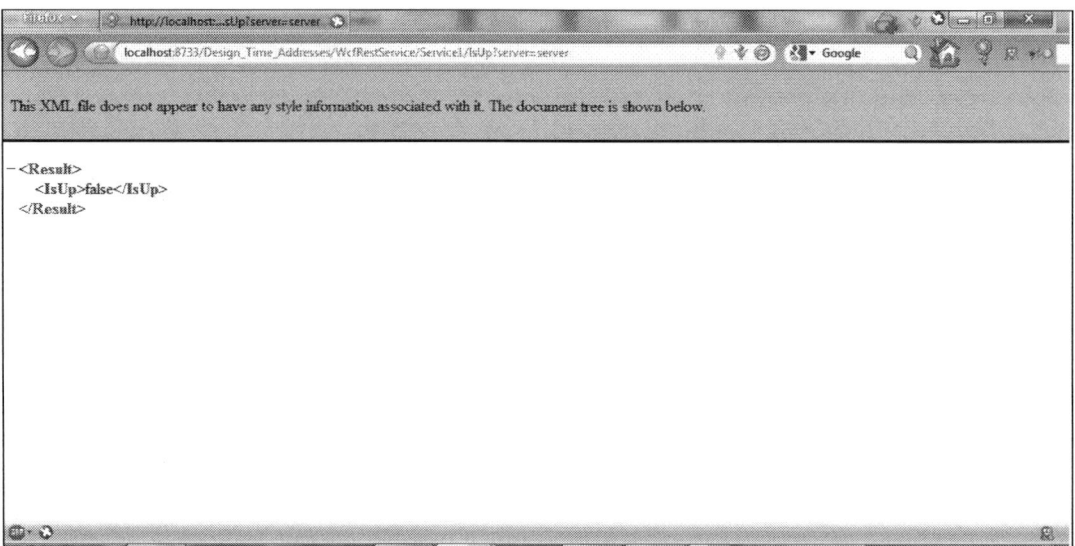

21. Next, provide a valid connection string. You will see a message similar to the one shown in the following screenshot:

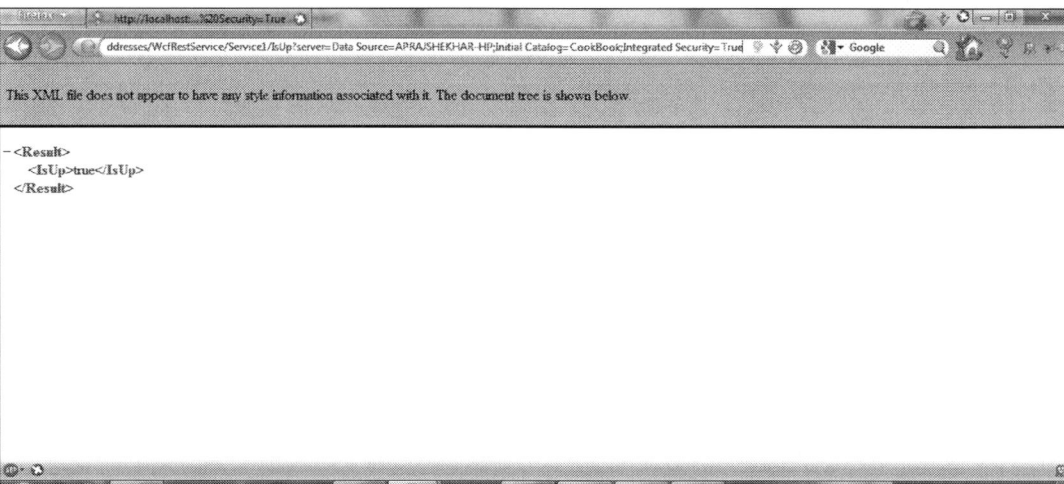

How it works...

The core of the REST implementation lies in `IPingService` and `App.config`. First, let us look at `IPingService`, specifically the `IsDbUp` method. We decorated the `IsDbUp` method with not only `[ServiceContract]` but also with `[WebGet]`:

```
[OperationContract]
[WebGet(UriTemplate="IsUp?server={connectionString}",
ResponseFormat=WebMessageFormat.Xml)]
Result IsDbUp(string connectionString);
```

In the preceding code, we pass the template for the REST call using `UriTemplate`. The second parameter of the attribute is the expected format of the result. The parameter is `ResponseFormat`. The `ResponseFormat` can either be XML or JSON. We set the value of the `ResponseFormat` to XML.

Just decorating a method with `[WebGet]` would not make a service RESTful. You need to make changes to `App.config`. The first change we made was changing the binding property of `<endpoint>` to webHttpBinding:

```
<service name="WcfRestService.PingService">
   <endpoint address="" binding="webHttpBinding"
contract="WcfRestService.IPingService">
      <identity>
        <dns value="localhost" />
      </identity>
   </endpoint>
   <endpoint address="mex" binding="webHttpBinding"
contract="IMetadataExchange" />
   <host>
     <baseAddresses>
        <add baseAddress="http://localhost:8733/Design_Time_Addresses/
WcfRestService/Service1/" />
     </baseAddresses>
   </host>
</service>
```

This tells .NET framework that the service is not going to use SOAP. Next, we added behavior to tell the framework that HTTP methods should be treated as CRUD requests for the service.

```
<behaviors>
  <endpointBehaviors>
    <behavior>
      <webHttp/>
    </behavior>
  </endpointBehaviors>
```

WCF Recipes

Apart from the details discussed here, there is no difference between the RESTful services and normal services. Hence, the `IsDbUp` method given in this recipe is not different from the `IsDbUp` method we implemented in the previous recipe.

There's more...

You can use `WebPut` and `WebPost` for updating and adding content using WCF REST services.

Handling exceptions using FaultContract and FaultException

Exceptions in applications are common. How they are handled differentiates the good applications from the bad ones. In case of services, the exceptions should be communicated to the clients so that clients can take the appropriate action. For WCF services, handling the exceptions become more important as compared to the other applications. The reason is that once an exception occurs, the underlying channel goes into the faulted state, and hence the server and client will not be able to communicate with each other. In WCF, this can be achieved using `FaultContract` and `FaultException`.

In this recipe, we will enhance the ping server by adding a check for the null string passed as the value of argument. If it is null, a `FaultException` exception will be thrown and the client can catch it and display the error.

How to do it...

1. Launch Visual Studio 2012 and open `WcfDbPingService.sln`.
2. Add a new class to the `WcfDbPingService` project. Name it `PingException`.
3. Decorate it with `[DataContract]`.
4. Add properties as detailed in the following table and decorate them with `[DataMember]`:

Name	Data type
Title	String
Message	String
InnerException	String
StackTrace	String

Chapter 6

5. Once done, `PingException` will be similar to the following code:

```
[DataContract]
class PingException
{
   [DataMember]
   public string Title;
   [DataMember]
   public string Message;
   [DataMember]
   public string InnerException;
   [DataMember]
   public string StackTrace;
}
```

6. In the `IPingService`, decorate `IsDbUp` with `[FaultContract]` as shown in the following highlighted code:

```
[ServiceContract]
public interface IPingService
{
   [OperationContract]
   [FaultContract(typeof(PingException))]
   bool IsDbUp(string connectionString);
}
```

7. Next, open `PingService` and add the following code to the `IsDbUp` method of `PingService` before the `try` statement:

```
if (string.IsNullOrEmpty(connectionString))
{
   PingException ex = new PingException();
   ex.Title = "Error Function:IdDbUp()";
   ex.Message = "Argument is null.";
   ex.InnerException = " ";
   ex.StackTrace = " ";
   throw new FaultException<PingException>(ex,"Reason: Argument is null");
}
```

8. Update the service reference of `PingDbTestApp`.

9. Open `PingDbTestForm` and modify the Click event handler of the **Ping** button as shown in the following code:

```
private void btnPing_Click(object sender, EventArgs e)
{
  try
  {
  PingServiceReference.PingServiceClient client = new PingServiceReference.PingServiceClient();
    bool result = client.IsDbUp(txtConnString.Text);
    lblResult.Text = "Database with connection string " + txtConnString.Text + " is up? " + result;
  }
  catch (FaultException<PingServiceReference.PingException> ex)
  {
    MessageBox.Show(ex.Detail.Message);
  }
}
```

10. Run `PingDbTestApp` by navigating to **Debug | Run in new instance**.
11. Click on the **Ping** button without entering the connection string in the textbox.
12. You will see a message similar to the one shown in the following screenshot:

How it works...

The first step in using `FaultContract` is defining `PingException` as a data contract, as shown in the following code:

```
[DataContract]
class PingException
{
    [DataMember]
    public string Title;
    [DataMember]
    public string Message;
```

```
        [DataMember]
        public string InnerException;
        [DataMember]
        public string StackTrace;
}
```

We did this so that not only can the client discover the kind of exception to be thrown, but the server can also pass on the details of the exception to the client. Next, we used the `PingExecption` as an argument to `FaultContract` in `IPingService`, as highlighted in the following code:

```
[ServiceContract]
public interface IPingService
{
   [OperationContract]
   [FaultContract(typeof(PingException))]
   bool IsDbUp(string connectionString);
}
```

To tell `[FaultContract]` to use our class to transfer the exception details to the client, we need to pass the type information of our class. We did that in the previous code by using the `typeof` statement. Next, in `PingService`, we checked whether the argument is null or empty. If it is empty, then create an instance of `PingException`, populate it with the required values, and throw a new `FaultException` using an instance of `PingException`.

```
if (string.IsNullOrEmpty(connectionString))
{
   PingException ex = new PingException();
   ex.Title = "Error Function:IdDbUp()";
   ex.Message = "Argument is null.";
   ex.InnerException = " ";
   ex.StackTrace = " ";
   throw new FaultException<PingException>(ex,"Reason: Argument is null");
}
```

Remember to throw `FaultException`. Otherwise, the exception may not be received by the client. At the client side, we caught `FaultException` and displayed the details to the user:

```
private void btnPing_Click(object sender, EventArgs e)
{
 try
   {
   PingServiceReference.PingServiceClient client = new PingServiceReference.PingServiceClient();
   bool result = client.IsDbUp(txtConnString.Text);
```

WCF Recipes

```
      lblResult.Text = "Database with connection string " + txtConnString.
   Text + " is up? " + result;
   }
   catch (FaultException<PingServiceReference.PingException> ex)
   {
      MessageBox.Show(ex.Detail.Message);
   }
}
```

One point to remember is to catch `FaultException` and not the type of exception detail. In the previous code we have caught the `FaultException` exception of type `PingException` and not `PingException` itself.

Uploading files using Stream

File upload has become a common and desired functionality for any web application/service as well as the libraries on which they are built. WCF is no exception. Until Version 4.0, WCF provided only the buffered mode for uploading the file. From Version 4.0 onwards, WCF started to provide the streaming mode. In the buffered mode, the entire file needs to be uploaded to the server before the WCF service can access it. In the streaming mode, the service can access the file before it is completely uploaded. The streamed mode is very useful when you need the service to process files of large sizes that cannot be buffered.

In this recipe, we will see how to implement and configure a service that can be used to upload files using the streaming mode.

How to do it...

1. Launch Visual Studio 2012. Create a project of type **WCF Service Library**. Name it `WcfFileUploadService`.
2. Add a new class and name it `UploadDetails`.
3. Open the `Result` class. Decorate the class with `[MessageContract]`.
4. Make it `public`.
5. Add the properties shown in the following table:

Name	Data type
FileName	String
Data	Stream

6. Decorate `FileName` with `[MessageHeader]`.
7. Decorate the data with `[MessageBodyMember]`.

8. After the modifications, the `UploadDetails` class will be similar to the following code:

   ```
   [MessageContract]
   public class UploadDetails
   {
     [MessageHeader]
     public string FileName { get; set; }
     [MessageBodyMember]
     public Stream Data { get; set; }
   }
   ```

9. Rename `IService` to `IUploadService` and `Service` to `UploadService`.
10. Open the `IUploadService` class and remove the existing code.
11. Add a method that accepts `UploadDetails` as the parameter and returns `void`, to the `IPingService` class. Name it `Upload`. Its signature will be:

    ```
    void Upload(UploadDetails details);
    ```

12. Decorate it with `[OperationContract]`. The interface will be similar to:

    ```
    [ServiceContract]
    public interface IUploadService
    {
      [OperationContract]
      void Upload(UploadDetails details);
    }
    ```

13. Next, open the `UploadService` class that implements `IUploadService`. Remove the existing code from the class.
14. Implement the `Upload` method of `IUploadService`.
15. Add the following code to the `Upload` method:

    ```
    using (FileStream fs = new FileStream(@"C:\Downloads\"+details.FileName, FileMode.Create))
    {
      int bufferSize = 1 * 1024 * 1024;
      byte[] buffer = new byte[bufferSize];
      int bytes;

      while ((bytes = details.Data.Read(buffer, 0, bufferSize)) > 0)
      {
        fs.Write(buffer, 0, bytes);
        fs.Flush();
      }

    }
    ```

16. In the previous code replace `C:\Downloads` with the path where you have read/write permissions as the code attempts to create the image file in the previously mentioned path.

17. Now, open `App.config`. Add the following binding just before the `<services>` section:

```xml
<bindings>
  <basicHttpBinding>
    <binding
            name="UploadServiceBinding"
            messageEncoding="Text"
            transferMode="Streamed"
            maxBufferSize="65536"
            maxReceivedMessageSize="5242880">
    </binding>
  </basicHttpBinding>
</bindings>
```

18. Update the `<service>` section so that it looks similar to the following code:

```xml
<service name="WcfFileUploadService.UploadService">
  <endpoint address="" binding="basicHttpBinding"
  bindingConfiguration="UploadServiceBinding"
  contract="WcfFileUploadService.IUploadService">
    <identity>
      <dns value="localhost" />
    </identity>
  </endpoint>
  <endpoint address="mex" binding="mexHttpBinding"
  contract="IMetadataExchange" />
  <host>
    <baseAddresses>
      <add baseAddress="http://localhost:8733/Design_Time_
  Addresses/WcfFileUploadService/Service1/" />
    </baseAddresses>
  </host>
</service>
```

19. Add a new project of type **Windows Forms Application** and name it `UploadServiceTestApp`.

20. Rename `Form1.cs` to `UploadTestForm.cs`.

21. Switch to the Design mode. Design the form so that it looks similar to the following screenshot:

Chapter 6

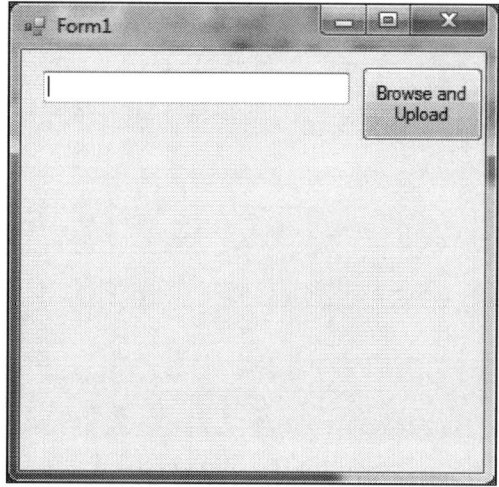

22. Name the controls as shown in the following table:

Control	Name	Description
Textbox	txtFile	To display path of selected file
Button	btnBrowse	To call the upload service

23. Add a reference to `UploadService` and name it `UploadServiceReference`.
24. Double-click on **btnBrowse** to add a Click event handler.
25. In the event handler add the following lines of code:

```
OpenFileDialog diagOpen = new OpenFileDialog();
if (diagOpen.ShowDialog() == System.Windows.Forms.DialogResult.OK)
 {
   try
   {
      txtFile.Text = diagOpen.FileName;
      UploadServiceReference.UploadServiceClient client = new
UploadServiceReference.UploadServiceClient();
      client.Upload(Path.GetFileName(txtFile.Text), File.
Open(txtFile.Text,
      FileMode.Open));
      MessageBox.Show("Upload successful");
   }
   catch (Exception)
   {
       MessageBox.Show("Upload failed");
    }
 }
```

26. Run the application by navigating to **Debug | Run in new instance**. You will see the following screen:

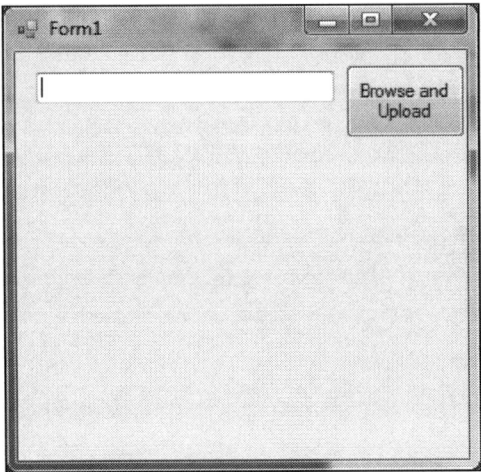

27. Click on the **Browse and Upload** button and select a file to upload.
28. If the upload is successful, you will see the following message on the screen:

29. If unsuccessful, the following message will be displayed:

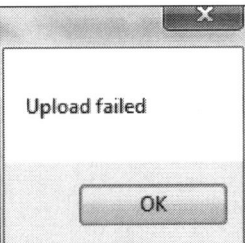

How it works...

To use the streaming mode for uploads, the service should have a method that accepts a parameter of type `Stream`. One point to keep in mind is that the method having `Stream` as parameter should neither have any other parameter nor have a return type. Otherwise the service will not run. This is the reason why we configured the `UploadDetails` class as `MessageContract`:

```
[MessageContract]
public class UploadDetails
{
  [MessageHeader]
  public string FileName { get; set; }
  [MessageBodyMember]
  public Stream Data { get; set; }
}
```

In the preceding code, we have decorated `FileName` with `[MessageHeader]` and not with `[MessageBodyMember]`. The reason is that `Data` is a type of `Stream`. If `MessageContract` contains `MessageBodyMember` of type `Stream`, other properties should be a part of `MessageHeader`. In other words, there can be only one `MessageBodyMember` if the property is of type `Stream`. All other properties must be a part of `MessageHeader`.

In the `Upload` method of `UploadService`, we opened a new `FileStream` to write the file to a folder. Then, we used it to write down the data contained in the instance of the `Stream` class of `UploadDetails`:

```
using (FileStream fs = new FileStream(@"C:\Downloads"+details.
FileName, FileMode.Create))
{
  int bufferSize = 1 * 1024 * 1024;
  byte[] buffer = new byte[bufferSize];
  int bytes;

  while ((bytes = details.Data.Read(buffer, 0, bufferSize)) > 0)
  {
    fs.Write(buffer, 0, bytes);
    fs.Flush();
  }

}
```

WCF Recipes

To tell the .NET runtime that we intend to use the streaming mode, we added a new binding named `UploadServiceBinding`. In the binding, we set `messageEncoding` to `Text` and `transferMode` to `Streamed`. Then we set the maximum buffer size and the upper limit of the message size. The size of the message determines the maximum size that can be uploaded:

```xml
<bindings>
  <basicHttpBinding>
    <binding
            name="UploadServiceBinding"
            messageEncoding="Text"
            transferMode="Streamed"
            maxBufferSize="65536"
            maxReceivedMessageSize="5242880">

    </binding>
  </basicHttpBinding>
</bindings>
```

Since we want to use HTTP itself for transfer, we use `<basicHttpBinding>` instead of custom binding. In the `<service>` section, we set `bindingConfiguration` to `UploadServiceBinding`, as highlighted in the following code:

```xml
<service name="WcfFileUploadService.UploadService">
  <endpoint address="" binding="basicHttpBinding"
  bindingConfiguration="UploadServiceBinding"
  contract="WcfFileUploadService.IUploadService">
    <identity>
      <dns value="localhost" />
    </identity>
  </endpoint>
  <endpoint address="mex" binding="mexHttpBinding"
  contract="IMetadataExchange" />
  <host>
    <baseAddresses>
      <add baseAddress="http://localhost:8733/Design_Time_Addresses/WcfFileUploadService/Service1/" />
    </baseAddresses>
  </host>
</service>
```

In `UploadTestForm`, we called the `Upload` method of the service with the name of the file selected and its content as an instance of `FileStream`:

```
txtFile.Text = diagOpen.FileName;
UploadServiceReference.UploadServiceClient client = new
UploadServiceReference.UploadServiceClient();
client.Upload(Path.GetFileName(txtFile.Text), File.Open(txtFile.Text,
FileMode.Open));
```

Chapter 6

In interface and implementation we have passed `MessageContract` as a parameter to the `Upload` method. However, while calling the same method, we passed the filename and the instance of the `Stream` class as arguments to `UploadMethod`. The marshalling of the arguments to `MessageContract` is done by .NET at runtime, transparently at the server side.

You should not use the transfer mode as `Streamed` and encoding as `MOTM` simultaneously in the binding. Using both of them simultaneously will create problems during the upload of files. The reason for the problems and ways to handle them are out of the scope of this book.

Securing a service using role-based security

Security is the primary concern for any application or service. The WCF services are no exception. There are many ways to secure a service. One of them is based on the "who can access what" principle. In other words, only those users who have certain privileges can access certain services or service methods. The privileges are defined via roles. Windows has certain built-in roles, such as Administrators, Users, Guest, and so on. We can configure the access to the service methods based on these roles so that any user who does not have that specific role will not be able to execute the method.

In this recipe, we will configure `PingService` so that only those users who have the Administrator's role will be able to call it. For others, it will give an "Access Denied" exception.

How to do it...

1. Launch Visual Studio 2012 and open `WcfDbPingService.sln`.
2. Open the `PingService` class.
3. Decorate the `IsDbUp` method with `[PrincipalPermission]` as shown in the following code:

```
[PrincipalPermission(SecurityAction.Demand,Role="Administrators")]
public bool IsDbUp(string connectionString)
{
 bool isUp = true;
 if (string.IsNullOrEmpty(connectionString))
 {
  PingException ex = new PingException();
  ex.Title = "Error Function:IdDbUp()";
  ex.Message = "Argument is null.";
  ex.InnerException = " ";
  ex.StackTrace = " ";
```

WCF Recipes

```
    throw new FaultException<PingException>(ex,"Reason: Argument is
null");
  }
  try
  {
    SqlConnection connection = new SqlConnection(connectionString);
    connection.Open();
    connection.Close();
  }
  catch (SqlException)
  {
    isUp = false;
  }
    return isUp;
}
```

4. Next, open App.config and replace the `<customBinding>` section with the following:

```
<wsHttpBinding >
  <binding name="Secured_IPingService">
    <security mode="Message">
      <message clientCredentialType="Windows"/>
    </security>
  </binding>
</wsHttpBinding>
```

5. Modify the `<service>` section as follows:

```
<service name="WcfDbPingService.PingService">
   <endpoint address="" binding="wsHttpBinding"
            bindingConfiguration="Secured_IPingService"
            contract="WcfDbPingService.IPingService">
     <identity>
         <dns value="localhost" />
     </identity>
   </endpoint>
   <endpoint address="mex" binding="mexHttpBinding"
            contract="IMetadataExchange" />
   <host>
      <baseAddresses>
         <add baseAddress="http://localhost:8733/Design_Time_
Addresses/WcfDbPingService/Service1/" />
     </baseAddresses>
   </host>
</service>
```

Chapter 6

6. Update the service reference of `PingDbTestApp`. If you get any error while updating, remove the existing reference and add again.

7. Open `PingDbTestForm`. In the `btnPing_Cick` method, add a `catch` clause for `AccessDeniedException` to display the access denied error. After modification, the method will be similar to the following code:

```
private void btnPing_Click(object sender, EventArgs e)
{
  try
    {
      PingServiceReference.PingServiceClient client = new PingServiceReference.PingServiceClient();
      bool result = client.IsDbUp(txtConnString.Text);
      lblResult.Text = "Database with connection string " + txtConnString.Text + " is up? " + result;
    }
    catch (FaultException<PingServiceReference.PingException> ex)
    {
      MessageBox.Show(ex.Detail.Message);
    }
    catch (System.ServiceModel.Security.
SecurityAccessDeniedException ex)
    {
      MessageBox.Show(ex.Message);
    }
}
```

8. Run `PingDbTestApp`. Click on the **Ping** button. You will see the following access denied message:

9. Close `PingDbTestApp`. Right-click on `WcfDbPingService`. Navigate to **Debug | Run in a new instance**.

10. Navigate to the `bin\debug` folder of `PingDbTestApp`. Run `PingDbTestApp.exe` as the Administrator.

WCF Recipes

11. Click on the **Ping** button after entering a valid connection string. You will see the following screen:

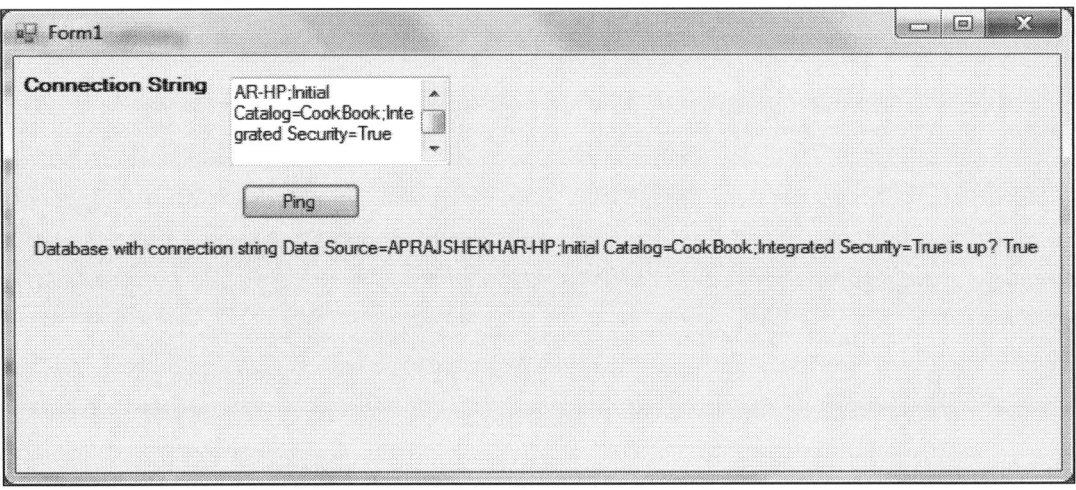

How it works...

To make the IsDbUp service method accessible to a user with a specific role, we performed two actions. First, we decorated the IsDbUp with [PrincipalPermission].Then we passed Demand as SecurityAction and Administrators as Role similar to the following code:

```
[PrincipalPermission(SecurityAction.Demand,Role="Administrators")]
public bool IsDbUp(string connectionString)
{
  bool isUp = true;
  if (string.IsNullOrEmpty(connectionString))
  {
  PingException ex = new PingException();
  ex.Title = "Error Function:IdDbUp()";
  ex.Message = "Argument is null.";
  ex.InnerException = " ";
  ex.StackTrace = " ";
  throw new FaultException<PingException>(ex,"Reason: Argument is null");
  }
  try
  {
  SqlConnection connection = new SqlConnection(connectionString);
  connection.Open();
```

```
        connection.Close();
    }
    catch (SqlException)
    {
    isUp = false;
    }
    return isUp;
}
```

Second, in App.config, we replaced customBinding with wsHttpBinding. Then we added a <security> section to it and set its mode to Message. By doing this we ensured that the message itself is secured. If we had used Transport as mode, the security while delivering the message would be ensured. However, the security of the message—including the headers and the body of the message—is not ensured:

```
<wsHttpBinding >
   <binding name="Secured_IPingService">
      <security mode="Message">
         <message clientCredentialType="Windows"/>
      </security>
   </binding>
</wsHttpBinding>
```

Next, we added a <message> section and set its clientCredentialType to Windows. This tells the runtime to look for the role as a part of the Windows credentials being sent:

```
<wsHttpBinding >
   <binding name="Secured_IPingService">
      <security mode="Message">
         <message clientCredentialType="Windows"/>
      </security>
   </binding>
</wsHttpBinding>
```

Then we changed the bindingConfiguration and binding attributes of the <endpoint> section, which is within the <service> section, to the binding we created:

```
<service name="WcfDbPingService.PingService">
   <endpoint address="" binding="wsHttpBinding"
             bindingConfiguration="Secured_IPingService"
             contract="WcfDbPingService.IPingService">
      <identity>
         <dns value="localhost" />
      </identity>
   </endpoint>
   <endpoint address="mex" binding="mexHttpBinding"
             contract="IMetadataExchange" />
```

```xml
<host>
    <baseAddresses>
      <add baseAddress="http://localhost:8733/Design_Time_
Addresses/WcfDbPingService/Service1/" />
    </baseAddresses>
  host>
</service>
```

At the client side, we included a `catch` clause for `AccessDeniedException`:

```csharp
private void btnPing_Click(object sender, EventArgs e)
{
 try
   {
    PingServiceReference.PingServiceClient client = new
    PingServiceReference.PingServiceClient();
    bool result = client.IsDbUp(txtConnString.Text);
    lblResult.Text = "Database with connection string " +
    txtConnString.Text + " is up? " + result;
   }
   catch (FaultException<PingServiceReference.PingException> ex)
   {
     MessageBox.Show(ex.Detail.Message);
   }
   catch (System.ServiceModel.Security.SecurityAccessDeniedException
ex)
   {
     MessageBox.Show(ex.Message);
   }
}
```

7
WPF Recipes

In this chapter we will cover:

- Implementing the Model and Repository pattern
- Implementing View Model
- Implementing View commands and binding data to View
- Using the live data shaper for live sorting
- Playing videos using MediaElement
- Using Ribbon control to display the video player controls

Introduction

Windows Presentation Framework (**WPF**) needs no introduction. It provides a unified programming model to develop Windows clients that incorporate User Interface, media, and documents so that developers can use them without depending upon third-party libraries. The focus of this chapter will be on the patterns used with WPF along with new controls introduced in Version 4.5. We will start off with the **Model-View-View Model** (**MVVM**) pattern. The first recipe will cover Model implementation. In the second recipe we will see how to implement View Model. The third recipe will be about View and commands. Then we will focus on the live data shaper in the fourth recipe. The next recipe will deal with playing videos using WPF. The last recipe will be about the Ribbon control that has become part of WPF in .NET 4.5. Live data shaper and Ribbon controls are new to .NET 4.5.

Please keep in mind that we are going to use the database developed in *Chapter 5, ADO.NET Recipes*.

WPF Recipes

Implementing the Model and Repository patterns

The MVVM pattern provides a way to separate the UI logic from business and presentation logic. It does so by dividing the application into three components – Model, View, and View-Model. Model represents the data. View is the visual representation of the data and View-Model contains the presentation logic for the Model to be used by the View. We shall look at each of these components in detail, starting with the Model in this recipe.

Model is a class that represents the data. A Model cannot exist on its own. The data it represents must be pulled from a data source and mapped to the Model. That is where the Repository pattern comes into the picture. In this recipe we will implement both the Model and Repository patterns.

The Model will hold the data related to the user, which includes ID, name, and so on; and Repository will connect to a SQL Server and retrieve the data.

How to do it...

1. Launch SQL Server Management Studio 2012.
2. Add a new table to the `CookBook` database and name it `tb_User`.
3. Add the following columns to the `tb_User` table:

Name	Data type	Is Identity Column
ID	int	Yes
User_name	nvarchar	No
Email_id	nvarchar	No
First_name	nchar	No
Last_name	nchar	No

4. Next, add a stored procedure that will get user data from `tb_User` and name it `GetUsers`. The procedure will be as follows:

   ```
   USE [CookBook]
   GO

   /****** Object:  StoredProcedure [dbo].[GetUsers]    Script Date: 02-08-2012 20:32:59 ******/
   SET ANSI_NULLS ON
   GO

   SET QUOTED_IDENTIFIER ON
   GO
   ```

Chapter 7

```
CREATE PROCEDURE [dbo].[GetUsers]
   AS
BEGIN
   -- SET NOCOUNT ON added to prevent extra result sets from
   -- interfering with SELECT statements.
   SET NOCOUNT ON;

   SELECT [Id]
       ,[User_name]
       ,[Email_id]
       ,[First_name]
       ,[Last_name]
     FROM [dbo].[tb_User]

END

GO
```

5. Press *F5* to execute the procedure.
6. Launch Visual Studio 2012. Create a project of type **WPF Application** and name it `WpfMVVM`.
7. Add another project of type **Class Library** and name it `Model`.
8. Add a reference to `Microsoft.SqlServer.ConnectionInfo.dll` and save the solution.
9. Delete `Class1.cs` of the `Model` project.
10. Add a new class. Name it `User` and make it public.
11. Add the following properties to the `User` class:

Name	Data type
ID	int
UserName	String
Email	String
FirstName	String
LastName	String

12. After adding the properties, the `User` class will be as follows:

```
public class User
{
   public int ID { get; set; }
   public string UserName { get; set; }
   public string Email { get; set; }
```

```csharp
        public string FirstName { get; set; }
        public string LastName { get; set; }
    }
```

13. Add an interface to the `Model` project and name it `IDataRepository`.
14. Add a method to `IDataRepository` that returns a collection of `User` instances and name it `GetUsers`.
15. After the addition of the method, the interface will be similar to the following code:

```csharp
public interface IDataRepository
{
    ObservableCollection<User> GetUsers();
}
```

16. Add a new class and name it `SqlDataRepository`.
17. Modify the `SqlDataRepository` class so that it implements `IDataRepository`.
18. Add the following code to the `GetUsers` method:

```csharp
public ObservableCollection<User> GetUsers()
{
    ObservableCollection<User> users = null;
    using (SqlConnection connection = new
      SqlConnection(ConfigurationManager.ConnectionStrings["local"].
ConnectionString))
    {
        connection.Open();
        SqlCommand command = new SqlCommand();
        command.Connection = connection;
        command.CommandType = CommandType.StoredProcedure;
        command.CommandText = "GetUsers";
        using (IDataReader reader = command.ExecuteReader())
        {
            users = MapUsers(reader);
        }
    }
    return users;
}
```

19. Next, add a private method that accepts `IDataReader` as a parameter and returns the collection of the `User` instances. Name it `MapUsers`. Its signature will be:

```csharp
private ObservableCollection<User> MapUsers(IDataReader reader)
{
}
```

20. Add the following code to the `MapUsers` method:

    ```
    ObservableCollection<User> users = new
    ObservableCollection<User>();
    if (reader != null)
    {
     while (reader.Read())
      {
        User user = new User();
        user.ID = Convert.ToInt32( reader["Id"]);
        user.UserName = reader["User_name"].ToString();
        user.Email = reader["Email_id"].ToString();
        user.FirstName = reader["First_name"].ToString();
        user.LastName = reader["Last_name"].ToString();
        users.Add(user);
      }
    }
    return users;
    ```

21. Next, add a new project of test project type and name it `ModelViewModelTests`.
22. Add a reference to the `Model` project.
23. Rename the existing test class to `DataRepositoryTest`.
24. Rename the `Test1` method to `TestGetUsers`.
25. Add the following code to the `TestGetUsers` method:

    ```
    IDataRepository repository = new SqlDataRepository();
    ObservableCollection<User> users = repository.GetUsers();
    Assert.IsNotNull(users);
    Assert.IsTrue(users.Count > 0);
    ```

26. Add an `App.config` file to `ModelViewModelTests`.
27. Add connection string details as shown in the following code:

    ```
    <connectionStrings>
       <add name="local" connectionString="Data Source=APRAJSHEKHAR-
    HP;Initial Catalog=CookBook;Integrated Security=True"/>
    </connectionStrings>
    ```

28. Run the test. If it runs successfully, you will see a test report as shown in the following screenshot:

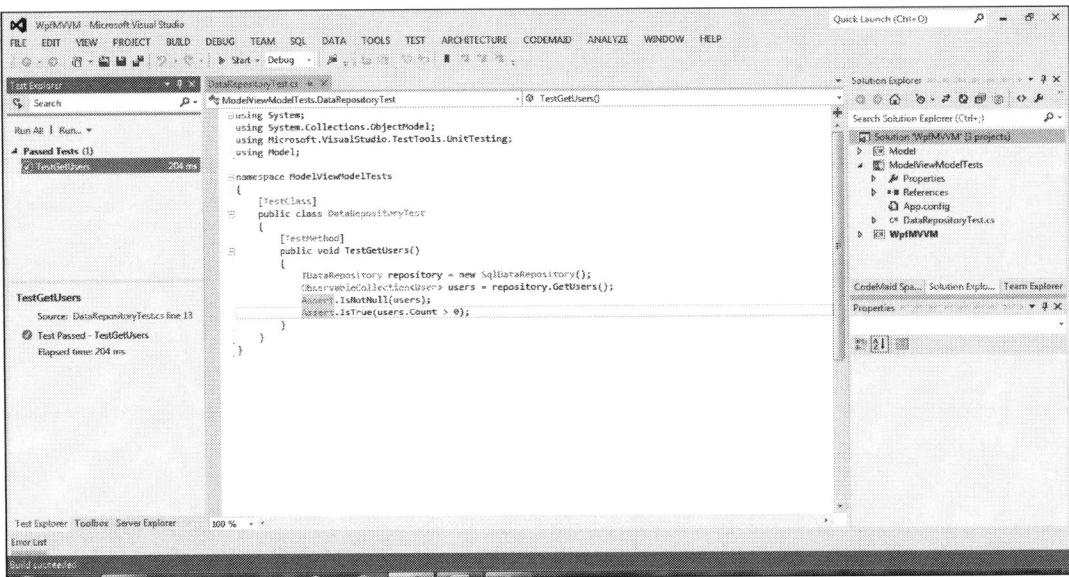

29. If the test fails, you will see the following report:

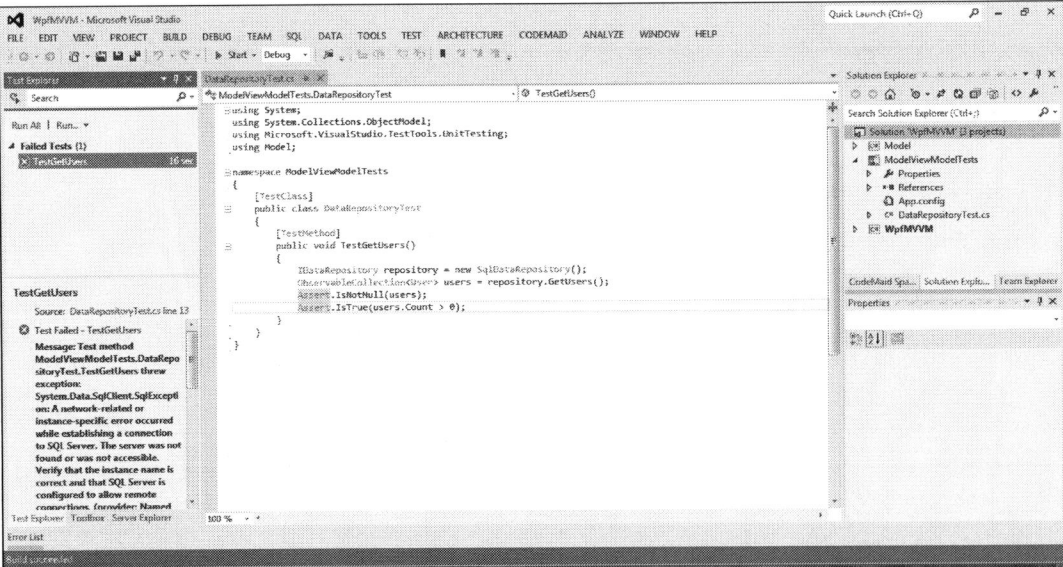

How it works...

In the last section, we accomplished three things – we created a model class (`User`) that reflects the table's columns, implemented the logic (`MapUsers` method) to map class instances to the rows of the table, and developed an adapter class (`SqlDataRepository`) that provides the bridge between data retrieval and mapping. Let us look at them starting with the `User` class.

We created a table named `tb_User`. The functionality of the `User` class is that other components can make use of the data in `tb_User` without knowing the details of the table. That is the reason why the properties of the `User` class have names similar to the columns of the table, as shown in the following table:

Name of the property	Name of the column
ID	Id
Email	Email_id
UserName	User_name
FirstName	First_name
LastName	Last_name

 Keep in mind that this is a convention and not a hard-and-fast rule.

Next is `SqlDataRepository`, which acted as an adapter for data retrieval and mapping. By definition, any class that acts in such a fashion implements the Repository pattern. The Repository pattern, simply put, has an interface that defines the operations for a data source, and a class that implements the interface for a specific type of database server where the data source resides. In our case, the data source is the `tb_User` table and it is in MS SQL Server 2012. In the `IDataRepository` interface we defined the `GetUsers` operation:

```
public interface IDataRepository
{
   ObservableCollection<User> GetUsers();
}
```

In `SqlDataRepository`, we implemented `IDataRepository` for MS SQL Server 2012 so that we can retrieve the data from `tb_User` using the stored procedure:

```
public class SqlDataRepository:IDataRepository
{
   public ObservableCollection<User> GetUsers()
   {
```

```csharp
      ObservableCollection<User> users = null;
      using (SqlConnection connection = new SqlConnection(ConfigurationM
anager.ConnectionStrings["local"].ConnectionString))
    {
      connection.Open();
      SqlCommand command = new SqlCommand();
      command.Connection = connection;
      command.CommandType = CommandType.StoredProcedure;
      command.CommandText = "GetUsers";
      using (IDataReader reader = command.ExecuteReader())
        {
          users = MapUsers(reader);
        }
    }
    return users;
   }
}
```

In the preceding code we have made a call to the `MapUsers` method. This is the method that maps the row retrieved from the table to the instance of the `User` class:

```csharp
    private ObservableCollection<User> MapUsers(IDataReader reader)
    {
      ObservableCollection<User> users = new ObservableCollection<User>();
      if (reader != null)
      {
        while (reader.Read())
        {
        User user = new User();
        user.ID = Convert.ToInt32( reader["Id"]);
        user.UserName = reader["User_name"].ToString();
        user.Email = reader["Email_id"].ToString();
        user.FirstName = reader["First_name"].ToString();
        user.LastName = reader["Last_name"].ToString();
        users.Add(user);
        }
      }
      return users;
    }
```

In the preceding code, we iterated through each row, retrieved the data from the columns, and populated the instances of the `User` class with the retrieved data. Then we added the instances to `ObservableCollection`. The reason for using `ObservableCollection` will become clear in the next recipe.

For our application, `MapUsers` is the Data Mapper. A **Data Mapper** is a pattern that defines how rows are mapped to the instances of the Model. The mapping can be implemented in a simple format as we did earlier, or it can be implemented by pushing the mapping details to an external file. That is what ORM libraries, such as NHibernate do. For our recipe, the simple implementation sufficed.

Implementing View Model

MVVM, **View Model** (**VM**) acts as a glue and controller between View and Model. It also interacts with those libraries and services that help in CRUD (Create, Retrieve, Update, and Delete) operations on the Model.

In this recipe we will implement a View Model for our Model class, `User`. The View Model will also contain logic to pass data to and receive data from View. It will also interact with the data repository we implemented in our previous recipe.

How to do it...

1. Launch Visual Studio 2012 and open `WpfMVVM.sln`.
2. Add a new folder to the `WpfMVVM` project. Name it `View Model`.
3. Add a new class to the `View Model` folder. Name it `UserViewModel`.
4. Add a reference to the Model project.
5. Add a private variable of type `IDataRepository`. Name it `_repository`:

   ```
   private IDataRepository _repository;
   ```

6. Add another private variable of type collection of `User`. Name it `_users`:

   ```
   private ObservableCollection<User> _users;
   ```

7. Next, add a no-argument/default constructor. Set `_repository` as the new instance of `SqlDataRepository` inside the constructor:

   ```
   public UserViewModel()
   {
     _repository = new SqlDataRepository();
   }
   ```

8. Add a private method that returns a collection of the `User` class and name it `GetUsers`. Its signature will be:

   ```
   private ObservableCollection<User> GetUsers()
   {
   }
   ```

9. Add the following code to the `GetUsers` method:

   ```
   return _repository.GetUsers();
   ```

10. Next, modify `UserViewModel` so that it implements the `INotifyPropertyChanged` interface:

    ```
    public class UserViewModel:INotifyPropertyChanged
    {
    ...
    }
    ```

11. Add a public variable of the `PropertyChangedEventHandler` delegate of type event. Name it `PropertyChanged`:

    ```
    public event PropertyChangedEventHandler PropertyChanged;
    ```

12. Add a getter and setter (together known as mutator) for `_users`. Call `GetUsers` from the getter:

    ```
    public ObservableCollection<User> Users
    {
      get
      {
        return GetUsers();
      }
      set
      {
        _users = value;
      }
    }
    ```

13. Raise the `PropertyChanged` event from the setter for `_users`:

    ```
    public ObservableCollection<User> Users
    {
      get
      {
      return GetUsers();
      }
      set
      {
      _users = value;
      if (PropertyChanged != null)
        {
          PropertyChanged(this, new PropertyChangedEventArgs("Users"));
        }
      }
    }
    ```

How it works...

View Model interacts with two layers. One of them is a data access or business logic layer. In our recipe, the Model project acts as a data access layer. So, we instantiated `SqlDataRepository` within the constructor and assigned it to the `IDataRepository` variable:

```
public UserViewModel()
{
  _repository = new SqlDataRepository();
}
```

Then we used the `_repository` to get a list of users from the SQL Server in the `GetUsers` method:

```
private ObservableCollection<User> GetUsers()
{
  return _repository.GetUsers();
}
```

The other layer that View Model interacts with is View. To make View Model work seamlessly with View, we need a way for View Model to tell View whenever there is a change in data. Therefore, we implemented the `INotifyPropertyChanged` interface. It contains one event – `PropertyChangedEventHandler`. We need to fire this event whenever data is set using any of the setters in View Model. In `UserViewModel`, we did this in the setter for the `Users` property:

```
public ObservableCollection<User> Users
{
  get
  {
    return GetUsers();
  }
  set
  {
    _users = value;
    if (PropertyChanged != null)
    {
    PropertyChanged(this, new PropertyChangedEventArgs("Users"));
    }
  }
}
```

If any of the controls in View are bound to this property, .NET will notify them when we raise the `PropertyChanged` event. Thus, View Model acts as a glue between View and business logic/data logic services.

Implementing View commands and binding data to View

In MVVM, if View wants to communicate with View Model, it is through commands. Commands are essentially classes that implement the `ICommand` interface. However, creating a separate class for each command required by the View makes the code base unnecessarily large. In this recipe we will develop a generic command class; the instances of which can be used by different View controls, such as buttons, to invoke a specific logic within View Model.

We will also look at how to bind data present in View Model to a control in View. We will accomplish this by binding user data in `UserViewModel` to the `DataGrid` control in `MainWindow.xaml`, which is our View.

How to do it...

1. Launch Visual Studio 2012. Open `WpfMVVM.sln`.
2. Add a new folder to `WpfMVVM` project. Name it `Commands`.
3. Add a new class to the `Commands` folder. Name it `DelegateCommand`.
4. Modify `DelegateCommand` so that it implements the `ICommand` interface.

   ```
   public class DelegateCommand:ICommand
   {
       public bool CanExecute(object parameter)
       {
         throw new NotImplementedException();
       }

        public event EventHandler CanExecuteChanged;

       public void Execute(object parameter)
       {
         throw new NotImplementedException();
       }
   }
   ```

5. Add a private variable of type `Action`. Name it `_commandMethod`:

   ```
   private Action _commandMethod;
   ```

6. Add a parameterized constructor that accepts `Action` as a parameter. Assign the parameter to `_commandMethod`:

   ```
   public DelegateCommand(Action commandMethod)
   {
     _commandMethod = commandMethod;
   }
   ```

7. Replace the statements in the `CanExecute` method with the following code:

   ```
   return true;
   ```

8. Replace the statements in `ExecuteMethod` with the following statement:

   ```
   _commandMethod.Invoke();
   ```

9. Open the `UserViewModel` class. Add the properties shown in the following table:

Name	Type	Description
Load	DelegateCommand	To load user data into the `DataGrid`
Clear	DelegateCommand	To clear the `DataGrid`

10. The properties would be similar to the following:

    ```
    public DelegateCommand Load { get; set; }
    public DelegateCommand Clear { get; set; }
    ```

11. Add a private method that returns `void`. Name it `LoadUsers`. Call `GetUsers` within it:

    ```
    private void LoadUsers()
    {
        Users = GetUsers();
    }
    ```

12. Add another private method that returns `void`. Name it `ClearUsers`. Clear the list of users and assign the empty list to the `Users` property within it:

    ```
    private void ClearUsers()
    {
      _users.Clear();
      Users = _users;
    }
    ```

13. Add the following statements to the constructor:

    ```
    Load = new DelegateCommand(LoadUsers);
    Clear = new DelegateCommand(ClearUsers);
    ```

14. Open `MainWindow.xaml`. Design it so that it looks similar to the following screenshot:

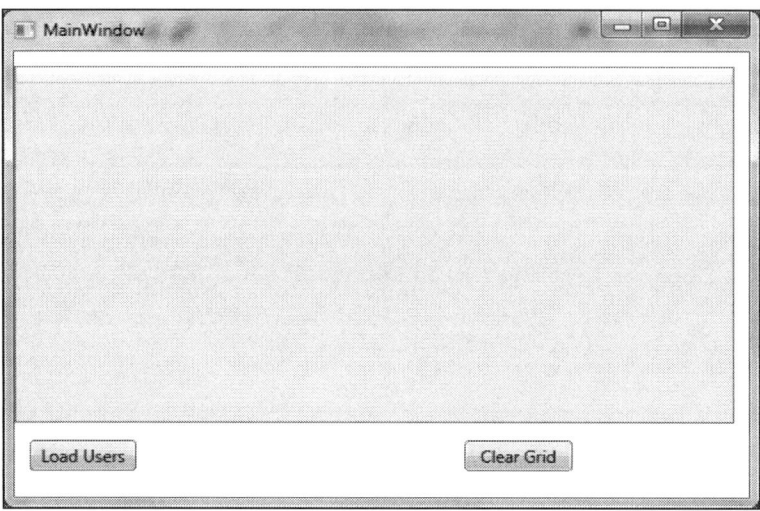

15. Modify the `DataGrid` tag so that it binds to the `Users` property:

    ```
    <DataGrid Margin="0,10,10,0" VerticalAlignment="Top" Grid.
    ColumnSpan="2"  Height="250" ItemsSource="{Binding Path=Users}"/>
    ```

16. Modify the `Load` and `Clear` buttons' tags so that they bind to the `Load` and `Clear` commands, respectively:

    ```
    <Button Content="Load Users"    HorizontalAlignment="Left"
            Command="{Binding Path=Load}"  Margin="11,11,0,0" Grid.
    Row="1"
            VerticalAlignment="Top" Width="75"/>

    <Button Content="Clear Grid"   Command="{Binding Path=Clear}"
          HorizontalAlignment="Left" Margin="43,11,0,0" Grid.Row="1"
          VerticalAlignment="Top" Width="75" Grid.Column="1"/>
    ```

17. Open `MainWindow.xaml.cs` and add the following to the constructor after the call to `InitializeComponents`:

    ```
    DataContext = new UserViewModel();
    ```

18. Open `App.config`. Add the connection strings section so that it is similar to the following:

    ```
    <connectionStrings>
       <add name="local" connectionString="Data Source=APRAJSHEKHAR-
    HP;Initial Catalog=CookBook;Integrated Security=True"/>
    </connectionStrings>
    ```

19. Run the application. You will see the following screenshot:

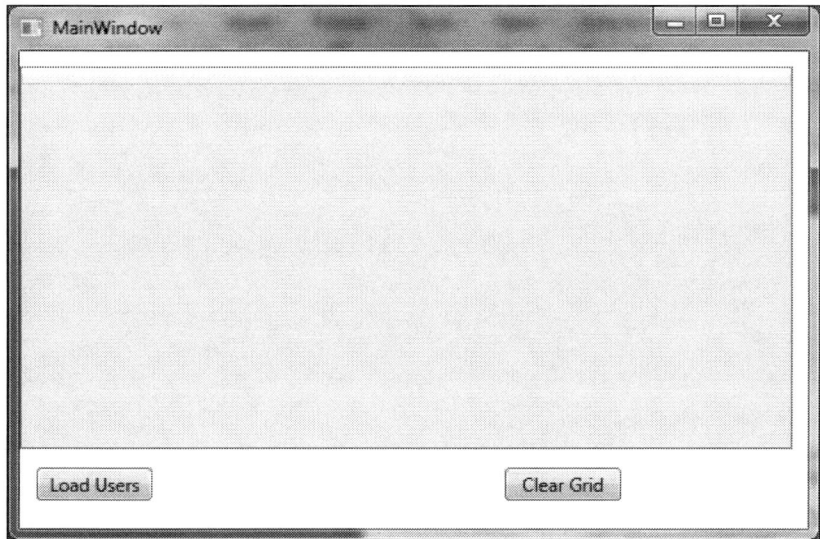

20. Click on the **Load Users** button. You will see the following screenshot:

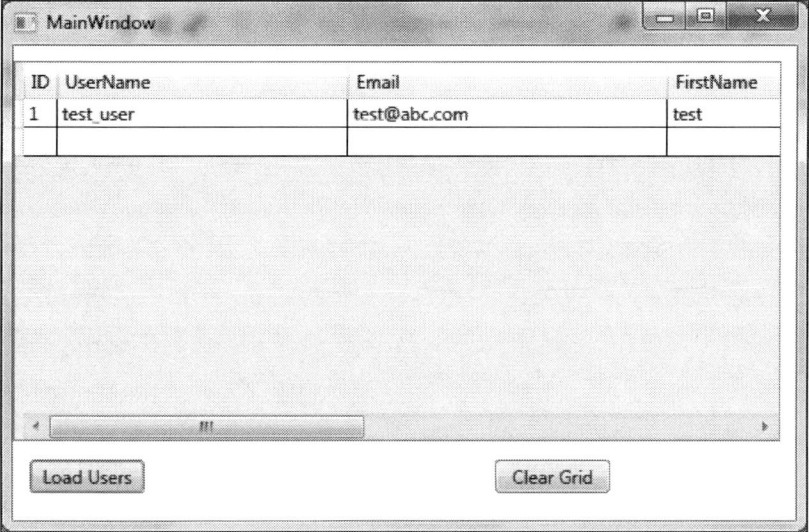

21. Click on the **Clear Grid** button. The screen will be similar to the following screenshot:

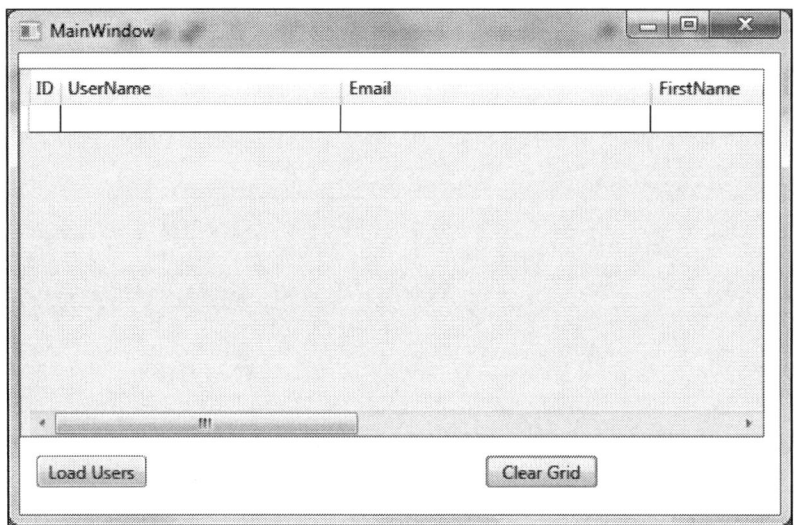

How it works...

The `DelegateCommand` command and binding that happens in `MainWindow.xaml` are the centerpieces of this recipe. Let us start with `DelegateCommand`. The main part of `DelegateCommand` is the `_commandMethod` variable. It is of type `Action`. We have used it to hold the method to be executed. The method to be executed is set via the constructor:

```
public DelegateCommand(Action commandMethod)
{
    _commandMethod = commandMethod;
}
```

So when we created an instance of `DelegateCommand` in the constructor of `UserViewModel`, we had passed the name of the method as an argument:

```
Load = new DelegateCommand(LoadUsers);
```

Once the previous code is executed, the `_commandMethod` variable in `DelegateCommand` would hold a reference to the `LoadUsers` method in `UserViewModel`.

The other two methods in `DelegateCommand`, `CanExecute` and `Execute`, are from the `ICommand` interface. `CanExecute` tells the runtime whether the command can be executed or not. A command, in our case, is the reference to the method held by `_commandMethod`. We are simply returning `true`, which runtime translates as "execute the command". Now the `Execute` method comes into the picture. When the runtime calls `Execute`, the method referred to by `_commandMethod` gets executed. This happens because of the following statement:

```
_commandMethod.Invoke();
```

For example, if `_commandMethod` contained a reference to `LoadUsers` then the previous statement would call the `LoadUsers` method and execute it.

In `UserViewModel`, we have two properties defined as follows:

```
public DelegateCommand Load { get; set; }
public DelegateCommand Clear { get; set; }
```

We instantiate them as shown in the following code:

```
public UserViewModel()
{
    _repository = new SqlDataRepository();
    Load = new DelegateCommand(LoadUsers);
    Clear = new DelegateCommand(ClearUsers);
}
```

So, when `Load` is executed the `LoadUsers` method will be invoked, and when `Clear` is executed `ClearUsers` will be invoked. Now, in the constructor of `MainWindow`, we set its `DataContext` to an instance of `UserViewModel`:

```
DataContext = new UserViewModel();
```

By doing so, we are telling the runtime where to look for the binding properties and commands. In `MainWindow.xaml`, which is our View, we bound `ItemSource` of `DataGrid` to the `Users` property of `UserViewModel`:

```
<DataGrid Margin="0,10,10,0" VerticalAlignment="Top" Grid.
ColumnSpan="2" Height="250"
                ItemsSource="{Binding Path=Users}"/>
```

In the preceding code, `{Binding Path=Users}` tells the runtime to look for the property named `Users` in `UserViewModel`. Similarly, we bound the `Command` attribute of `Button` to the `Load` and `Clear` properties:

```
<Button Content="Load Users" HorizontalAlignment="Left"

Command="{Binding Path=Load}"
                 Margin="11,11,0,0" Grid.Row="1"
VerticalAlignment="Top" Width="75"/>
        <Button Content="Clear Grid"
  Command="{Binding Path=Clear}"
                 HorizontalAlignment="Left" Margin="43,11,0,0" Grid.
Row="1" VerticalAlignment="Top" Width="75" Grid.Column="1"/>
```

As a result of binding the `Command` attribute to the properties of type `DelegateCommand`, we are ensuring that the `LoadUsers` and `Clear` methods of `UserViewModel` get executed when the **Load** and **Clear** buttons are clicked.

Using the live data shaper for live sorting

Data shaping means processing the data by sorting, grouping, or filtering the data being displayed. Live data shaping takes this one step forward and does the processing on live data. In the case of live data, the new data is being added continuously or the existing data is being changed continuously. Before Version 4.5 of .NET, shaping of live data meant adding custom logic so that sorting and grouping do not go wrong. .NET 4.5 provides a new collection type, which negates the requirement of custom logic for shaping live data.

In this recipe, we will use the new collection type to enable sorting of asset data based on the values that change continuously.

How to do it...

1. Launch Visual Studio 2012. Add a new project of type **WPF Application** and name it `LiveDataShaping`.
2. Add a new folder. Name it `Entities`.
3. Add a new class to the `Entities` folder. Name it `Asset`.
4. Add the following properties to the class:

Name	Data type
ID	int
Name	String
Region	String
Value	String

5. Modify the class so that it implements the `INotifyPropertyChanged` interface.

   ```
   public class Asset : INotifyPropertyChanged
   {
   }
   ```

6. Set the `PropertyChanged` event to empty `delegate`:

   ```
   public event PropertyChangedEventHandler PropertyChanged = delegate { };
   ```

7. Modify the `value` property so that it does not use the automatic property feature and raises the `PropertyChanged` event in its setter:

   ```
   private double _currentValue;
   public double Value
   {
     get
     {
   ```

```
      return _currentValue;
    }
    set
    {
      _currentValue = value;
      PropertyChanged(this, new PropertyChangedEventArgs("Value"));
    }
  }
}
```

8. Open `MainWindow.xaml.cs`. Add a `private` variable of type collection `Asset`. Name it `_items`:

   ```
   private ObservableCollection<Asset> _items = new
   ObservableCollection<Asset>();
   ```

9. Next, add a `private` variable of type `DispatcherTimer`. Name it `_timer`:

   ```
   private DispatcherTimer _timer = new DispatcherTimer();
   ```

10. Add a `private` method that returns the collection of `Asset`. Name it `GenerateTestData`. Its signature will be as follows:

    ```
    private ObservableCollection<Asset> GenerateTestData()
    {
    }
    ```

11. Add the following code to the `GenerateTestData` method:

    ```
    ObservableCollection<Asset> temp = new
    ObservableCollection<Asset>();
    temp.Add(new Asset() { ID = 1, Name = "ASD", Region = "Mumbai",
    Value = 1000 });
    temp.Add(new Asset() { ID = 2, Name = "AS Hotel", Region =
    "Chennai", Value = 11000 });
    temp.Add(new Asset() { ID = 3, Name = "AD Cafe", Region =
    "Kolkatta", Value = 10000 });
    temp.Add(new Asset() { ID = 4, Name = "Landmark", Region =
    "Mumbai", Value = 50000 });
    temp.Add(new Asset() { ID = 5, Name = "ASD II", Region =
    "Kolkatta", Value = 400 });
    return temp;
    ```

12. In the constructor, add the following code after the call to `InitializeComponent`:

    ```
    _items = GenerateTestData();
    ICollectionViewLiveShaping view = (ICollectionViewLiveShaping)
    CollectionViewSource.GetDefaultView(_items);

    view.IsLiveSorting = true;
    view.LiveSortingProperties.Add("Value");
    ```

WPF Recipes

```
dgAsset.ItemsSource = (IEnumerable)view;

Random random = new Random();
_timer.Interval = TimeSpan.FromSeconds(1);
_timer.Tick += (s, e) =>
{
  foreach (var item in _items)
    item.Value += random.NextDouble() * 1000 - 500;
};
_timer.Start();
```

13. Open `MainWindow.xaml`. Add `DataGrid`. Name it `dgAsset`:

    `<DataGrid x:Name="dgAsset" IsReadOnly="True" />`

14. Run the application. You will see the following screenshot:

    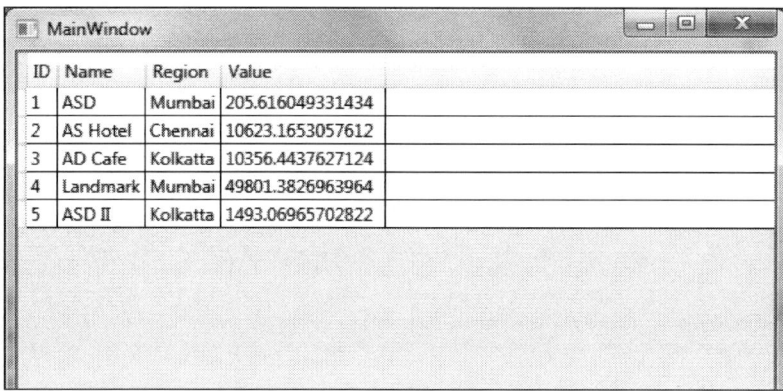

15. Click on the **Value** column so that it is sorted in descending order. You will see the following screenshot:

    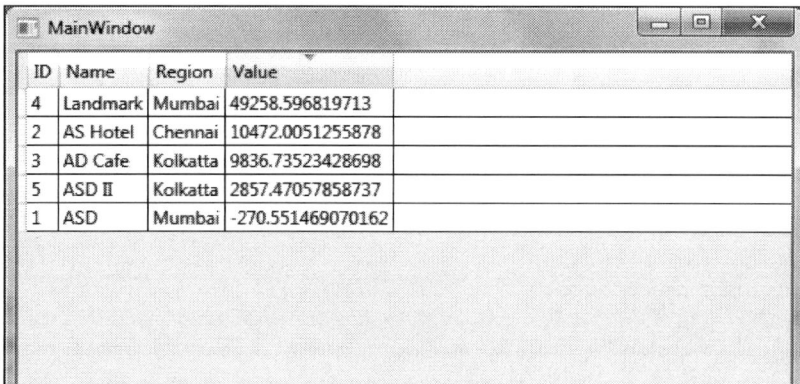

How it works...

The load of shaping live data is taken by the `ICollectionViewLiveShaping` interface. .NET provides us a default implementation for `ICollectionViewLiveShaping` via `CollectionViewSource`. By calling the `GetDefaultView` method of `CollectionViewSource` and passing the `Asset` collection as argument, we have instantiated the default implementation provided by .NET:

```
ICollectionViewLiveShaping view = (ICollectionViewLiveShaping)
CollectionViewSource.GetDefaultView(_items);
```

Then we set `IsLiveSorting` to `true`:

```
view.IsLiveSorting = true;
```

Next, to tell `ICollectionViewLiveShaping` that the sorting has to be done on the `Value` property, we added it to the `LiveSortingProperties` collection of `ICollectionViewLiveShaping`:

```
view.LiveSortingProperties.Add("Value");
```

After that we assigned `view` to `DataGrid`:

```
dgAsset.ItemsSource = (IEnumerable)view;
```

Since `ItemSource` accepts only objects derived from `IEnumerable`, we type-casted the `ICollectionViewLiveShaping` variable view to `IEnumerable`. We used `DispatchTimer` and `Random` to simulate live data:

```
Random random = new Random();
_timer.Interval = TimeSpan.FromSeconds(1);
_timer.Tick += (s, e) =>
{
 foreach (var item in _items)
  item.Value += random.NextDouble() * 1000 - 500;
};
_timer.Start();
```

Playing videos using MediaElement

The `MediaElement` control provides an easy way to play videos in WPF applications. Essentially, `MediaElement` wraps Windows Media Player. So any video that Windows Media Player can play, `MediaElement` can also play.

In this recipe we will use `MediaElement` to create a simple video player with four basic functionalities: load, play, pause, and stop.

WPF Recipes

How to do it...

1. Launch Visual Studio 2012. Create a new project of type **WPF Application**. Name it `WpfMediaPlayer`.
2. Add a reference to `System.Window.Forms`.
3. Open `MainWindow.xaml`. Switch to design mode.
4. Design it so that it looks similar to the following screenshot:

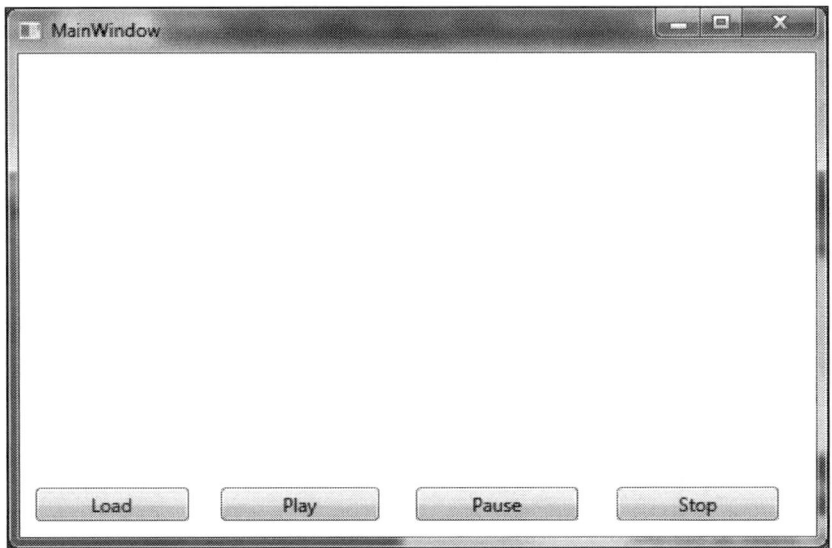

5. Name the controls as detailed in the following table:

Control	Name	Description
MediaElement	mePlayer	To display the video
Button	btnLoad	To load the file and set the source of mePlayer
Button	btnPlay	To play the video
Button	btnPause	To pause the video
Button	btnStop	To stop the video

Chapter 7

6. Set the `UnloadedBehavior` and `LoadedBehavior` attributes of `MediaElement`:

   ```
   <MediaElement x:Name="mePlayer" Grid.ColumnSpan="5" Height="239"
   Margin="10,10,10,0" VerticalAlignment="Top"
   UnloadedBehavior="Manual" LoadedBehavior="Manual"/>
   ```

7. Double-click on `btnLoad` to add the Click event handler.

8. Add the following code:

   ```
   OpenFileDialog diagOpen = new OpenFileDialog();
   if (diagOpen.ShowDialog() == System.Windows.Forms.DialogResult.OK)
   {
      mePlayer.Source = new Uri(diagOpen.FileName);
      mePlayer.Play();
      mePlayer.Pause();
   }
   ```

9. Open `MainWindow.xaml`. Switch to design mode. Add event handlers for `btnPlay`, `btnPause`, and `btnStop`.

10. In the event handler for `btnPlay` add the following highlighted code:

    ```
    private void btnPlay_Click(object sender, RoutedEventArgs e)
    {
       mePlayer.Play();
    }
    ```

11. In the event handler for `btnPause` add the following highlighted code:

    ```
    private void btnPause_Click(object sender, RoutedEventArgs e)
    {
       mePlayer.Pause();
    }
    ```

12. In the event handler for `btnStop` add the following highlighted code:

    ```
    private void btnStop_Click(object sender, RoutedEventArgs e)
    {
       mePlayer.Stop();
    }
    ```

WPF Recipes

13. Run the application. Click on the Load button and select a file. You will see the following screenshot:

14. Test the application by clicking on the **Play**, **Pause**, and **Stop** buttons.

How it works...

`MediaElement` leverages the functionalities provided by Windows Media Player. Due to this we need not worry about the "heavy lifting" activities such as loading the file, initializing the decoder, rendering the video, and so on. The first step in using `MediaElement` is setting its `Source` property to a video file:

```
mePlayer.Source = new Uri(diagOpen.FileName);
mePlayer.Play();
mePlayer.Pause();
```

In the preceding code we called `Play()` and `Pause()` so that the first frame of the video is displayed. To call `Play` and `Pause` just after setting the `Source` property, we have to set `LoadedBehavior` and `UnloadedBehavior` to `Manual`. We did that in the XAML code:

```
<MediaElement x:Name="mePlayer" Grid.ColumnSpan="5" Height="239"
Margin="10,10,10,0" VerticalAlignment="Top"
UnloadedBehavior="Manual" LoadedBehavior="Manual"/>
```

As you have seen in the previous code, the `Play` method starts playing the video. We have used the `Play` method in the Click event handler of `btnPlay`:

```
private void btnPlay_Click(object sender, RoutedEventArgs e)
{
  mePlayer.Play();
}
```

Similarly, we called the `Pause` and `Stop` methods of `MediaElement` to pause the video and stop playing the video. In the Click event handler of `btnPause` we called the `Pause` method:

```
private void btnPause_Click(object sender, RoutedEventArgs e)
{
  mePlayer.Pause();
}
```

In the Click event handler of `btnStop` we called the `Stop` method:

```
private void btnStop_Click(object sender, RoutedEventArgs e)
{
  mePlayer.Stop();
}
```

Using Ribbon control to display the video player controls

Until .NET 4.5, Ribbon control for WPF existed as a separate download. In Version 4.5 of .NET, Ribbon control and its corresponding child controls have been included as a part of the framework itself so that a separate download is not required. Ribbon and its child controls include `RibbonButton`, `RibbonButtonGroup`, `RibbonTab`, and so on.

In this recipe, we will modify the video player created in the last recipe so that the video control buttons are displayed using Ribbon control.

How to do it...

1. Launch Visual Studio 2012. Open the solution named `WpfMediaPlayer`.
2. Open `MainWindow.xaml`.
3. Remove the `Load`, `Play`, `Pause`, and `Stop` buttons.

WPF Recipes

4. Move `MediaElement` to the bottom. Once done, the UI will look as shown in the following screenshot:

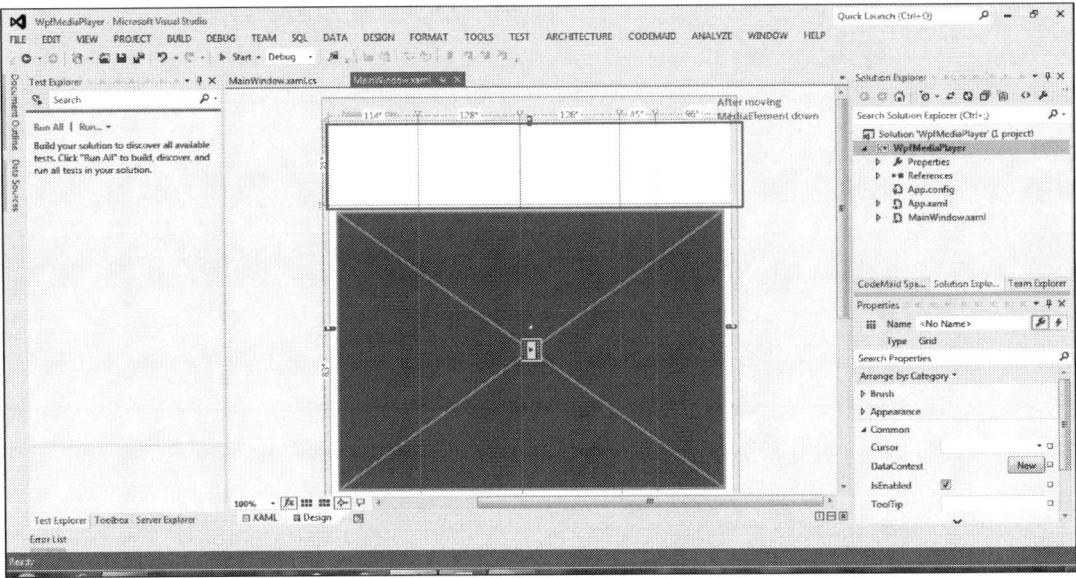

5. Switch to the **XAML** view. Add the `Ribbon` control to the main `Grid` so that it is placed on the top of the window, above `MediaElement`. The markup will be as follows:

```
<Ribbon HorizontalAlignment="Left" Margin="10,0,0,0"
VerticalAlignment="Top" Grid.ColumnSpan="5" Width="489"
Height="108">
</Ribbon>
```

6. Add `RibbonTab` to the `Ribbon` control. Set its header to `Video Controls`. The markup will be as highlighted in the following code:

```
<Ribbon HorizontalAlignment="Left" Margin="10,0,0,0"
VerticalAlignment="Top" Grid.ColumnSpan="5" Width="489"
Height="108">
    <RibbonTab Header="Video Controls" HorizontalAlignment="Left"
Height="57" VerticalAlignment="Top" Width="487">

    </RibbonTab>
</Ribbon>
```

7. Add `RibbonGroup` to `RibbonTab`. The markup will be similar to the highlighted markup in the following code:

```
<Ribbon HorizontalAlignment="Left" Margin="10,0,0,0"
VerticalAlignment="Top" Grid.ColumnSpan="5" Width="489"
Height="108">
   <RibbonTab Header="Video Controls" HorizontalAlignment="Left"
Height="57" VerticalAlignment="Top" Width="487">
   <RibbonGroup Header="" Height="57" Margin="0"
VerticalAlignment="Top" Width="251">

   </RibbonGroup>
   </RibbonTab>
</Ribbon>
```

8. Next, add four buttons to `RibbonGroup`. Lay them out so that they look similar to the following screenshot:

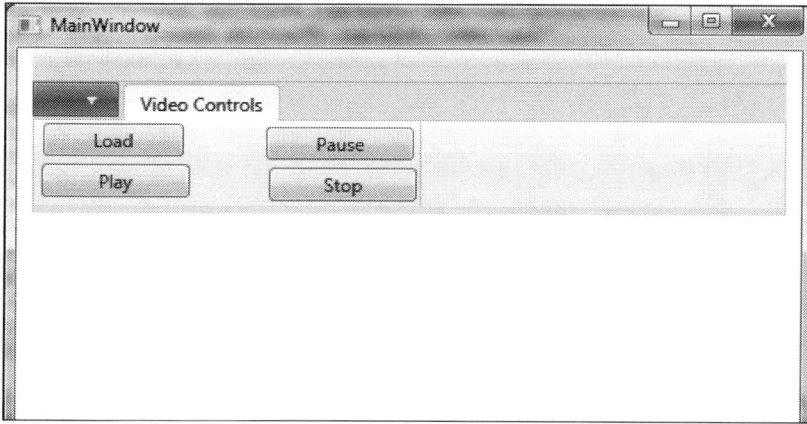

9. Now name them according to the following table:

Control	Name	Description
Button	btnLoad	To load the file and set the source of `mePlayer`
Button	btnPlay	To play the video
Button	btnPause	To pause the video
Button	btnStop	To stop the video

WPF Recipes

10. Set btnLoad_Click as the value of the Click attribute of btnLoad.
11. Set btnPlay_Click as the value of the Click attribute of btnPlay.
12. Set btnPause_Click as the value of the Click attribute of btnPause.
13. Set btnStop_Click as the value of the Click attribute of btnStop.
14. The markup for the buttons will be similar to the highlighted markup shown in the following code:

```xml
<Ribbon HorizontalAlignment="Left" Margin="10,0,0,0"
VerticalAlignment="Top" Grid.ColumnSpan="5" Width="489"
Height="108">
   <RibbonTab Header="Video Controls" HorizontalAlignment="Left"
Height="57" VerticalAlignment="Top" Width="487">
      <RibbonGroup Header="" Height="57" Margin="0"
VerticalAlignment="Top" Width="251">
  <Button x:Name="btnLoad" Content="Load" Margin="0,0,-91,0"
   Click="btnLoad_Click"/>
  <Button x:Name="btnPlay" Content="Play"
   RenderTransformOrigin="0.5,2.045" Margin="-1,27,-95,-27"
   Click="btnPlay_Click"/>
  <Button x:Name="btnPause" Content="Pause"
   RenderTransformOrigin="0.5,2.045" Margin="144,2,-240,-2"
   Click="btnPause_Click"/>
  <Button x:Name="btnStop" Content="Stop"
   RenderTransformOrigin="0.5,2.045" Margin="146,29,-242,-29"
   Click="btnStop_Click"/>
     </RibbonGroup>
   </RibbonTab>
</Ribbon>
```

15. Run the application. Click on **Load** and select a video file. You will see the following screenshot:

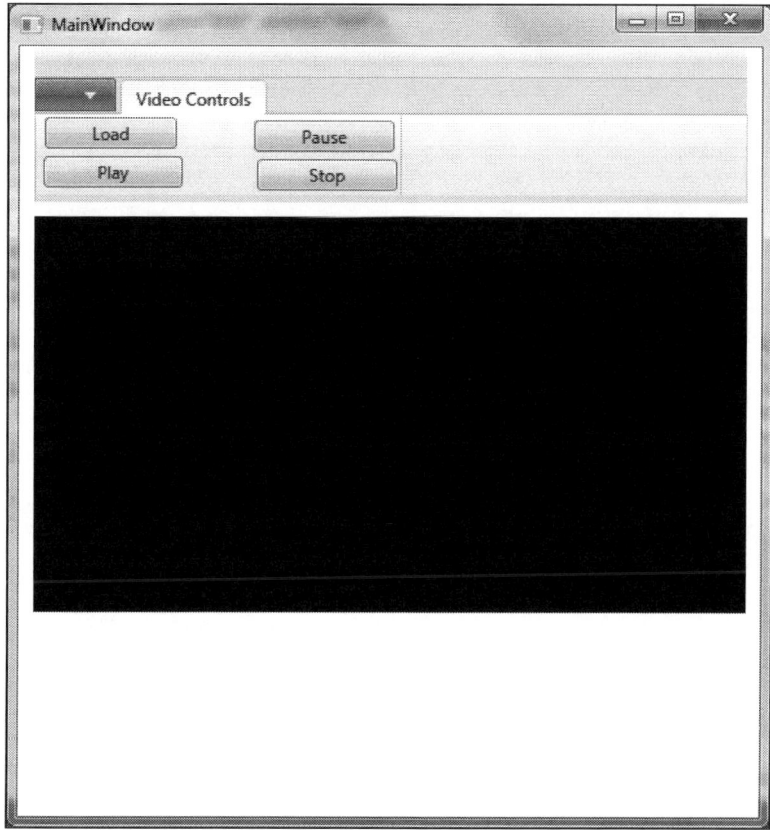

16. Test the play, pause, and stop functionalities.

WPF Recipes

How it works...

The main point to keep in mind regarding the Ribbon control is that to display the buttons (or for that matter any other control) properly, you will need to use `RibbonGroup`. The same is true for `RibbonTab`. That is the reason we placed `RibbonGroup` within `RibbonTab` and the `Button` controls within `RibbonGroup`:

```xml
<Ribbon HorizontalAlignment="Left" Margin="10,0,0,0"
VerticalAlignment="Top" Grid.ColumnSpan="5" Width="489" Height="108">
  <RibbonTab Header="Video Controls" HorizontalAlignment="Left"
Height="57" VerticalAlignment="Top" Width="487">
    <RibbonGroup Header="" Height="57" Margin="0"
VerticalAlignment="Top" Width="251">
      <Button x:Name="btnLoad" Content="Load" Margin="0,0,-91,0"
        Click="btnLoad_Click"/>
      <Button x:Name="btnPlay" Content="Play"
        RenderTransformOrigin="0.5,2.045" Margin="-1,27,-95,-27"
        Click="btnPlay_Click"/>
      <Button x:Name="btnPause" Content="Pause"
        RenderTransformOrigin="0.5,2.045" Margin="144,2,-240,-2"
        Click="btnPause_Click"/>
      <Button x:Name="btnStop" Content="Stop"
        RenderTransformOrigin="0.5,2.045" Margin="146,29,-242,-29"
        Click="btnStop_Click"/>
    </RibbonGroup>
  </RibbonTab>
</Ribbon>
```

Since `Ribbon`, `RibbonTab`, and `RibbonGroup` act as containers, we can directly add the event handlers for the buttons as evident in the preceding code.

8
ASP.NET Recipes – II

In this chapter we will cover:

- ▶ Preventing cross-site injection using the anti-XSS library
- ▶ Adding Google Map functionality using Map Helper
- ▶ Third-party authentication of users using Google
- ▶ Implementing unobtrusive validation

Introduction

In this chapter we will look at the advanced features provided by ASP.NET. The first recipe will use built-in anti-XSS library to prevent cross-site scripting. The next recipe will be about enabling map functionalities using Google Maps and Map Helper. The third recipe will focus on using third-party authentication services. The last recipe will tell you how to use the Validation helper to implement client- and server-side validation. All the recipes deal with new features provided by ASP.NET 4.5. The first recipe deals with new features of the ASP.NET application (ASPX pages), while the remaining three deal with new features of ASP.NET Web Sites (CSHTML pages). This chapter assumes that you know the basics of ASP.NET Web Sites and CSHTML pages. Also, except for the first recipe, the recipes work well only with Internet Explorer 9 and higher.

ASP.NET Recipes – II

Preventing cross-site injection using the anti-XSS library

Cross-site scripting (**XSS**) is the process of injecting HTML or JavaScript fragments into a website. When these fragments are executed, they can do anything from redirecting the user to another site without his/her knowledge to accessing the cookies of the user and thus hijacking his/her session. Developers have been using the anti-XSS library for .NET to safeguard their websites from XSS. With Version 4.5, .NET has incorporated the anti-XSS library into ASP.NET.

In this recipe, we will develop a page for entering comments and displaying it. We will use anti-XSS functionality to make the comment display page safe from XSS.

How to do it...

1. Launch Visual Studios 2012.
2. Create a project of type **ASP.NET Web Forms Application**. Name it `AntiXss`.
3. Remove `Default.aspx` and `AboutUs.aspx`, as we will not be using them.
4. Add a new ASPX page. Name it `Default.aspx`.
5. Open `Default.aspx` and switch to the **Design** tab.
6. Design the page so that it looks as follows:

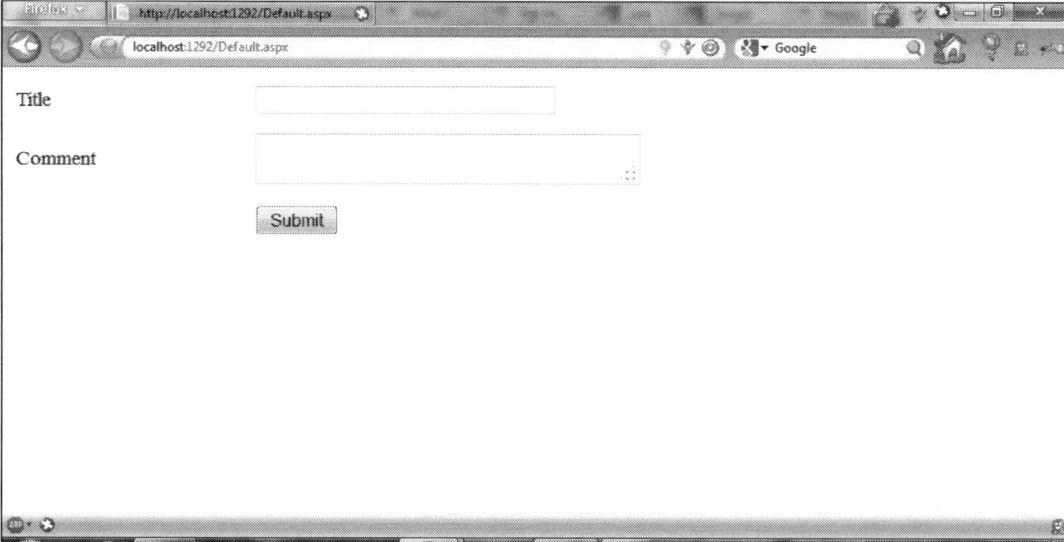

Chapter 8

7. Name the controls as shown in the following table:

Control	Name	Description
Textbox	txtTitle	To enter titles for the comments
Textbox	txtComment	To enter the comment
Button	btnSubmit	To submit the comment

8. Add another ASPX page. Name it CommentsDisplay.aspx. Open it in design mode.
9. Design the page so that it looks similar to the following screenshot:

10. Name the controls as given in the following table:

Control	Name	Description
Literal	ltlTitle	To display the title of the comment
Literal	ltlComments	To display the comment
Literal	ltlUnsafeComments	To display comments that are not guarded against XSS

11. Open Default.aspx in design mode. Double-click on btnSubmit to add a Click event handler.

211

12. In the event handler, add the following code:

    ```
    Session.Add("title", txtTitle.Text);
    Session.Add("comment", txtComments.Text);
    Server.Transfer("~/CommentsDisplay.aspx");
    ```

13. Next, open `CommentsDisplay.aspx.cs`. In the `Page_Load` method, add the following code:

    ```
    ltlTitle.Text = System.Web.Security.AntiXss.AntiXssEncoder.HtmlEncode((string)Session["title"],false);
    ltlComments.Text = System.Web.Security.AntiXss.AntiXssEncoder.HtmlEncode( (string)Session["comment"], false);
    ltlUnsafeComments.Text = (string)Session["comment"];
    ```

14. Set `Default.aspx` as the startup page. Run the application.

15. In the **Title** textbox, enter the following code:

    ```
    <b>Title</b>
    ```

16. In the **Comment** textbox, enter the following code:

    ```
    <script>window.alert("XSS successful");</script>
    ```

17. You will see a screen similar to the following screenshot:

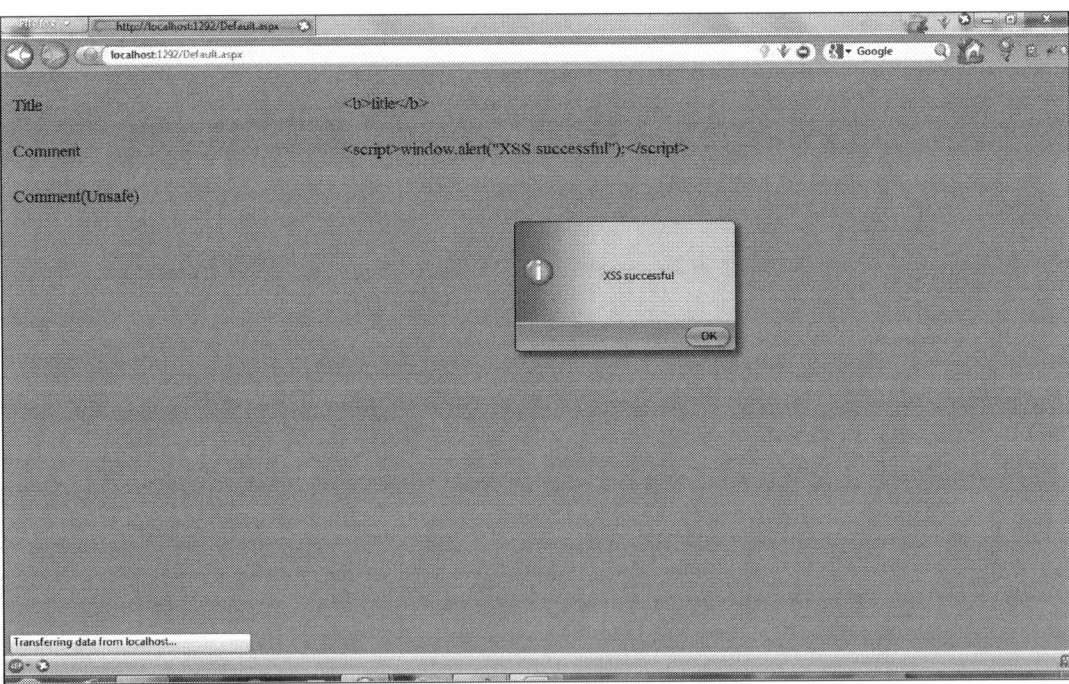

How it works...

The code that handles XSS is in the `Page_Load` method of `CommentsDisplay.aspx.cs`, specifically, the following statements:

```
ltlTitle.Text = System.Web.Security.AntiXss.AntiXssEncoder.
HtmlEncode((string)Session["title"],false);
ltlComments.Text = System.Web.Security.AntiXss.AntiXssEncoder.
HtmlEncode( (string)Session["comment"], false);
```

In the preceding statements, we called the `HtmlEncode` method of the `AntiXssEncoder` class with the string we want to encode. The string is the comments entered in the previous page. The `HtmlEncode` method replaces `<` and `>` with `&lt;` and `&gt;` respectively, so that the `<script>window.alert("XSS successful");` snippet becomes as follows:

```
&lt;script&gt;window.alert("XSS successful"); &lt;/script&gt;
```

This changed snippet is not executed by the browser. Hence, XSS fails.

Adding Google Map functionality using Map Helper

Nowadays, displaying maps as a part of your website has become a requirement. The reason can be anything from helping customers locate your store to providing the transit path of a package. ASP.NET 4.5 makes displaying maps easier by providing Map Helpers that can be installed using the `NuGet` package manager.

In this recipe, we will see how to use Map Helper and Google Maps. We will be using the Razor V2 View engine.

Getting ready

You will need to update the `NuGet` package manager by going to **Tools | Extensions and Updates**. If `NuGet` is not installed, then install it by going to **Tools | Extensions and Updates**.

How to do it...

1. Create a new **Web Site** project. Name it `MapDisplay`.
2. Install ASP.NET Web Helpers Library by going to **WEBSITE | Manage NuGet Packages...**.
3. Add a new **Content Page** (**Razor v2**) page. Name it `DisplayMap`.

4. Open `DisplayMap.cshtml`. Design it so that it looks similar to the following screenshot:

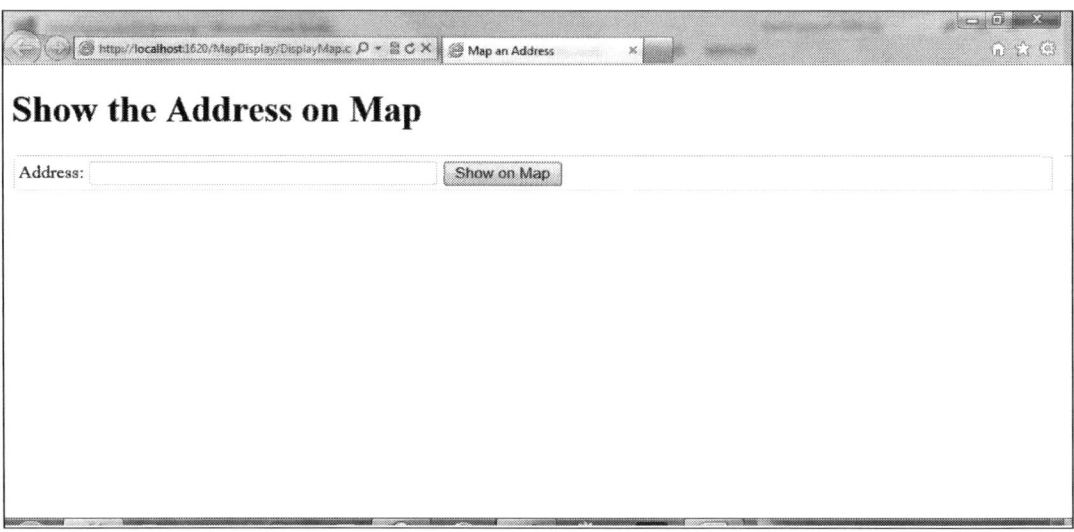

5. Provide the name and values for the controls as detailed in the following table:

Control	Type	Name	Value	Description
Input	text	address	@Request["address"]	To enter the address that needs to be displayed on the map, and to display the entered address once the query is submitted
Input	submit		Show on Map	To submit the request

6. Add the following code after the `<form>` section:

```
@if(IsPost) {
@Maps.GetGoogleHtml(Request.Form["address"],
   width: "400",
   height: "400")
}
```

7. Run the application. Enter the name of the place or address in the textbox. Click on the **Show on Map** button. You will see a map similar to the one in the following screenshot:

Chapter 8

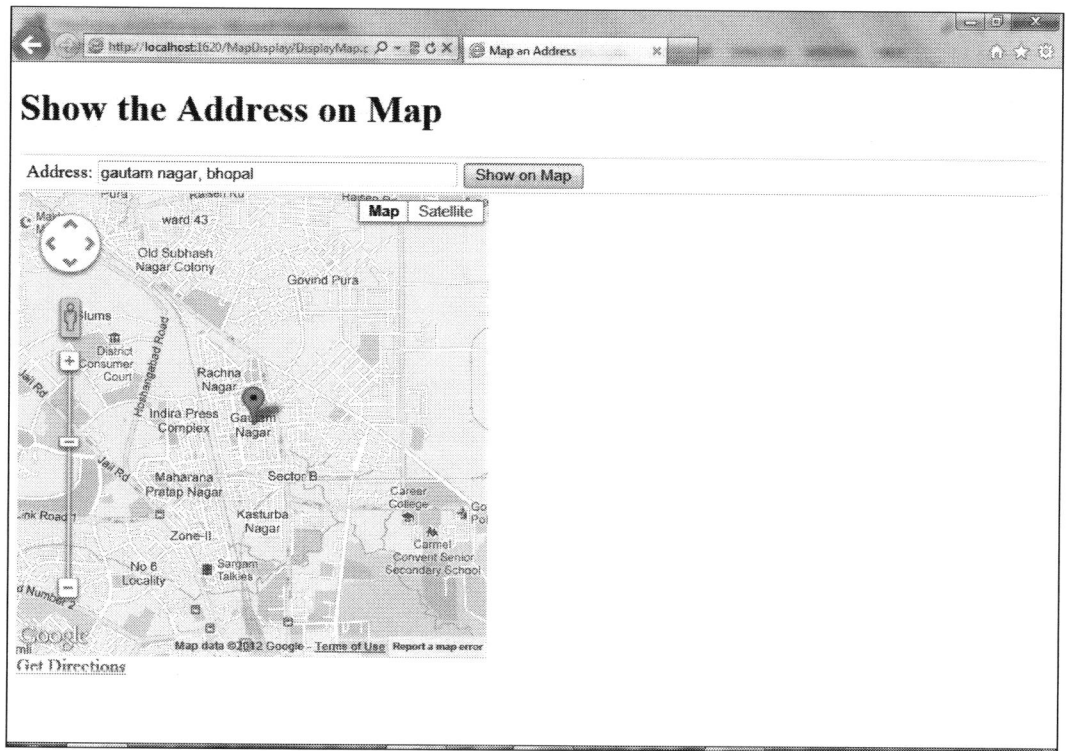

How it works...

The following code in `DisplayMap.cshtml` does the heavy lifting of calling the Google Map API and displaying the result:

```
@Maps.GetGoogleHtml(Request.Form["address"],
width: "400",
height: "400")
```

In the previous code we called the `GetGoogleHtml` method of Map Helper. Then, we passed the value present in the address field by accessing it through the `Form` collection of the `Request` object. The previous code is within the `if` statement that checks whether the request is a postback request:

```
@if(IsPost) {
@Maps.GetGoogleHtml(Request.Form["address"],
  width: "400",
  height: "400")
}
```

If it is a postback request call the Map Helper; otherwise do not call it.

Third-party authentication of users using Google

Before Version 4.5, ASP.NET Web Pages used to provide functionality to authenticate users using third parties such as Google, Live, Facebook, Twitter, or similar third parties, through installable helpers. These helpers were categorized as Open Authentication (OAuth) helpers. However, with Version 4.5, `OAuth` helpers have become part of the standard ASP.NET Web Pages library. In this recipe, we will see how to use `OAuth` helpers to enable Google authentication in a website.

How to do it...

1. Create a new **Web Site** project. Name it `GoogleAuthentication`.
2. Open `_AppStart.cshtml`. Add the following code after the call to `WebSecurity.InitializeDatabaseConnection`:

   ```
   OAuthWebSecurity.RegisterOpenIDClient(BuiltInOpenIDClient.Google);
   ```

3. Next, open `Login.cshtml`, which is in the `Account` folder.
4. Uncomment the following code:

   ```
   <fieldset>
     <legend>Log in using another service</legend>
     <input type="submit" name="provider" id="facebook" value="Facebook"
        title="Log in using your Facebook account." />
     <input type="submit" name="provider" id="twitter" value="Twitter"
        title="Log in using your Twitter account." />
     <input type="submit" name="provider" id="windowsLive"
        value="WindowsLive" title="Log in using your Windows Live account." />
   </fieldset>
   ```

5. Add the following to the `<fieldset>` tag:

   ```
   <input type="submit" name="provider" id="google" value="Google"
   title="Log in using your Google account." />
   ```

6. Open `AssociateServiceAccount.cshtml`, which is present in the `Account` folder. Add the following to `<fieldset>`:

   ```
   <input type="submit" name="provider" id="google" value="Google"
   title="Log in using your Google account." />
   ```

7. Open `Default.cshtml`. Run the application.

—— *Chapter 8*

8. Click on the **Log in** link. You will see the following page:

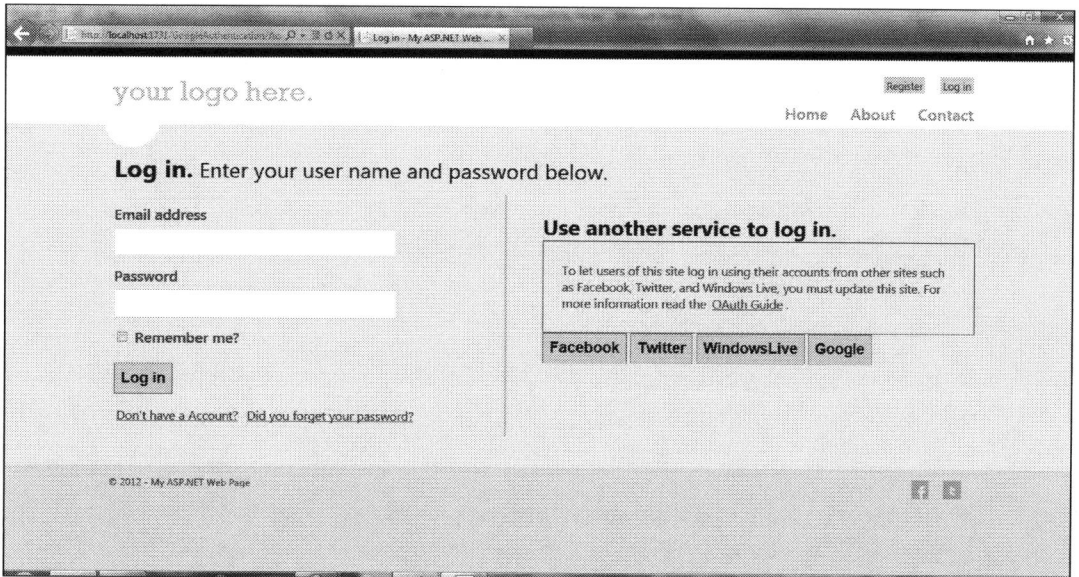

9. Click on the **Google** button and you will see the following page, which asks you to provide your Google credentials to log in:

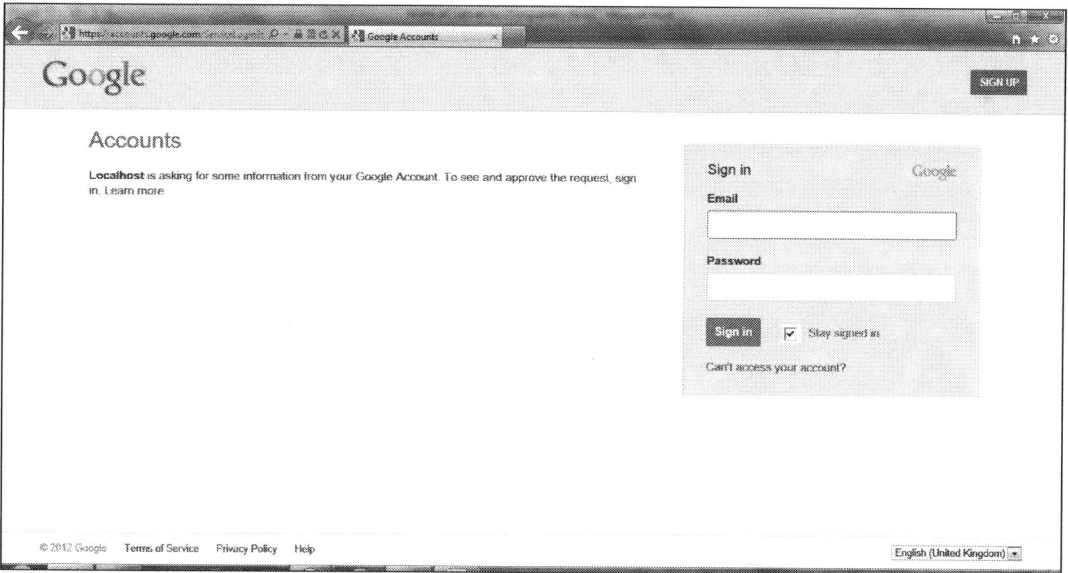

How it works...

The entire process of implementing Google authentication is done by the `OAuthWebSecurity` class. All we had to do was tell it that we want to use Google authentication by calling `RegisterOpenIDClient`, as we did in `_AppStart.cshtml`:

```
OAuthWebSecurity.RegisterOpenIDClient(BuiltInOpenIDClient.Google);
```

Then we displayed the button that takes us to the Google sign-in page by uncommenting `<fieldset>` in `Login.cshtml` and adding a button for Google, as highlighted in the following code:

```
<fieldset>
  <legend>Log in using another service</legend>
  <input type="submit" name="provider" id="facebook" value="Facebook"
      title="Log in using your Facebook account." />
  <input type="submit" name="provider" id="twitter" value="Twitter"
        title="Log in using your Twitter account." />
  <input type="submit" name="provider" id="windowsLive"
        value="WindowsLive" title="Log in using your Windows Live account." />
  <input type="submit" name="provider" id="google" value="Google"
      title="Log in using your Google account." />
</fieldset>
```

Implementing unobtrusive validation

In previous versions of ASP.NET Web Pages, you had to manually check each field and add the error message to the `ModelState` class. However, Version 4.5 of .NET (ASP.NET Web Pages Version 2) introduced the Validation helper, which can not only help your server-side validation but also provide unobtrusive client-side validation. In this recipe, we will enhance the Map Display application by adding the required field validation to the address field.

How to do it...

1. Open the `MapDisplay` website.
2. Open `DisplayMap.cshtml`. Add the following code to the top of the page, above the `DOCTYPE` section:

    ```
    @{
        Validation.RequireField("address", "Address is required");
    }
    ```

3. Next, add the following code to the `<head>` section:

```
<script src="~/Scripts/jquery.validate.js" type="text/javascript"></script>
<script src="@Href("~/Scripts/jquery.validate.unobtrusive.min.js")"></script>
```

4. Modify the `address` textbox so that it looks similar to the following markup:

```
<input style="width: 300px" type="text" name="address" value="@Request["address"]" @Validation.For("address")/>
```

5. Next, add the following `<div>` section after the `<div>` section containing the `address` textbox:

```
<div>
  @Html.ValidationMessage("address")
</div>
```

6. Modify the `if` statement containing the call to the Map Helper, as shown in the following code:

```
@if(IsPost && Validation.IsValid()) {
    @Maps.GetGoogleHtml(Request.Form["address"],
        width: "400",
        height: "400")
}
```

7. Run the application. Click on the **Show On Map** button without entering anything in the textbox. You will see the following screen:

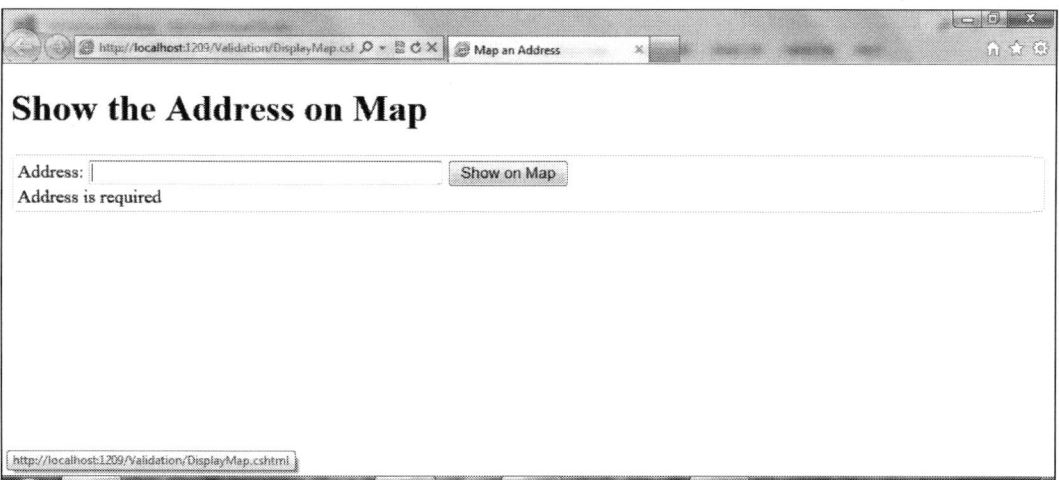

8. Next, enter a valid address in the textbox. You will see the following screen:

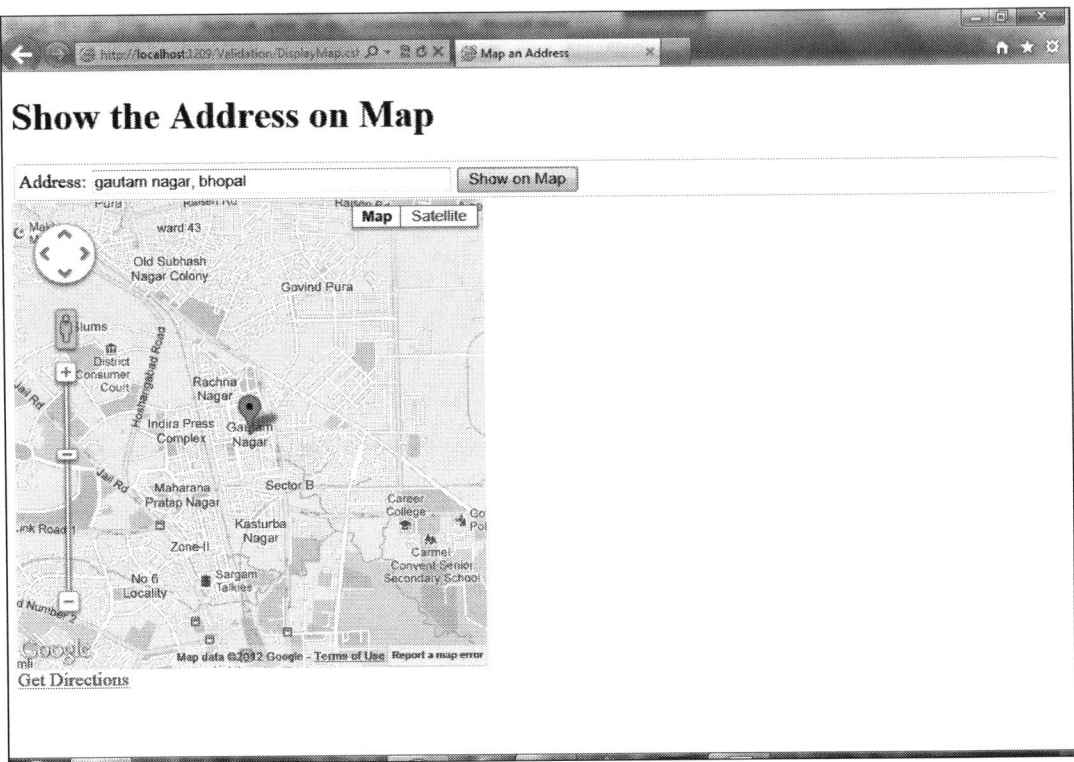

How it works...

In this recipe, we have implemented both server-side and client-side validation. The first thing we did was to tell the `Validation` helper that we want to validate the address field. That is what we did with the following code:

```
@{
    Validation.RequireField("address", "Address is required");
}
```

The previous code is for server-side validation. Next, we added the `<script>` section for unobtrusive validation:

```
<script src="~/Scripts/jquery.validate.js" type="text/javascript">
</script>
<script src="@Href("~/Scripts/jquery.validate.unobtrusive.min.js")">
</script>
```

In the previous code, the link to `jquery.validate.unobtrusive.min.js` is generated after the `cshtml` file is compiled. Next, we told the helper that we want to validate the address field. We did this by adding `@Validation.For` to the address field. We also passed the name of the field to `@Validation.For`:

```
<input style="width: 300px" type="text" name="address" value="@
Request["address"]" @Validation.For("address") />
```

The last step for client-side validation is displaying the error messages, which we did by using `@Html.ValidationMessage`:

```
<div>
    @Html.ValidationMessage("address")
</div>
```

For server-side validation, we called the `IsValid()` method of the `Validation` helper in the `if` statement:

```
@if(IsPost && Validation.IsValid()) {
    @Maps.GetGoogleHtml(Request.Form["address"],
        width: "400",
        height: "400")
}
```

The map helper is displayed only if `IsValid()` returns `true`.

9
Silverlight Recipes

In this chapter we will cover:

- Using Pivot control to present asset data
- Accessing webcams
- Using client-side storage for saving a draft of the user registration data

Introduction

Silverlight helps developers create rich web clients. This is similar to WPF in the sense that it helps in developing content and feature-rich desktop applications. However, Silverlight applications run in a sandboxed environment within the web browser. In other words, as a developer you will not have access to certain functionalities that are present in WPF. These limitations include restricted access to DirectX for better graphics, limited access to webcams, and so on. With Version 5, new features have been included that help overcome these limitations. In this chapter we will look at some of these new functionalities. The *Using Pivot control to present asset data* recipe will be about Pivot control introduced in Version 5. Then we will see how to use webcams to capture live images. The *Using client-side storage for saving a draft of the user registration data* recipe will introduce you to isolated storage APIs, using which you can save data onto the client's system.

Using Pivot control to present asset data

The Pivot view makes interacting with data easy for the user. Until Version 5 of Silverlight (.NET 4.0 and below), PivotViewer control needed to be installed separately. However, with Silverlight 5 and .NET 4.5, it is supplied as part of the core distribution. In this recipe, we will see how to use PivotViewer control to display asset-related data.

Silverlight Recipes

How to do it...

To use Pivot control to present asset data, perform the following steps:

1. Launch Visual Studio 2012. Create a project of the type **Silverlight Application**. Name it `Pivot`.
2. Add a new folder. Name it `Entities`.
3. Add a new class to the `Entities` folder. Name it `Asset`.
4. Add the following properties to the class:

Name	Data type
ID	int
Name	string
Region	string
Value	double

5. Open `MainWindow.xaml`. Add the following statements in the `<Grid>` section:

    ```xml
    <sdk:PivotViewer x:Name="pvAsset">

      <!--Setting PivotProperties-->
      <sdk:PivotViewer.PivotProperties>
         <sdk:PivotViewerStringProperty Id="PName" Options="CanFilter"
            DisplayName="Name" Binding="{Binding Name}" />
         <sdk:PivotViewerStringProperty Id="PRegion" Options="CanFilter"
            DisplayName="Region" Binding="{Binding Region}" />

      </sdk:PivotViewer.PivotProperties>

        <!--Setting data-->
        <sdk:PivotViewer.ItemTemplates>
          <sdk:PivotViewerItemTemplate>
            <Border Width="200" Height="200" Background="Blue">
               <StackPanel Orientation="Vertical">
                <TextBlock Text="{Binding Name}" FontSize="16"
                  Foreground="White" />
    ```

```xml
                <TextBlock Text="{Binding Value}" FontSize="16"
                  Foreground="White" />
                </StackPanel>
                </Border>
              </sdk:PivotViewerItemTemplate>
            </sdk:PivotViewer.ItemTemplates>
        </sdk:PivotViewer>
```

6. Open `MainWindow.xaml.cs`. Add a private method that returns `ObservableCollection<Asset>`. Name it `GenerateTestData`. Its signature will be as follows:

```
private ObservableCollection<Asset> GenerateTestData()
{
}
```

7. Add the following code to `GenerateTestData`:

```
ObservableCollection<Asset> temp = new
ObservableCollection<Asset>();
temp.Add(new Asset() { ID = 1, Name = "ASD", Region = "Mumbai",
Value = 1000 });
temp.Add(new Asset() { ID = 2, Name = "AS Hotel", Region =
"Chennai", Value = 11000 });
temp.Add(new Asset() { ID = 3, Name = "AD Cafe", Region =
"Kolkatta", Value = 10000 });
temp.Add(new Asset() { ID = 4, Name = "Landmark", Region =
"Mumbai", Value = 50000 });
temp.Add(new Asset() { ID = 5, Name = "ASD II", Region =
"Kolkatta", Value = 400 });
temp.Add(new Asset() { ID = 5, Name = "ASD III", Region =
"Kolkatta", Value = 1400 });
return temp;
```

8. Add the following statement to the constructor, after the call to `InitializeComponent`:

```
pvAsset.ItemsSource = GenerateTestData();
```

Silverlight Recipes

9. Run the application. You will see the output as shown in the following screenshot. Test the application by selecting the regions.

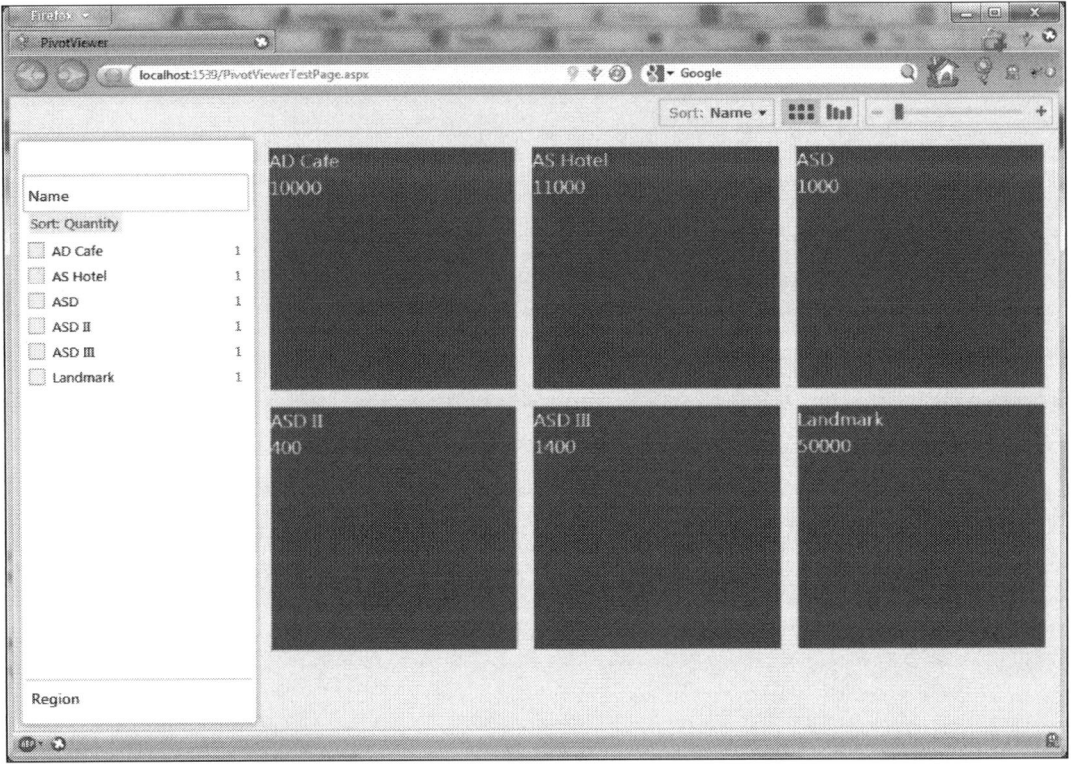

How it works...

To display a pivot using PivotViewer control, two steps are required. First, set the properties that the user can use to filter the data and control the pivot. We did this using the PivotProperties property of PivotViewer. We wanted to set the filter on the Name and Region properties of the Asset class.

```
<sdk:PivotViewer.PivotProperties>
    <sdk:PivotViewerStringProperty Id="PName" Options="CanFilter"
        DisplayName="Name" Binding="{Binding Name}" />
    <sdk:PivotViewerStringProperty Id="PRegion" Options="CanFilter"
        DisplayName="Region" Binding="{Binding Region}" />

</sdk:PivotViewer.PivotProperties>
```

Chapter 9

In the preceding code, we used `PivotViewerStringProperty` during runtime to signify that the property is of type `string`, it can be used to filter the data, and that it has to be bound to the `Name` and `Region` properties.

The second step is to tell PivotViewer control how to display the data when the filters are applied. That can be done using `PivotViewItemTemplate`. We used `StackPanel` and `TextBlock` within `PivotViewItemTemplate` for representing the data as shown in the following code:

```xml
<sdk:PivotViewerItemTemplate>
    <Border Width="200" Height="200" Background="Blue">
      <StackPanel Orientation="Vertical">
       <TextBlock Text="{Binding Name}" FontSize="16"
         Foreground="White" />
       <TextBlock Text="{Binding Value}" FontSize="16"
         Foreground="White" />
      </StackPanel>
    </Border>
</sdk:PivotViewerItemTemplate>
```

`StackPanel` and `TextBlock` are basic ways to display data. Any kind of transformations and controls can be used to display the data.

Accessing webcams

In certain scenarios, you may have to access the webcam of the client. From Silverlight 4 onwards, the API to access webcams have become simpler to use. In this recipe, we will see how to use webcams to display live images.

How to do it...

1. Launch Visual Studio 2012. Create a new project of the type **Silverlight Application**. Name it `WebCam`.

2. Open `MainPage.xaml`. Add the following code to the `<Grid>` section:

   ```xml
   <Rectangle RadiusX="5" RadiusY="5" x:Name="rectCam" Height="285"
   HorizontalAlignment="Left" Margin="10,10,0,0" Stroke="Black"
   StrokeThickness="1" VerticalAlignment="Top" Width="383"
   Fill="Black" />

   <Button Content="Start Webcam" Height="23"
   HorizontalAlignment="Left" Margin="68,330,0,0" Name="btnStart"
   VerticalAlignment="Top" Width="94"/>
   ```

Silverlight Recipes

```
<Button Content="Stop Webcam" Height="23"
HorizontalAlignment="Left" Margin="284,330,0,0" Name="btnStop"
VerticalAlignment="Top" Width="99" />
```

3. The page should look similar to the following screenshot:

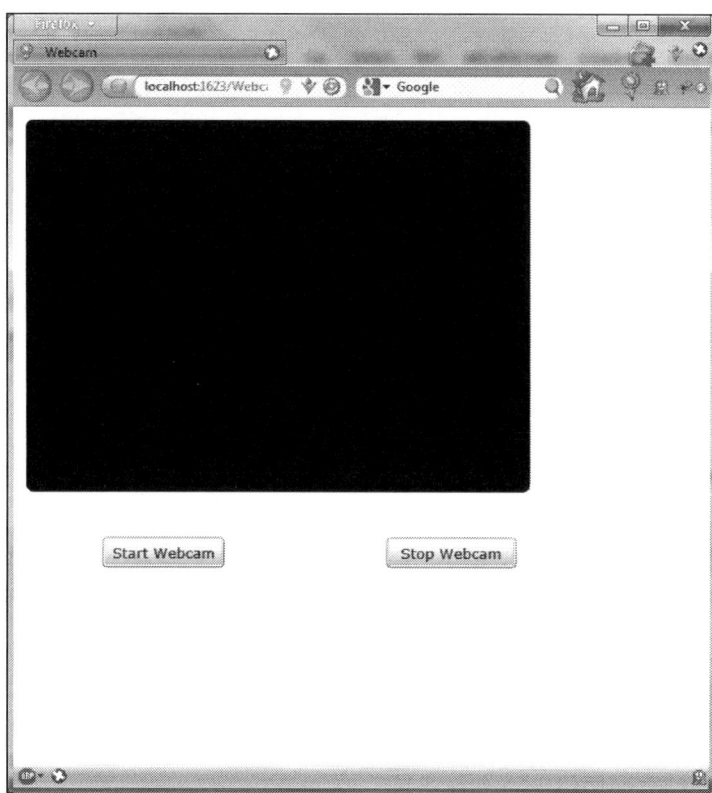

4. Open `MainPage.xaml.cs`. Add a private variable of the type `CaptureSource`. Name it `_captureSource`.

   ```
   private CaptureSource _captureSource = null;
   ```

5. Add a method of the type `void`. Name it `StartWebCam`. Its signature will be as follows:

   ```
   private void StartWebCam()
   {
   }
   ```

Chapter 9

6. Add the following code to `StartWebCam`:
    ```
    if (_captureSource==null)
    {
      _captureSource = new CaptureSource();
    }
    if (_captureSource.State== CaptureState.Stopped)
    {
     _captureSource.VideoCaptureDevice =
     CaptureDeviceConfiguration.GetDefaultVideoCaptureDevice();
     VideoBrush previewBrush = new VideoBrush();
     previewBrush.SetSource(_captureSource);
     rectCam.Fill = previewBrush;
     _captureSource.Start();
    }
    ```

7. Open `MainPage.xaml` in the design mode. Double-click on the **Start Webcam** button to add a Click event handler.

8. Add the following code to the event handler:
    ```
    if (!CaptureDeviceConfiguration.AllowedDeviceAccess)
    {
     if (!CaptureDeviceConfiguration.RequestDeviceAccess())
       {
          MessageBox.Show("Cannot access the webcam");
       }
    }
    else
    {
       StartWebCam();
    }
    ```

9. Open `MainPage.xaml` in the design mode. Double-click on the **Stop Webcam** button to add a Click event handler.

10. Add the following code to the event handler:
    ```
    if (_captureSource != null && _captureSource.State ==
    CaptureState.Started)
    {
      _captureSource.Stop();
    }
    ```

11. Run the application. Test the application by clicking on the **Start Webcam** and **Stop Webcam** buttons.

Silverlight Recipes

How it works...

The first step in accessing a webcam is finding out whether we have permission to access it or not. To do so, we used the `AllowDeviceAccess` property and the `RequestDeviceAccess()` method of the `CaptureDeviceConfiguration` class in the Click event handler of `btnStart`.

```
if (!CaptureDeviceConfiguration.AllowedDeviceAccess)
{
  if (!CaptureDeviceConfiguration.RequestDeviceAccess())
    {
      MessageBox.Show("Cannot access the webcam");
    }
}
```

If we get a false value for any of them, we show a message to the user and stop the process. If we get a true value for both, we need to initialize the `CaptureSource` variable. That's what we did in the `StartWebCam` method.

```
_captureSource = new CaptureSource();
```

Then set the `VideoCapture` property of `_capture` using the `GetDefaultVideoCaptureDevice()` method of `CaptureDeviceConfiguration`.

```
_captureSource.VideoCaptureDevice =
    CaptureDeviceConfiguration.GetDefaultVideoCaptureDevice();
```

Next, we need a brush using which we can draw (the output of webcam) on the `Rectangle` control. Hence, we instantiated `VideoBrush`, set its source to `_captureSource`, and then set the `Fill` property of the `Rectangle` control to the instance of `VideoBrush`.

```
VideoBrush previewBrush = new VideoBrush();
previewBrush.SetSource(_captureSource);
rectCam.Fill = previewBrush;
```

Once we have the `Brush` instance, we can start capturing the image using the webcam.

```
_captureSource.Start();
```

To stop the capturing of images, we first checked whether `_captureSource` has been instantiated or not. If it is instantiated, we need to check whether the capturing is going on. If both are true, we call the `Stop()` method of `_captureSource` to stop the capturing.

```
if (_captureSource != null && _captureSource.State == CaptureState.
Started)
{
  _captureSource.Stop();
}
```

Using client-side storage for saving a draft of the user registration data

Isolated storage APIs provide a way to store limited amount of data at the client side. Using this functionality, we can save data such as search strings and usernames. In this recipe we will use the isolated storage API so that the user can save the data entered in the registration form on the client's system.

How to do it...

1. Create an application of the type **Silverlight Application** in Visual Studio 2012. Name it `ClientSidePersistance`.
2. Open `MainPage.xaml`. Design it so that it looks similar to the following screenshot:

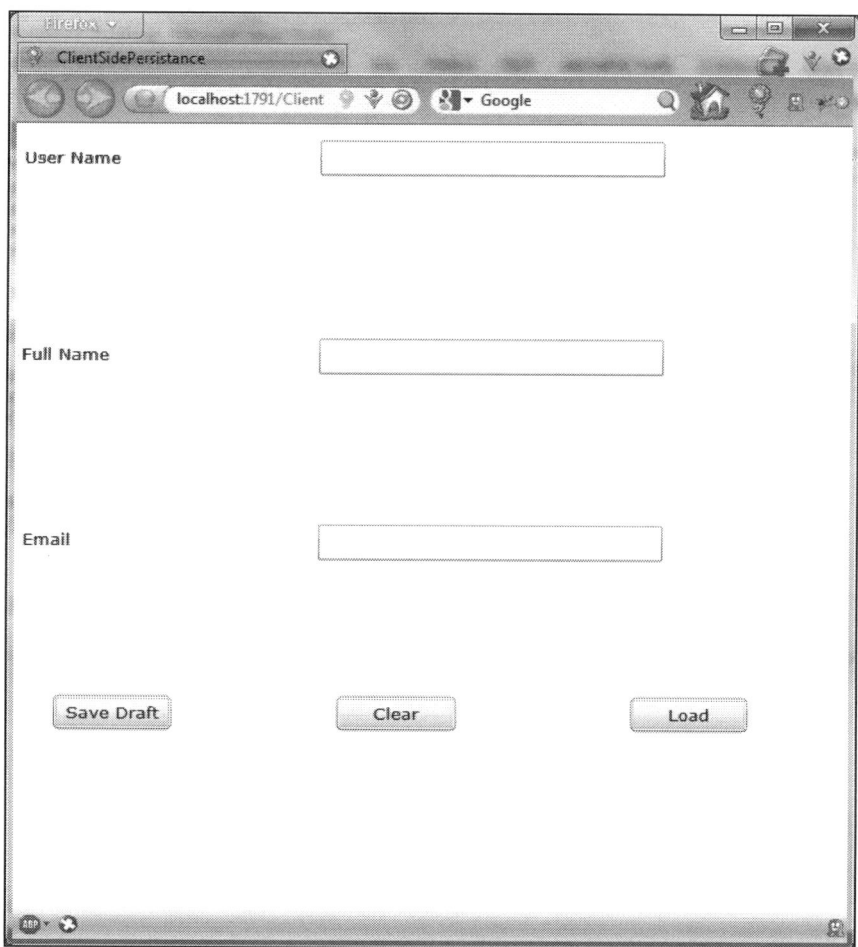

3. Name the controls as detailed in the following table:

Control	Name	Description
Textbox	txtUserName	To enter the username
Textbox	txtFullName	To enter the full name of the user
Textbox	txtEmail	To enter the e-mail address of the user
Button	btnDraft	To save the entered values in the user's system
Button	btnClear	To clear the values
Button	btnLoad	To load and display the saved values

4. Open `MainPage.xaml.cs`. Add a private variable of the type `IsolatedStorageSettings`. Name it `appSettings`.

5. Instantiate it using the `ApplicationSettings` property of `IsolatedStorageSettings` as shown in the following code snippet:

```
private IsolatedStorageSettings appSettings =
IsolatedStorageSettings.ApplicationSettings;
```

6. Add a Click event handler for `btnDraft`. Add the following code in the event handler:

```
appSettings.Add("username", txtUserName.Text);
appSettings.Add("fullname", txtFullName.Text);
appSettings.Add("email", txtEmail.Text);
```

7. Next, add a Click event handler for `btnClear`. Add the following code in the event handler:

```
txtEmail.Text = "";
txtFullName.Text = "";
txtUserName.Text = "";
```

8. Then, add a Click event handler for `btnLoad`. Add the following code in the event handler:

```
txtUserName.Text = appSettings["username"]!=null?
appSettings["username"].ToString():"";
txtFullName.Text = appSettings["fullname"]!=null?
appSettings["fullname"].ToString():"";
txtEmail.Text = appSettings["email"]!=null? appSettings["email"].
ToString():"";
```

9. Run the application. Enter values in the textboxes. Click on the **Save Draft** button.

10. Then click on **Clear**. The values will be cleared.

11. Now click on the **Load** button. The saved values will be displayed.

How it works...

The `IsolatedStorageSettings` class acts as a collection. So we can save our data using the `Add` method. The `Add` method takes `key` and `value` as parameters. To save our data, we called the `Add` method with a key and the text from the textbox as the value.

```
appSettings.Add("username", txtUserName.Text);
appSettings.Add("fullname", txtFullName.Text);
appSettings.Add("email", txtEmail.Text);
```

Similarly, we can access the saved value by using the key as an index. That's what we did in the `Click` event of the event handler of `btnLoad`.

```
txtUserName.Text = appSettings["username"]!=null?
appSettings["username"].ToString():"";
txtFullName.Text = appSettings["fullname"]!=null?
appSettings["fullname"].ToString():"";
txtEmail.Text = appSettings["email"]!=null? appSettings["email"].
ToString():"";
```

10
Entity Framework Recipes

In this chapter we will cover:

- Joining two entities using LINQ
- Uploading files using Entity Framework and stored procedures
- Managing connections manually for long-running tasks
- Using functions that return tables as return values

Introduction

Entity Framework is the technological successor to ADO.NET. It implements the **Object Relational Mapping** (**ORM**) pattern. So, you can access the tables through the classes that map to them. In this chapter, we will focus on the recipes that deal with using LINQ to join multiple entities, will call stored procedures using Entity Framework, and so on. We will start with using LINQ to join two entities that do not have navigation (foreign key) defined. The *Uploading files using Entity Framework and stored procedures* recipe will focus on calling stored procedures via Entity Framework to upload files. After that, we will look at handling connections manually. The *Using functions that return tables as return value* recipe will be about importing Table Valued Functions, which is a new feature in Version 5 of Entity Framework.

We will use the database, tables, and stored procedures developed in *Chapter 5*, *ADO.NET Recipes*.

Joining two entities using LINQ

If two tables are joined by a foreign key relationship, their corresponding entities will have a navigation defined between them. However, if the tables are not joined by a foreign key, navigation does not exist. Even then, if they have common columns/fields, they can be joined using LINQ. In this recipe, we will use LINQ to join entities representing `tb_Users` and `tb_FileStorage` to retrieve all the files uploaded by a particular user.

How to do it...

1. Launch SQL Server Management Studio 2012.
2. Add a new column to `tb_FileStorage`. Name it `User_ID` and set its data type to `int`.
3. Create a project of the type **Windows Forms Application** in Visual Studio 2012. Name it `TwoTableJoin`.
4. In **Solution Explorer**, right-click on the project and choose **New Item** from **Add**.
5. In the dialog that comes up, choose **ADO.NET Entity Data Model** and click on **Add** to launch the Entity Data Model wizard. Name it `CookBookModel`:

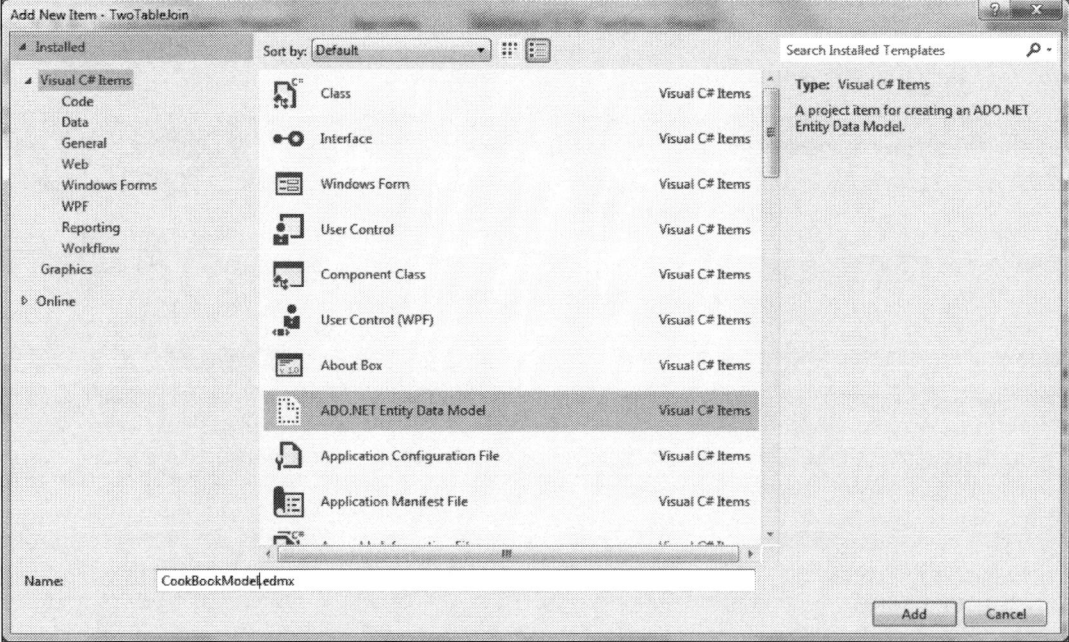

6. In the wizard, choose **Generate from database**, and click on **Next**.
7. Select the CookBook.dbo connection, which connects to CookBook. We had created this in the *Saving large files (BLOB) in MS SQL Server using ADO.NET* recipe in *Chapter 5, ADO.NET Recipes*.

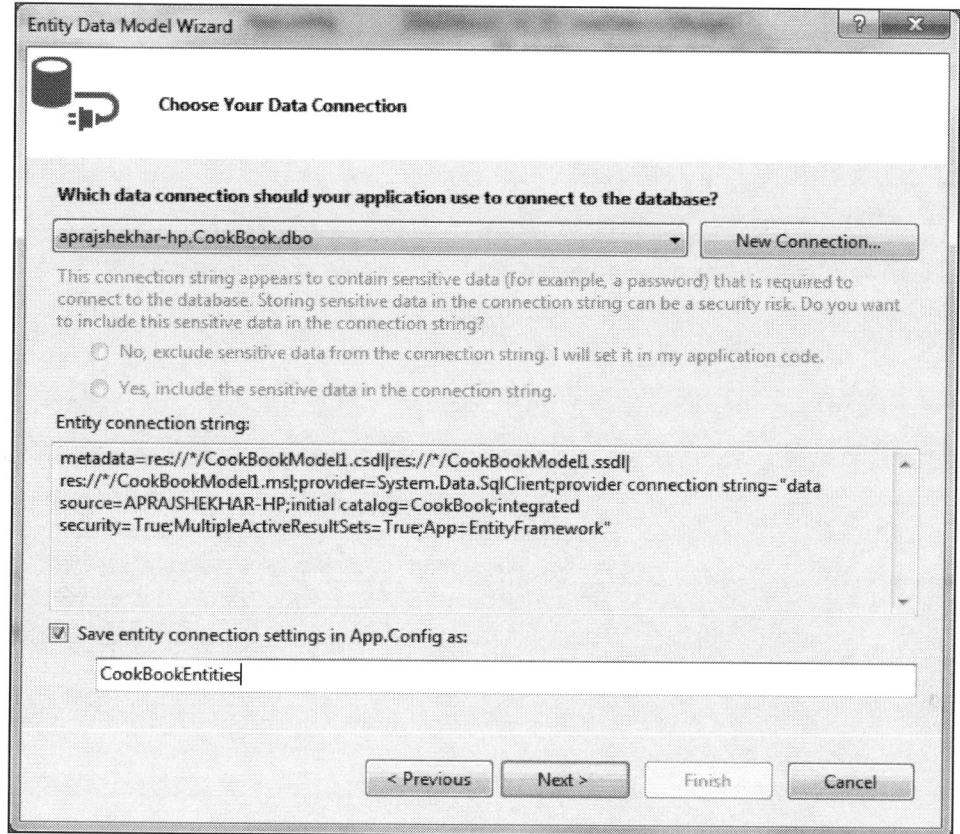

8. If the connection does not exist, create a new connection for the CookBook database.
9. Enter CookBookEntities in the **Save entity connection settings...** field. This will be the name of the main ORM class.

10. Click on **Next**. In the next screen, select all the tables and stored procedures. Click on **Finish**:

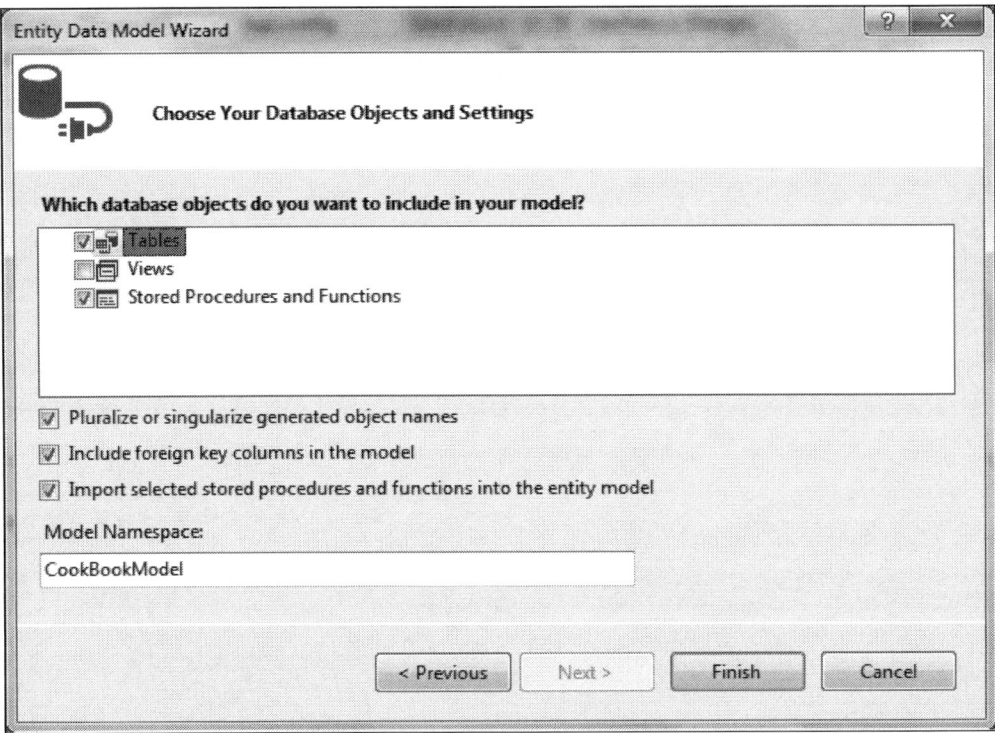

11. In the EDM designer, rename tb_Users to Users and tb_FileStorage to Files.
12. Rename Form1.cs to UserData.cs.
13. Open UserData.cs in the design mode. Design the form so that it looks similar to the following screenshot:

14. Name the controls as detailed in the following table:

Control	Name	Description
Textbox	txtUser	To enter ID of the user whose files need to be listed
Button	btnShow	To execute the logic for listing the files
DataGridView	dgvFiles	To display the files

15. Double-click on btnShow to add a Click event handler.
16. In the event handler, add the following code:

    ```
    using (CookBookEntities context = new CookBookEntities())
    {
      ObjectSet<User> users = context.Users;
      ObjectSet<Files> files = context.Files;
      int userID = Convert.ToInt32(txtUser.Text);
      var query =
          from user in users
          join file in files
          on user.Id equals file.User_ID
          where user.Id == userID
          select new
          {
            FileID = file.ID,
            FileName = file.File_name
          };
      var fileDetails = query.ToList();
      dgvFiles.DataSource = fileDetails;

    }
    ```

17. Run the application. In the textbox, enter the ID (for example 1) of a user who has entries in tb_FileStorage.
18. Click on Show. You will see the data grid populated.

How it works...

The core of the logic is in the following statement:

```
var query =
    from user in users
    join file in files
```

```
on user.Id equals file.User_ID
where user.Id == userID
select new
{
  FileID = file.ID,
  FileName = file.File_name
};
```

In the preceding code, the `user` identifier is used for the `users` set. Then, it is joined with the `files` set, whose identifier is `file`. The join is performed using the `Id` field of `user` and `User_ID` field of the `file` identifier. Now, we want file details of only those users whose IDs have been entered in the textbox. So, we used the `where` clause. The user should exist in the `users` set. Therefore, we used the `where` clause on `Id` of the user and not on files.

This provides us with the required data. However, we do not want to display all the fields. Hence, in the `select` clause, we created a new object with two fields, `FileID` and `FileName`. We assigned the ID of file to `FileID` and `File_name` of the file to `FileName`. So, when we execute the query, we get a list of objects that has two properties, `FileID` and `FileName`. One point to keep in mind is that the query is not executed until the following statement is run:

```
var fileDetails = query.ToList();
```

Uploading files using Entity Framework and stored procedures

Using Entity Framework, you can accomplish all of the **CRUD** (**Create**, **Retrieve**, **Update**, and **Delete**) operations without making calls to the stored procedures. However, in some cases, encapsulating CRUD operations within a stored procedure becomes necessary. In such scenarios, you can call a stored procedure from within your code as if you are calling any other method of C#.

In this recipe, we will use a stored procedure to upload image files to the database. We will call the stored procedures by using classes and methods generated by Entity Framework.

How to do it...

1. Create a project of the type **Windows Forms Application** in Visual Studio 2012. Name it `FileUpload`.
2. In **Solution Explorer**, right-click on the project and choose **Add | New Item**.
3. In the dialog, choose **ADO.NET Entity Data Model** and click **Add** to launch the Entity Data Model wizard. Name it `CookBookModel`:

Chapter 10

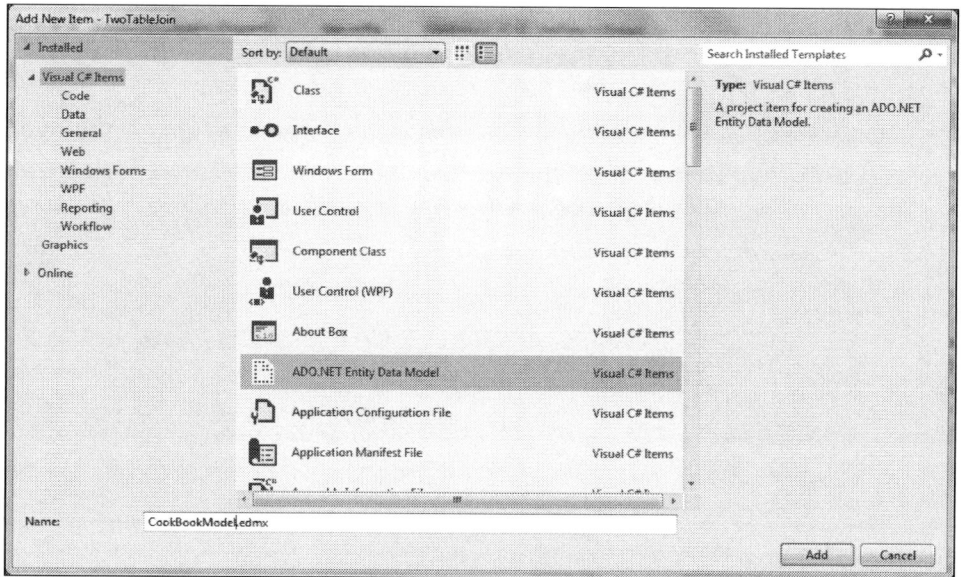

4. In the wizard, choose **Generate from database** and click on **Next**.
5. Select CookBook.dbo connection. We had created this in the *Saving large files (BLOB) in MS SQL Server using ADO.NET* recipe in *Chapter 5, ADO.NET Recipes*.

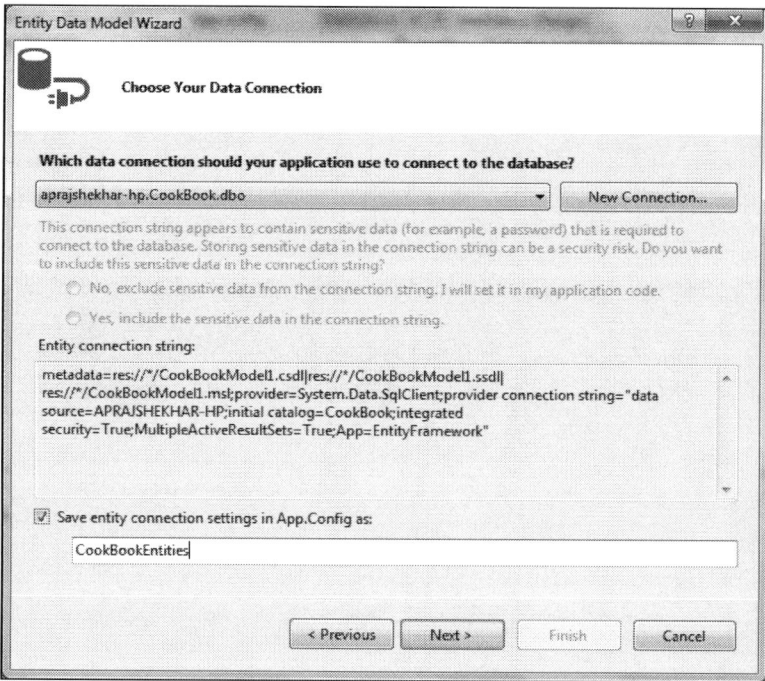

6. If the connection does not exist, create a new connection for the CookBook database.
7. Enter CookBookEntities in the **Save entity connection settings...** field. This will be the name of the main ORM class.
8. Click on **Next**. On the next screen, select all the tables and the stored procedure named **SaveFile**. Click on **Finish**.
9. Rename Form1.cs to UploadForm.cs.
10. Open UploadForm.cs in the design mode. Design the form so that it looks similar to the following screenshot:

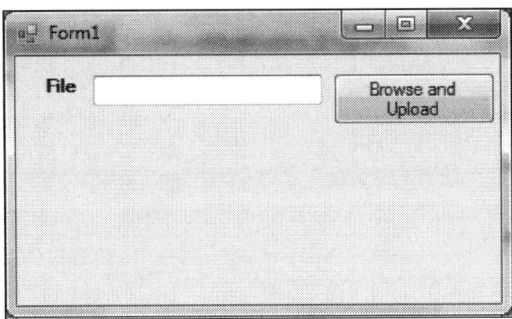

11. Name the controls as detailed in the following table:

Control	Name	Description
Textbox	txtPath	To display the path of the selected file.
Button	btnUpload	To select and upload the selected file.

12. Double-click on btnUpload to add a Click event handler.
13. In the event handler, add the following code:

```
OpenFileDialog diagFile = new OpenFileDialog();

if (diagFile.ShowDialog()==System.Windows.Forms.DialogResult.OK)
  {
    txtPath.Text = diagFile.FileName;
    using (CookBookEntities context = new CookBookEntities())
    {
      try
        {

        context.SaveFile(Path.GetFileNameWithoutExtension(txtPath.Text),
        GetBytesFromFile(txtPath.Text));
            MessageBox.Show("Upload Successful");
```

Chapter 10

```
        }
        catch (Exception ex)
        {
         MessageBox.Show(ex.Message);
        }
       }
     }
```

14. Next, add a private method that takes the file path as an argument and returns a `byte` array. Name it `GetBytesFromFile`. Its signature will be as follows:

    ```
    private byte[] GetBytesFromFile(string path)
    {
    }
    ```

15. Add the following code to `GetBytesFromFile`:

    ```
    byte[] data = null;

    FileInfo info = new FileInfo(path);
    long numBytes = info.Length;

    FileStream stream = new FileStream(path, FileMode.Open,
             FileAccess.Read);

    BinaryReader reader = new BinaryReader(stream);
    data = reader.ReadBytes((int)numBytes);
    return data;
    ```

16. Run the application. Click on the **Browse and Upload** button.
17. Select an image file and click on **OK**.

If the upload/save is successful, you will see a message box stating that the upload was successful. If the upload/save is not successful, then you will see a message box displaying the exception.

How it works...

The main difference between the version of Entity Framework shipped with Visual Studio 2012 and previous versions (versions before Version 4.5) is that, when you generate ORM for a stored procedure, you can accomplish it in one step—importing the stored procedure. In the versions before Version 4.5 of Entity Framework, two steps were involved. First, you had to import the stored procedure. Then, you had to perform a function import. The function import generated entities relate to the result returned by the stored procedure imported while generating the model.

Entity Framework Recipes

In Version 5 of Entity Framework, the function import step is carried out while generating the model. You can still customize the default return types that are provided when the model is generated. In our case, we do not require a customized return type. Therefore, we skipped the (optional) step of customizing the return type.

The generated function, named `SaveFile`, takes two parameters—the name of the image file to be saved and the byte array containing the data. We retrieved the file name using the `GetFileNameWithoutExtension` method of the `Path` class. For the `byte` array, we used `FileStream` and `BinaryReader` to read the file contents into the byte array, as shown in the following code:

```
FileStream stream = new FileStream(path, FileMode.Open,
        FileAccess.Read);

BinaryReader reader = new BinaryReader(stream);
data = reader.ReadBytes((int)numBytes);
```

With the filename and byte array thus retrieved, we called the `SaveFile` method of the `CookBookEntities` class:

```
try
    {
  context.SaveFile(Path.GetFileNameWithoutExtension(txtPath.Text),
  GetBytesFromFile(txtPath.Text));
    MessageBox.Show("Upload Successful");
    }
    catch (Exception ex)
    {
    MessageBox.Show(ex.Message);
    }
```

In the preceding code, the call to `SaveFile` is encapsulated in `try/catch`. We did this so that if there is a failure to upload the file due to some exception, we can display it to the user.

Managing connections manually for long-running tasks

Entity Framework manages connections by itself. In other words, you as a developer need not open and close connections manually. However, there are scenarios where you would want to manage the opening and closing of connections manually. Saving large-sized files to a database is one such scenario.

In this recipe, we will look at the steps required in managing connections manually. To do so, we will use the application developed in the previous recipe.

How to do it...

1. Open `FileUpload.sln` in Visual Studio 2012.
2. Open `UploadForm.cs` in the view code mode.
3. In the `btnUpload_Click` method, replace the `using` statement with the following statement:

   ```
   CookBookEntities context = new CookBookEntities();
   ```

4. Next, add the following `if` block inside the `try` block, above the call to the `SaveFile` method:

   ```
   if (context.Connection.State != ConnectionState.Open)
   {
    context.Connection.Open();
   }
   ```

5. Now, add the following `finally` block after the `catch` block:

   ```
   finally
   {
      context.Dispose();
   }
   ```

6. Once the modifications are done, the `btnUpload_Click` method will be similar to the following code:

   ```
   OpenFileDialog diagFile = new OpenFileDialog();

   if (diagFile.ShowDialog() == System.Windows.Forms.DialogResult.OK)
   {
      txtPath.Text = diagFile.FileName;
      CookBookEntities context = new CookBookEntities();

   try
   {
    if (context.Connection.State != ConnectionState.Open)
    {
       context.Connection.Open();
    }
      context.SaveFile(Path.GetFileNameWithoutExtension(txtPath.Text),
      GetBytesFromFile(txtPath.Text));
   MessageBox.Show("Upload Successful");
   }
   catch (InvalidOperationException ex)
   {
      MessageBox.Show(ex.Message);
   }
   ```

```
            finally
            {
                context.Dispose();
            }
        }
    }
```

7. Run the application and click on the **Browse and Upload** button.
8. Select an image file and click on **OK**.

If the save is successful, you will see a message box stating that the upload is successful. If the save is not successful, you will see a message box displaying the exception message.

How it works...

In the previous recipes, we used the `using` statement so that we do not have to manually dispose of the context object. One important point about the context object (`CookBookEntities`) is that, once its `Dispose` method is called, the connection is closed. So, to manually control the closing of the connection, we removed the following statement:

```
using (CookBookEntities context = new CookBookEntities())
```

In its place, we inserted the following code:

```
CookBookEntities context = new CookBookEntities();
```

Since we have removed the `using` statement, we have to manually open the connection and dispose of the object manually. To open the connection, we first have to check the state of the connection. If it is not in the opened state, we have to open the connection by calling the `Open` method of the `Connection` property. The `Connection` property is a `public` property of `CookBookEntities`. That is what we did in the following statements:

```
if (context.Connection.State != ConnectionState.Open)
{
    context.Connection.Open();
}
```

Next, we called the `Save` method to save the selected file:

```
context.SaveFile(Path.GetFileNameWithoutExtension(txtPath.Text),
GetBytesFromFile(txtPath.Text));
```

For this recipe, the preceding statement is a long-running task. It will either run successfully or end in an exception. Whichever be the case, we have to close the connection. To do so, we called the `Dispose` method of `CookBookEntities` in the `finally` method:

```
finally
{
    context.Dispose();
}
```

Calling `Dispose` internally calls the `Close` method of the `Connection` property thus closing the database connection.

Using functions that return tables as return values

In Microsoft SQL Server 2008 and later versions, we could create functions that return tables as return values. These functions are known as **Table Valued Functions**. Until Entity Framework Version 5, there was no way to use such functions with Entity Framework. However, with Entity Framework 5 (Visual Studio 2012), it is possible to use Table Valued Functions.

In this recipe, we will see how to do so. The function that we will use will return the details of files uploaded by a user, and we will display the details on `DataGridView`.

How to do it...

1. Launch SQL Server Management Studio 2012.
2. Open the database named `CookBook`.
3. Next, add a Table Valued Function that will retrieve data from `tb_FileStorage`. Name it `GetUserDetails`. The function will be:

```sql
USE [CookBook]
GO

/****** Object:  UserDefinedFunction [dbo].[GetUserDetails]
Script Date: 24-10-2012 17:55:48 ******/
SET ANSI_NULLS ON
GO

SET QUOTED_IDENTIFIER ON
GO

CREATE FUNCTION [dbo].[GetUserDetails]
(
        -- Add the parameters for the function here
        @vID int
)
RETURNS TABLE
AS
RETURN
(
```

Entity Framework Recipes

```
            -- Add the SELECT statement with parameter references here
            SELECT * FROM tb_FileStorage WHERE tb_FileStorage.User_ID =
@vID
)

GO
```

4. Create a project of type `Windows Forms Application` in Visual Studio 2012. Name it `TableValuedFunction`.
5. In **Solution Explorer**, right-click on the project and choose **Add | New Item**.
6. In the dialog box, choose **ADO.NET Entity Data Model** and click on **Add** to launch the Entity Data Model wizard. Name it `CookBookModel`:

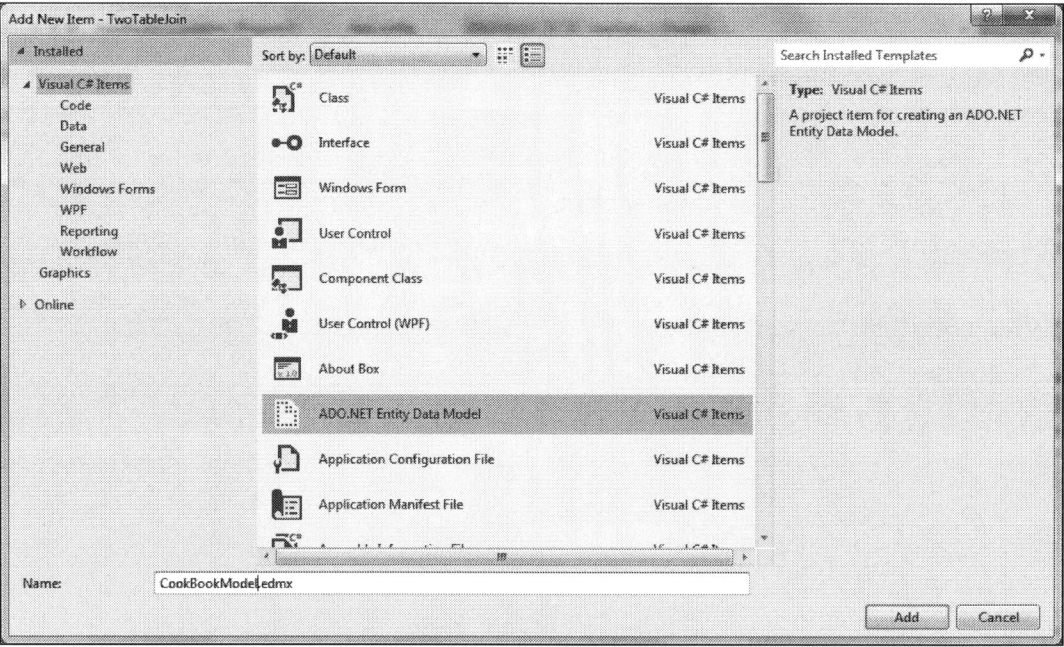

7. In the wizard, choose **Generate from database** and click on **Next**.

Chapter 10

8. Select the `CookBook.dbo` connection. We had created this in the *Saving large files (BLOB) in MS SQL Server using ADO.NET* recipe in *Chapter 5, ADO.NET Recipes*.

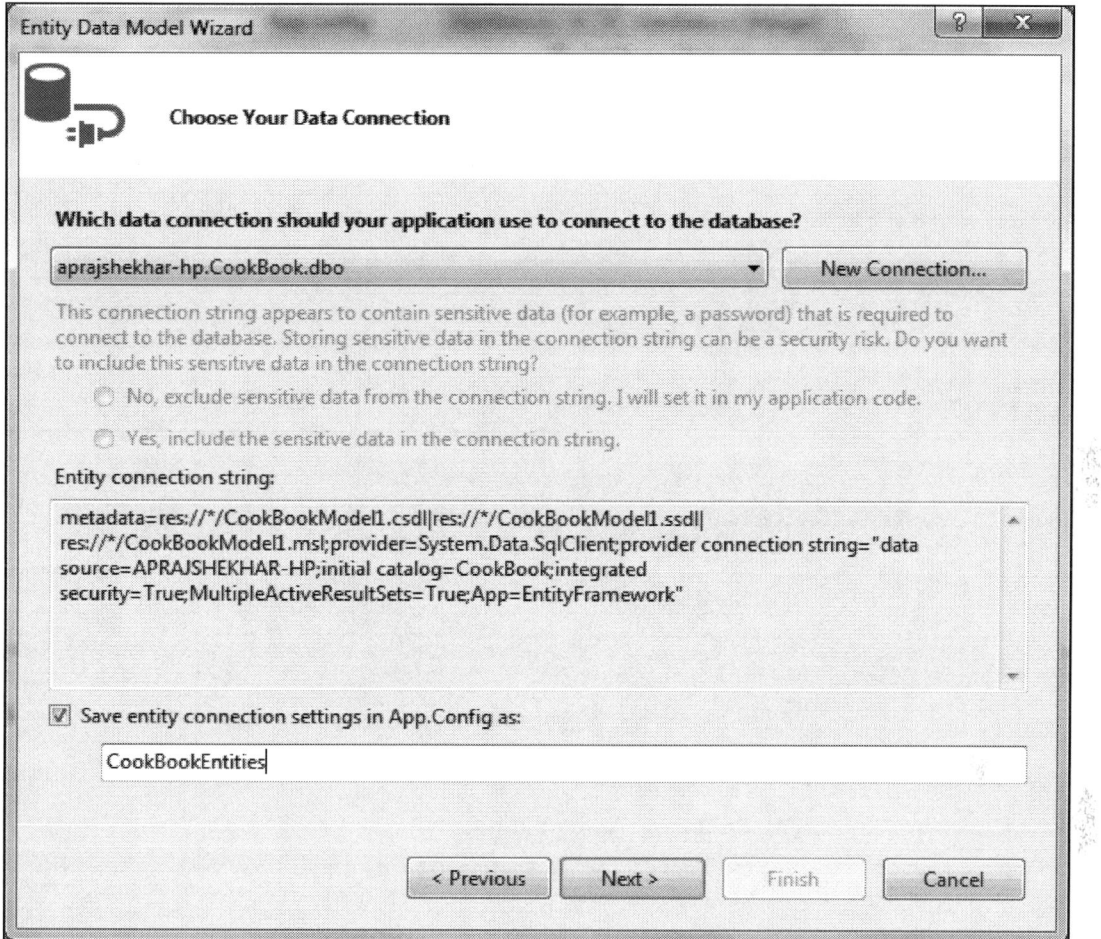

9. If the connection does not exist, create a new connection for the `CookBook` database.
10. Enter `CookBookEntities` in the **Save entity connection settings...** field. This will be the name of the main ORM class.

11. Click on **Next**. In the next screen that comes up, select all the tables and the function named **GetUserDetails**. Click on **Finish**:

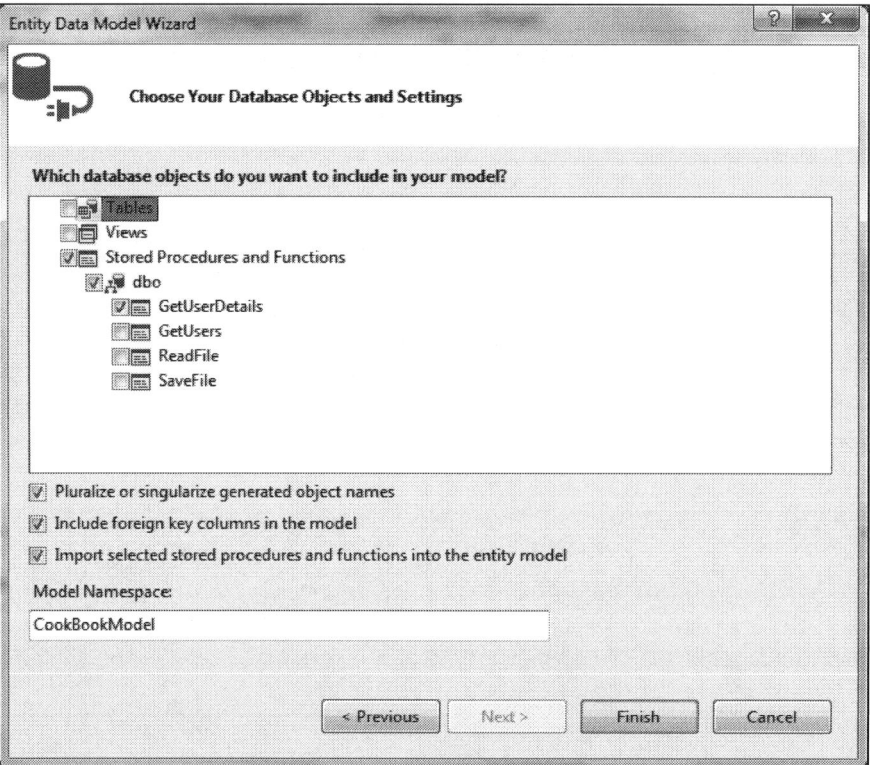

12. Open `CookBookModel.edmx` in the design mode.

13. In the **Model Browser** window, select **GetUserDetails** under the **Function Imports** section. Right-click on it and select **Edit**.

14. In the **Edit Function Import** dialog box, select **Entities** and choose **tb_FileStorage**:

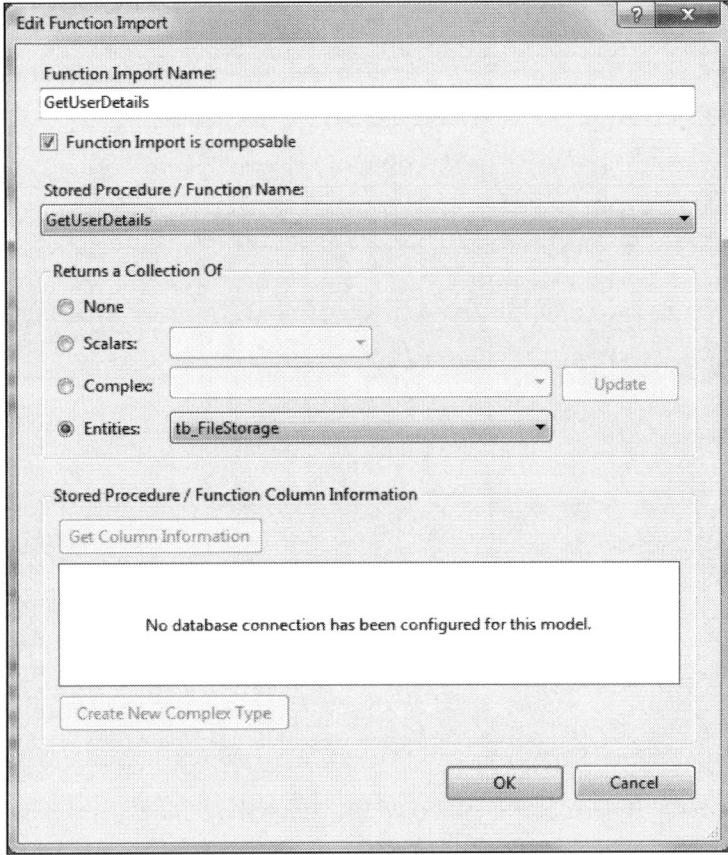

15. Rename `Form1.cs` to `UserDetails.cs`.

16. Open `UserDetails.cs` in the design mode. Design the form so that it looks similar to the following screenshot:

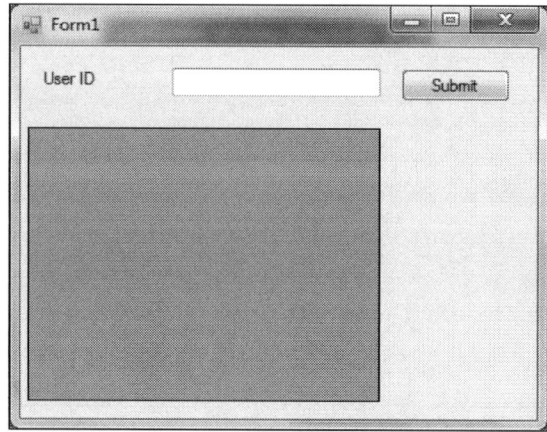

17. Name the controls as detailed in the following table:

Control	Name	Description
Textbox	txtUserID	To enter the ID of the user whose files need to be listed
Button	btnSubmit	To execute the logic for listing the files
DataGridView	dgvUserDetails	To display the files

18. Double-click on `btnShow` to add a Click event handler.
19. In the event handler, add the following code:

```
int userID = Convert.ToInt32(txtUserID.Text);
using (CookBookEntities context = new CookBookEntities())
{
   var result = context.GetUserDetails(userID);

   dgvUserDetails.DataSource = result;
}
```

20. Run the application.

21. Enter the user ID in the textbox and click on Submit. You will see the following screen:

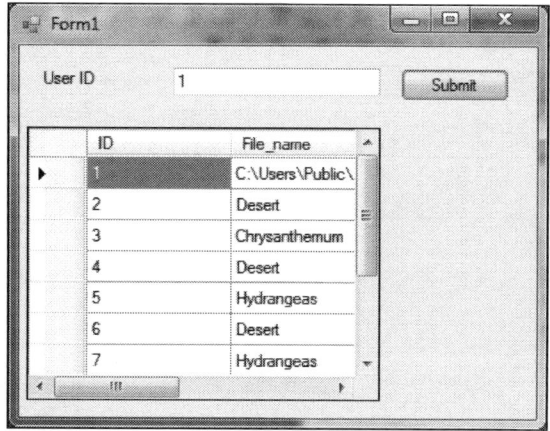

How it works...

The heavy lifting to map the method to the Table Valued Function of the database is done by the Entity Framework in step 11. The function generated by the framework maps to a complex entity type. However, we want to use the tb_FileStorage entity, which is mapped to the tb_FileStorage table. Hence, in step 14, we chose the tb_FileStorage entity. Once that mapping is done, calling the method with the value entered by the user is pretty straightforward:

```
int userID = Convert.ToInt32(txtUserID.Text);
using (CookBookEntities context = new CookBookEntities())
{
   var result = context.GetUserDetails(userID);

   dgvUserDetails.DataSource = result;
}
```

The retrieved value is then assigned as data source to DataGridView.

Index

Symbols

@Html.ValidationMessage 221
.NET 5

A

AddOrRemove method 60
AddOrRemoveRows method 58
ADO.NET
   used, for large file retrieving from SQL Server 134-138
   used, for large file saving in MS SQL Server 129-133
Age property 120
anti-XSS library
   used, for cross-site injection preventing 210-213
ApplicationSettings property 232
ASP.NET
   about 105
   advanced features 209
ASP.NET 4.5 105
ASPX page and Silverlight application communication
   implementing 119-127
asset data
   presenting, Pivot control used 223-227
Asynchronous file I/O
   about 33-37
   using, for directory-to-directory copy 33-37

B

background threads
   handling, in window forms 88-93
BeginInvoke method 93
Binary Large Objects. *See* **BLOB**
BLOB 129
Blog property 120
btnParse button 40
btnPing_Cick method 175
btnUpload_Click method 245

C

Click event 233
client-side storage
   used, for registration data draft saving 231-233
client-side validation
   implementing 218-221
collection size based rows
   adding, table layout creating 52-57
commit 143
Connection property 246
connections
   managing manually 244-246
ContactDetailsAdded event 51
ContinueWith method 104
CopyDirectoryAsync method 38
CopyToAsync method 38

Create, Retrieve, Update, and Delete. *See* CRUD
cross-site injection
  preventing, anti-XSS library used 210-213
Cross-site scripting. *See* XSS
CRUD 157, 240
custom attributes
  about 22
  creating 22-24
  processing, via reflection 27-33
  working 25-27
custom binding
  implementing, in WCF 151-156
customBinding 177
custom validation attribute
  creating, validation logic used 10-15
custom XML configuration files
  modifying, DataSet used 145-149

D

data annotations 10
DataGridView
  about 61-66
  creating dynamically 61-66
  working 67-70
data parallelism 100
DataSet
  used, for custom XML configuration files modifying 145-149
data shaping 196
DirectX
  used, for video player creating 71-76
Dob property 120
DoRotate method 102
draft functionality 105
dynamic programming
  used, for JSON accessing 38-43

E

Email property 120
entity
  joining, LINQ used 236-239
Entity Framework
  used, for file uploading 240-244
EventArgs class 46

event with generic values as payload
  creating 46-52
exceptions
  handling, FaultContract used 162-165
  handling, FaultException used 162-165

F

FaultContract
  used, for exception handling 162-165
FaultException
  used, for exception handling 162-165
files
  uploading, Stream used 166-170
FormatErrorMessage method 21

G

GenerateColumns method 69
GenerateTestData method 197
GetConstructors method 31
GetDefaultVideoCaptureDevice() method 230
GetDetails method 32
GetGoogleHtml method 215
GetProperty() method 33
GetUsers method 189
Google
  used, for third-party user authentication 216-218
Google Map
  about 213
  adding, Map Helper used 213-215

H

HTML5 client storage
  used, for user registration page draft saving 109-114
HTML5 controls
  used, for user registration page creating 105-109
HtmlEncode method 213

I

ID property 120
InitializeComponent method 62
Invoke method 126
IsUsernameUnique method 9

J

JSON
  accessing, dynamic programming used 38-43

K

key
  delivery 42
  order 42

L

LINQ
  used, for entity joining 236-239
ListFiles method 97
live data shaper
  using 196-198
  working 199
Load from DB button 136
LoadUsers method 195
localized validation message
  generating, XML used 16-19
localStorage property 113

M

MakeTransparent method 104
Map Helper
  about 213
  used, for Google Maps adding 213-215
MapUsers method 186
MediaElement
  used, for videos playing 199-203
model 180
model pattern
  implementing 180-184
  working 185-187
Model-View-View Model. *See* **MVVM**
MS SQL Server
  large files saving, ADO.NET used 129-133
MVVM 179

O

object binding
  to controls, strongly-typed data controls used 114-119

Object Relational Mapping. *See* **ORM**
Operation property 60
ORM 235

P

parallelized bulk image processing operations
  chaining 101-104
parallel programming
  about 77
  used, for bulk image processing speedup 98-101
Phone property 120
Pivot control
  used, for asset data presentation 223-227
Plain Old CLR Object. *See* **POCO**
Play method 203
POCO 10
predicate feature 10
Producer-Consumer race condition
  about 82
  handling 83, 84
  working 86-88
PropertyChanged event 189, 196
public static method 33

R

Read method 82
ReadXml method 148
RegisterScriptableObject method 126
RemoveRow method 58
Repository pattern
  about 6, 180
  implementing 180-184
  used, for validation logic implementing 6-10
  working 185-187
Representational State Transfer. *See* **REST**
RequestDeviceAccess() method 230
REST 157
REST WCF service
  about 157
  creating 157-159
  working 161
Ribbon control
  used, for video player control display 203-208

role-based security
  used, for service securing 173-178
rollback 143

S

service
  securing, role-based security used 173-178
setResult function 127
SetUser method 127
shared resource
  about 78
  creating 78, 79
  working 80-82
Show On Map button 219
Silverlight 223
Silverlight and ASPX page application communication
  implementing 119-127
SQL Server
  large files, retrieving from ADO.NET 134-138
StartBulkProcessing method 104
Stop() method 230
stored procedures
  used, for file uploading 240-244
Stream
  used, for files uploading 166-170
  working 171, 172
strongly-typed data controls
  used, for object binding to controls 114-119

T

table layout
  Class Library project, using 52-57
  creating 52, 57-61
TableLayoutPanel 52
table valued functions
  about 247
  using 247-253
  working 253
task parallelism 100
TextMode values
  txtAge 109
  txtBlog 109
  txtDob 109
  txtEmail 109

  txtPhone 109
third-party user authentication
  Google, using 216-218
threading 77
threads, WPF
  handling 93-96
  working 96, 97
transactions
  about 138
  used, for database consistency maintenance 138-144

U

Upload method 172
UserName property 120
user registration page
  creating, HTML5 controls used 105-109
user registration page draft
  saving, HTML5 client storage used 109-114
Users property 191
utility 57

V

validation attribute
  extending, for localization 19-22
validation logic
  implementing, Repository pattern used 6-10
  used, for custom validation attribute creating 10-15
ValueChanged event 74
video player
  creating, DirectX used 71-76
  Windows Forms used 71-76
video player controls
  displaying, Ribbon control used 203-208
videos
  playing, MediaElement used 199-203
View
  commands, implementing 190-195
  data, binding to 190-195
View Model. *See* **VM**
VM
  about 187
  implementing 187, 188
  working 189

W

WCF
  about 151
  custom binding, implementing 151-156
webcams
  about 227
  accessing 227-229
  working 230
Windows Communication Framework. *See* WCF
Windows Forms
  background threads, handling 88-93
  used, for video player creating 71-76

Windows Presentation Framework. *See* WPF
WPF
  about 179
  threads, handling 93-96

X

XML
  used, for localized validation message generation 16-19
XSS 210

**Thank you for buying
.NET Framework 4.5 Expert Programming Cookbook**

About Packt Publishing

Packt, pronounced 'packed', published its first book "*Mastering phpMyAdmin for Effective MySQL Management*" in April 2004 and subsequently continued to specialize in publishing highly focused books on specific technologies and solutions.

Our books and publications share the experiences of your fellow IT professionals in adapting and customizing today's systems, applications, and frameworks. Our solution-based books give you the knowledge and power to customize the software and technologies you're using to get the job done. Packt books are more specific and less general than the IT books you have seen in the past. Our unique business model allows us to bring you more focused information, giving you more of what you need to know, and less of what you don't.

Packt is a modern, yet unique publishing company, which focuses on producing quality, cutting-edge books for communities of developers, administrators, and newbies alike. For more information, please visit our website: www.PacktPub.com.

About Packt Enterprise

In 2010, Packt launched two new brands, Packt Enterprise and Packt Open Source, in order to continue its focus on specialization. This book is part of the Packt Enterprise brand, home to books published on enterprise software – software created by major vendors, including (but not limited to) IBM, Microsoft and Oracle, often for use in other corporations. Its titles will offer information relevant to a range of users of this software, including administrators, developers, architects, and end users.

Writing for Packt

We welcome all inquiries from people who are interested in authoring. Book proposals should be sent to author@packtpub.com. If your book idea is still at an early stage and you would like to discuss it first before writing a formal book proposal, contact us; one of our commissioning editors will get in touch with you.

We're not just looking for published authors; if you have strong technical skills but no writing experience, our experienced editors can help you develop a writing career, or simply get some additional reward for your expertise.

Microsoft .NET 4.5 Quickstart

ISBN: 978-1-84968-698-3 Paperback: 210 pages

Over 50 simple but incredibly effective recipes to get updated to exciting new features in .NET 4.5 Framework

1. Designed for the fastest jump into .NET 4.5, with a clearly designed roadmap of progressive chapters and detailed examples

2. A great and efficient way to get into .NET 4.5 and not only understand its features but clearly know how to use them, when, how and why

3. Covers Windows 8 XAML development, .NET Core (with Async/Await & reflection improvements), EF Code First & Migrations, ASP.NET, WF, and WPF

OData Programming Cookbook for .NET Developers

ISBN: 978-1-84968-592-4 Paperback: 376 pages

70 fast-track, example-driven recipes with clear instructions and details for OData programming with .NET Framework

1. Master OData programming concepts and skills by implementing practical examples and apply them in real-world scenarios

2. Find simple and handy means to resolve common OData programming issues more effectively

3. Explore the new OData programming features in latest and future versions of WCF Data Service

Please check www.PacktPub.com for information on our titles

Microsoft Silverlight 5 Data and Services Cookbook

ISBN: 978-1-84968-350-0   Paperback: 662 pages

Over 100 practical recipes for creating rich, data-driven, business applications in Silverlight 5

1. Design and develop rich data-driven business applications in Silverlight and Windows Phone 7 following best practices
2. Rapidly interact with services and handle multiple sources of data within Silverlight and Windows Phone 7 business applications
3. Packed with practical, hands-on cookbook recipes, illustrating the techniques to solve particular data problems effectively within your Silverlight and Windows Phone 7 business applications

MVVM Survival Guide for Enterprise Architectures in Silverlight and WPF

ISBN: 978-1-84968-342-5   Paperback: 490 pages

Eliminate unnecessary code by taking advantage of the MVVM pattern—less code, fewer bugs

1. Build an enterprise application using Silverlight and WPF, taking advantage of the powerful MVVM pattern
2. Discover the evolution of presentation patterns—by example—and see the benefits of MVVM in the context of the larger picture of presentation patterns
3. Customize the MVVM pattern for your projects' needs by comparing the various implementation styles

Please check www.PacktPub.com for information on our titles

Made in the USA
Lexington, KY
07 January 2017